Praise for Michael Gurian

"Michael Gurian is a leading edge teacher with the rare ability to combine the personal, the practical, and the political in very accessible and powerful form. In *Saving Our Sons*, he has written a real page-turner. Its eight chapters take on one of the fundamental issues of our time—how we raise boys—from a science-based perspective that will catalyze new thinking and new strategies for families, schools, and communities in need. This is a very important book."

—Daniel Amen, M.D., author of
Unleashing the Power of the Female Brain and *The Brain Warrior's Way*

"Michael Gurian's *Saving Our Sons* is an immensely powerful mirror on the state of boyhood in America. Dr. Gurian's depiction of the problems and issues facing our sons is remarkable in its thoroughness. The book's tone is forceful but not strident, warm and engaging without sentimentality or hyperbole. Gurian provides practical solutions for each issue he explores—economic, social, emotional, political, and personal. This is a must read for every one in America and indeed the world who cares about and is caring for our boys."

—Troy Kemp, Executive Director of
The National Center for the Development of Boys

"Michael Gurian is America's most passionate advocate for boys."

—Michael Thompson, Ph.D., author of
It's a Boy! and coauthor of *Raising Cain*

"There is no one who understands the development of boys better than Michael Gurian."

—William Damon, Ph.D., professor of Education,
Stanford University, and author of *The Moral Child*

"Michael Gurian's work in gender is at the leading edge of our profession and can significantly affect the field of psychology."
—Tracey J. Shors, Ph.D., Department of Psychology, Center for Collaborative Neuroscience, Rutgers University

"Michael Gurian provides invaluable insight into how understanding our children's unique core natures can help us raise happy, successful, and emotionally fulfilled children."
—Harold S. Koplewicz, M.D., Former Chair, Department of Child and Adolescent Psychiatry, New York University School of Medicine; and founder and director of the Child Mind Institute

SAVING OUR SONS

PREVIOUS BOOKS BY MICHAEL GURIAN

Child Development and Parenting

The Purpose of Boys
Nurture the Nature
The Wonder of Girls
The Wonder of Boys
Raising Boys by Design
The Wonder of Children (previously published as *The Soul of the Child*)
A Fine Young Man
The Good Son
What Stories Does My Son Need?
(with Terry Trueman)
It's a Baby Boy!
It's a Baby Girl!
(by the Gurian Institute, with Adrian Goldberg, ACSW, Stacie Bering, MD)

Education

The Minds of Boys (with Kathy Stevens)
Boys and Girls Learn Differently!
(with Kathy Stevens, Patricia Henley, Terry Trueman)
The Boys and Girls Learn Differently Action Guide for Teachers
(with Arlette C. Ballew)
Strategies for Teaching Boys and Girls—Elementary Level Strategies for Teaching Boys and Girls—Secondary Level
(with Kathy Stevens, Kelley King)
Successful Single-Sex Classrooms (with Kathy Stevens, Peggy Daniels)

Psychology

Lessons of Lifelong Intimacy
The Wonder of Aging
How Do I Help Him?
What Could He Be Thinking?
Love's Journey
The Invisible Presence (previously published as Mothers, Sons and Lovers)
The Prince and the King

Business-Corporate

Leadership and the Sexes (with Barbara Annis)
The Leading Partners Workbook (with Katherine Coles, Kathy Stevens)

For Young Adult Readers

Understanding Guys
From Boys to Men

Saving Our Sons

A New Path for Raising Healthy and Resilient Boys

Dr. Michael Gurian

The *New York Times* Bestselling Author of
The Wonder of Boys and *The Minds of Boys*

With Special Sections on Motivating Boys
and Managing Their Technology Use

Dedication

For my father, Dr. Jay P. Gurian
In the memory of my mother, Julia Gurian
and
For my beloved family: Gail, Gabrielle, and Davita

Table of Contents

Preface.. ix

Part I: Confronting Our Boy Crisis

Chapter 1: Invisible Boys: The Case for Revolution....................... 3

Chapter 2: The Real Causes of Male Violence: Confronting the
Dominant Gender Paradigm 23

Chapter 3: Forward-to-Nature: Embracing the New Science of
Healthy Boyhood 55

Chapter 4: Protecting Our Sons: Ending Three Dangerous Attacks
on Boyhood.. 89

Part II: Saving Our Sons

Chapter 5: Male Nurturance: Supporting and Building Male
Emotional Intelligence.. 117

Chapter 6: The Science of Maturity: Ending the Male Motivation
and Maturity Gap.. 151

Chapter 7: The Digital Boy: Ensuring Seven Milestones of Male
Development in the Digital Age 183

Chapter 8: Saving Both Our Sons and Daughters: Toward a New
Gender Equity Paradigm 233
Epilogue.. 261

Acknowledgments 267
Notes and Resources.. 269
Bibliography.. 305
Appendix... 311
Index.. 319

Preface

IN THIRTY YEARS OF WORKING WITH CHILDREN, I have never been more worried than I am right now for our sons. Some boys are doing very well but millions are disappearing into violence, imprisonment, social withdrawal, listlessness, virtual worlds, and real life self-destruction. If we don't end this national pattern, our boys and young men will become increasingly destructive, both to others and themselves because nearly every social problem we face in our civilization today—unemployment, income equality, incarceration rates, religious extremism, domestic abuse, mental illness, health care inequities, and painful violence against women—intersects in some way with the state of boyhood in America.

This book provides a professional and personal blueprint for social revolution on behalf of our sons. Specifically, I have written this book to assist you in deploying these ideas and strategies in your home, school, neighborhood, and in our larger culture.

1. Many of the social systems within which we raise and care for our children—schools, neighborhoods, social programs, and families—have changed in the last fifty years such that males in general face *systematic neglect* despite our public presentation of males as inherently privileged.

2. To help boys survive and thrive we must alter our thinking to include all three parts of gender—*nature, nurture, and culture.* Our public, academic, and media attention to "masculine norms and gender stereotypes" is no longer enough help for boys (or girls) because these stereotypes and norms are not the primary causes of the problems our children face today.

3. As we look at all aspects of boyhood, we must make *nature* our starting point and baseline. There is a natural boy we can understand, assist, and protect, one boy at a time. Among the elements that assault this boy today are hidden *neurotoxins* that attack male genetics and socialization and, thus, can utterly derail male development yet often go unrecognized in our everyday lives. In this book I will help you find these neuro-

toxins and construct family plans to protect your boys from them.

4. A non-malicious but also not-benign *Dominant Gender Paradigm* has emerged in the last fifty years in "*The Big Three*" (our academic institutions, governmental/legislative agencies, and media) that deploys a number of superficial ideas about males that keep male life underserved, under-funded, and under-nurtured. I will show you ways to understand and confront this paradigm in your daily life and local community.

5. Ensuring gender equality for girls and women does not require *gender sameness.* In the new millennium, neuroscience shows us that males and females are not the same, though their brains overlap a great deal across a wide gender spectrum. We can now build equality without the false premise of sameness, and we must do so in order to help all children.

6. It's been difficult to revolutionize the lives of our boys, and thus our men, in part because we confuse the ordinary lives of the majority of males with the lives of alpha and criminal males. Hyper-focused on "the 10 percent" (the leader/alpha males and frightening/pathological males), we neglect the deep needs of the majority of our sons, which makes the boy crisis worse, and puts females in greater danger.

7. Now is the right time for revolution because there are now significant child development institutions already in existence around our nation and our world that show *specific success-data* for saving our sons. I'll provide examples of these proactive and revolutionary communities and schools throughout this book.

8. What we do now to help boys will help girls and women, because *their needs are interdependent.* The oppressor/enemy approach to women's rights popularized over the last fifty years has created a false impression of separation between women's and men's needs in order to uplift women. Now, however, the situation of our sons has become so dire we will not be able to advance the cause of girls' and women's equity any further without ending the cruelties and neglect our culture perpetrates on our males.

The social revolution I will ask you to advance involves some politics and a lot of practical strategies, both at home and in our communities. Thus this book will help you as parents, educators, and caregivers to take to the next level your efforts to raise your sons to become the good men you want them to be. I believe an advanced kind of parenting is essential in our complex technological world so this book provides you with science-based best practices for ensuring male maturity and developmental milestones from birth to 25 that fit our new millennium's technological and social revolutions.

If you've read any of my other books, you know that my work is multi-cultural. This book will not be a repeat of my previous books except that, like them, it includes current and new research from more than two dozen different countries and cultures.

At the same time, this book includes new research specifying the privation of many American boys because:

- Our American boys in general are not doing as well as boys in many other developed countries—we must understand and change that dangerous trend right now.
- Americans have always innovated when we realized that nothing but innovation could help us—as we innovate for boys now, our innovations can become useful to other parts of the world.
- America has become severely polarized in its politics of gender and that hurts both our sons and daughters—so we must build bridges.

This book is a bridge. Wherever you fit on the ideological spectrum, I hope the insights and suggested policies in these pages will inspire and resonate for you personally. If you have daughters, as I do, I hope you'll also feel inspired to spread this word and mission with personal vigor as well.

Ultimately, I hope you will leave this book understanding a boy in your life in a way akin to peering into his core self, his hidden nature—and I hope that journey into the natural boy will inspire you to become not just an effective and joyful parent, a powerful teacher, a committed community member, but also an invested advocate for boys in your own world.

The issues our boys experience today comprise a vast flood in the face of which our culture is building only tiny skiffs. Thank you for joining in this effort—this social revolution—on behalf of our children. We are all, truly, in this together, and what we do, in unity of purpose, to care for and save all our children will be the greatest reward we experience in a lifetime.

—Dr. Michael Gurian, Spokane, 2017

Part I

Confronting Our Boy Crisis

"Amid the general and sudden change of customs and of laws during revolution, when all people and all rules share one vast confusion, when citizens rise and fall at a previously unthought-of rate, and when equal power passes so quickly from hand to hand,...it is important to remember that ambitions are writ on a grand scale while this democratic revolution lasts...and although high ambitions swell...the characteristic of equality can actually be lost when the characteristics of equality become a fact."

—Alexis de Tocqueville, *Democracy in America*

Chapter 1

Invisible Boys: The Case for Revolution

> "There is a tribe of invisible boys who move around us like shadows—have you felt them? They cannot be seen except when they die; only then they become visible."
>
> —Nakasak, Eskimo poet

COLIN, 14, WALKED INTO MY OFFICE on a snowy day in February. He had been a late bloomer in some ways, and so his parents held him out of first grade for a year. This had been a good move, and he had been an A student, and a happy one, in elementary school. Now, however, toward the end of eighth grade, he was neither. He had been fighting with his mom and dad a lot, spending all day playing video games and scrolling through social media. He did very little homework or, when he did do it, he refused to hand it in. He got Ds regularly. I had met with his parents already, and heard key words I hear quite often in my counseling practice:

"He's unmotivated."

"He seems to be checking out of life. I can't read him anymore. Sometimes I don't know who he is."

"He's in a shell, he won't talk to us."

"He doesn't care any more about anything except his friends, his video games, his social media."

"He hates school."

"He's basically a good kid, but he fights us all the time or just pulls away."

"I can't tell if he needs more time with me or if I should just leave him alone," his father said.

"I'm losing him," his mom said tearfully.

Because of snow on the ground, Colin wore a blue down coat into my office. His hair was relatively well combed, but he wore the grim face of a boy forced into counseling. As I do with many of my male clients,

I asked him to take a walk with me to begin the therapeutic experience. Since Colin already had his coat on, I put mine on and we left the office. We walked down the hall and out the door into freshly fallen snow.

Walking past the cars in the parking lot toward a trail behind my office's brick building, I stopped and asked him, "Can you guess which car is mine?"

Colin took a few guesses. "I bet you drive that Subaru. You're all about the 'love' thing." (He referred, in this comment, to the Subaru commercials that emphasize the brand as "Love.")

"No," I responded, "that's not mine."

"Okay," he pondered, scanning cars, "that one." He pointed with an ironic tone at a new silver F-150 pickup.

"No," I chuckled, amused by his highly masculine choice, "but thanks."

He scanned further before settling on a blue minivan. Walking to it, he looked in the window, saw no car seats (I had some gray hair so he was doing some detective work) and seeing none, said, "This one."

I smiled with encouragement, enjoying his existential leaps and assumptions—with every guess, he was trying to measure me as a man and, thus, as a potential helper. Saying no, I suggested we keep walking and then he guess again when we found our way back here. He agreed and we walked away from the parking lot up a small hill and talked for ten minutes. As we gradually circled back to the parking lot, he opened up about himself somewhat, though still guardedly. When we got back to the parking lot we began the car-game again. Three guesses later, he ended up guessing correctly—I drove a ten-year-old silver Jeep Grand Cherokee.

"Does that car surprise you?" I asked as I waited for him to open the building's door. Once he did, I followed him into the building and we arrived at my office door.

"I guess it kind of surprises me, yeah," he said. "You don't look like the outdoors type."

I said nothing in response but already in these ten to fifteen minutes of initial time together I was setting up a relationship between us in which he would see that I respected him as a young male.

- I walked around the neighborhood with him rather than just making him sit down in a chair upon arrival so that he would feel immediately comfortable with the fact that this new potential mentor understood *boys*.

- I let his comment about who I was ("not the outdoors type") go unanswered so he could see that I didn't need to respond to masks and stereotypes. We both heard the message: "Now you know I'm not what I seem, and Colin, I know you aren't what you seem, either."
- I made him open the heavy front door of the building rather than opening the door for him to both show that I trusted his age and independence (i.e. would not do anything for him he could do for himself) and to assert my very important authority in the young male's eyes.
- We made a game of guessing what car I drove so that he could gain some control over the hierarchical experience of counseling—keep some power, have some choice-making, and realize that I did not mind him measuring me, since I would be constantly measuring him.
- I made this into a game because a lot of counseling and nurturance of males connects with game theory—puzzle solving, measuring one another, competition, confrontation, and social-emotional challenge rather than pure "words-for-feelings" (I will go much further into this later in this book).

As we sat down in our chairs in my office, Colin took his coat off. This, too, was an existential act: he had not taken his coat off before, in part, because he hadn't felt safe and so he kept "armor" on but now, fifteen minutes into our interaction, he not only took his coat off to acclimate to interior conditions but because he felt psychologically safer with me than before.

We sat down together, he on the couch and me on a chair kitty corner from him rather than right across from him (thus avoiding potential discomfort for him as a male with forced eye contact). I asked him questions that could give him the safety of concrete responses. I didn't ask him how he felt or anything about his feelings in that first session. But we went very deep into his life-situation. Pretty quickly it was clear that Colin knew he had a lack of purpose or motivation to do anything, that he was alienated from school work and his teachers. He even revealed that he felt guilty about disappointing his parents.

Counseling over a six-month period ultimately worked with Colin because it became a place where he could become visible: "see" not only who he was but, in measuring his assets and liabilities, make new decisions about who to become as a visible *man*.

Invisible American Boys

Colin is one of millions of disappearing American boys. In our population of 330 million are approximately 165 million males. Of these males, perhaps 5 million are alpha males who "run everything" (businesses, governments, city councils, school districts) and 5 million are criminal males about whom countless frightening stories are written or envisioned in our media. That leaves approximately 150 million other males. What about them?

Most are doing okay, we could say, but in this chapter I'll show that when we start peeling back the layers of male distress in America, we find at least 20 million males who can't be called "okay." These males are invisible to us until we see what is really happening with them: jobless or under-employed, ripped from families or leaving them hopelessly, living in basements or alleys or city parks, committing suicide, talking to themselves on bridges or on the streets, shooting one another or being shot, failing out of school and failing at marriage. Once we see them, we can see millions of males at the center of our most pressing social problems.

How will we fully see these boys and these men?

Did You Know?

- America has the highest rate of male incarceration per capita of any country in the world. Among males 17 or younger, the boy-to-girl ratio in correctional institutions is 9:1. Among 18-21 year olds, the ratio grows to 14:1. While boys of color are systematically moved from neighborhoods to schools to prisons, those prisons are populated mainly by white males, so this is an issue that includes race but goes beyond race, too—it goes to the heart of maleness in America.

- Suicide kills approximately 30,000 American boys and men per year, and males kill themselves at four times the rate of girls. Males of color are increasingly turning to suicide as a way out of despair, especially among returning veterans, and suicide among our males is now the second leading cause of death in America.

- Boys are twice as likely as girls to be victims of violence in America but in certain age groups, the ratio is 6:1. For instance, among adolescent children, six males die from violence for every one female. Boys of color in the inner city are considered "highly likely" to die from violent causes by or about age 25—the end of male adolescence.

- Boys receive two-thirds of the Ds and Fs in our schools but less than 40 percent of the As. Some boys, of course, test very well and are doing quite well, but overall, there is no racial or ethnic group in which boys are, in overall markers, doing better than girls. The well-known female gap in math/science is a 3-point gap while the male gap in literacy is a 10-point gap, leaving males 1 and 1/2 years behind females in literacy skills, and skewing all aggregate test scores toward much higher female and lower male performance.

- Boys are twice as likely as girls to be labeled "emotionally disturbed" and twice as likely to be diagnosed with a behavioral or learning disorder. One in every forty-two boys lives somewhere on the autism spectrum. This and other male-specific brain disorders are rising exponentially year by year.

- One in eleven Americans, most of them boys, are diagnosed with ADD/ADHD. Our Gurian Institute research in 2,000 schools show that at least one-third of schoolboys diagnosed with ADD/ADHD are misdiagnosed. While some boys do need medication, millions of males are being medicated unnecessarily, with some severe consequences for motivation and growth. Given that 80 percent of the world's Ritalin is used in the U.S., we have a particularly American problem.

- Boys are four times as likely as girls to be suspended or expelled from early childhood and K – 12 learning environments. Our Gurian Institute research shows America's schools, from Pre-K through college, struggling in these academic and behavioral markers in large part because teachers and staff have never received gender science-based training in male/female learning difference. Graduate schools that train teachers don't teach a Boys and Girls Learn Differently class to future teachers because they don't find it to be politically correct. But without this training, these hard-working people, mainly women, are often unable to manage and grow male energy and acumen.

- The latest educational research known as the PISA study (Programme for International Student Assessment) from the Organization of Economic Cooperation and Development (OECD) shows boys behind girls in most developmental, behavioral, academic, and social markers in *all industrialized countries*. Weekly and sometimes daily, I receive an email from a parent or professional in China, Japan, Qatar, Nigeria, Brazil, Vietnam, Australia, and many other countries asking, "What can we do to help our failing boys?" The boy crisis is a worldwide problem that is hitting America especially hard.

In 2015, the World Health Organization published a major study of men's and boys' health worldwide. In it the study's authors—from Europe, the U.S. and Asia—provided statistics and analysis from all continents, including the most comprehensive health study worldwide to date, the Global Burden of Disease Study led by the Institute for Health Metrics and Evaluation. This study corroborates the OECD's PISA study referred to above but takes it even further, into health markers.

The study concludes: "*In most of the world, girls and women are doing better than boys and men in both physical and mental health indicators.*" Even when statistics regarding female depression, eating disorders, and violence-against-females such as rape and genital mutilation are included, males are doing worse. Perhaps most surprising to people is the study's wide reach: the health and wellness gender gap favoring females exists in *all 72 industrialized countries, including countries like China or Oman* that we have tended to believe are 'still patriarchal,' and thus should be harder on females than males.

The WHO study asks us to see the world's invisible boys. "In most parts of the world, health outcomes among boys and men continue to be substantially worse than among girls and women. Yet this gender-based disparity in health has received little national, regional or global acknowledgement or attention from health policy-makers or health-care providers." The study concludes: "Including both women and men in efforts to reduce gender inequalities in health as part of the post-2015 sustainable development agenda would improve everyone's health and well-being."

Seeing Our Sons:
The First Action Step of Social Revolution

The first action step of our new social revolution will be to *see* the boy crisis all around us—both abroad and right here at home. Except for the WHO study, most of the statistics in the box you just read come from the largest meta-study I am aware of regarding male health in the U.S., a study you can access at www.whitehouseboysmen.org. Dr. Warren Farrell, Dr. Marty Nemko, Peter Moore (Executive Editor of *Men's Health*), and myself were lead authors on the study, and 34 other authors contributed. This group represented a bi-partisan wealth of scholars and researchers from many of the nation's best known academic institutions. We wrote the meta-analysis, the *Proposal to Create a White House Council on Boys and Men,* in order to help foment revolution in America, both in the grassroots and in the Oval Office.

This study is one of three major studies published recently that you can access and use in your communities. Two others are MIT economist David Autor and Melanie Wasserman's *Wayward Sons: The Emerging Gender Gap in Labor Markets and Education* (which I will feature in a moment), and "For Every One Hundred Girls," provided by Tom Mortenson of the Pell Institute. Mr. Mortenson has studied male life in America for more than forty years and presents comparative data for males and female in growth and learning in a unique and powerful format I will share with you here.

Repeat Grades, Suspensions, Expulsions, Violence, At Risk

For every 100 girls who repeat kindergarten, 194 boys repeat kindergarten.

For every 100 girls suspended from public elementary and secondary schools, 215 boys are suspended.

For every 100 girls expelled from public elementary and secondary schools, 297 boys are expelled.

For every 100 twelfth-grade girls who were threatened or injured with a weapon on school property, 175 boys were threatened or injured.

For every 100 twelfth-grade girls who offered, sold or were given an illegal drug on school property, 134 boys did the same.

Death Rates

For every 100 girls ages 10 to 14 years who die, 149 boys die.

For every 100 girls ages 15 to 19 years who die, 242 boys die.

For every 100 white, non-Hispanic girls ages 15 to 19 who die, 216 white, non-Hispanic boys the same age die.

For every 100 black girls ages 15 to 19 who die, 310 black boys the same age die.

For every 100 Asian girls ages 15 to 19 who die, 203 Asian boys the same age die.

For every 100 American Indian girls ages 15 to 19 who die, 180 American Indian boys die.

For every 100 Hispanic girls ages 15 to 19 who die, 287 Hispanic boys ages 15 to 19 die.

For every 100 girls ages 5 to 14 who commit suicide, 225 boys kill themselves.

For every 100 girls ages 15 to 24 who commit suicide, 433 boys commit suicide.

Learning and Physical Disabilities

For every 100 girls diagnosed with a special education disability, 217 boys are diagnosed with a special education disability.

For every 100 girls diagnosed with a learning disability, 276 boys are diagnosed with a learning disability.

For every 100 girls diagnosed with emotional disturbance, 324 boys are diagnosed with emotional disturbance.

For every 100 girls diagnosed with a speech impairment, 147 boys are similarly diagnosed.

For every 100 girls with multiple disabilities, 189 boys have multiple disabilities.

Further Disabilities

For every 100 girls less than 3 years old with a developmental delay, 165 boys have a developmental delay.

For every 100 girls 3 to 5 years old with a developmental delay, 154 boys are developmentally delayed.

For every 100 girls 6 to 14 years old who have difficulty doing regular schoolwork, 176 boys have difficulty doing regular schoolwork.

For every 100 girls 6 to 14 years old who have difficulty getting along with others, 183 boys have difficulty getting along with others.

For every 100 girls 6 to 14 years old with a learning disability, 160 boys have a learning disability.

For every 100 girls 6 to 14 years old with other developmental disability, 212 boys have other developmental disabilities.

For every 100 girls less than 15 years old with a severe disability, 191 boys have a severe disability.

For every 100 girls less than 15 years old with a disability that needs assistance, 195 boys have a disability that needs assistance.

(Throughout this book I will provide answers to frequently-asked-questions in a Box format that I hope you will find useful in social and family conversations, book groups, media reports, professional development workshops, town hall meetings, and policy discussions).

Question: I knew boys had a few issues in the U.S. but I thought girls are generally doing worse in education since most of our federal and state funding goes to helping girls in school. But you seem to be saying boys are the main students having trouble in education and school—is that really true?

Answer: Yes. In nearly every area of schooling, boys are behind—in grades, test scores, and extra-curricular leadership activities. Admitting this as a society is crucial to ending the systematic neglect of males in America.

For every 100 girls ages 9 to 11 years enrolled below modal grade, there are 130 boys enrolled below modal grade.

For every 100 girls ages 12 to 14 years enrolled below modal grade, there are 120 boys enrolled below modal grade.

For every 100 girls age 13 scoring 250 or above on the reading test of the National Assessment of Educational Progress, there are 90 boys scoring 250 or above.

For every 100 girls ages 15 to 17 years enrolled below modal grade, there are 130 boys enrolled below modal grade.

For every 100 twelfth-grade girls who participate in music, drama, or debate, 70 boys participate.

For every 100 twelfth-grade girls who participate in vocational clubs, 71 boys participate.

Colin suffered in a number of these categories—dropping out of school activities, avoiding homework, acting out and becoming a discipline problem. His parents were afraid he might have a learning disability. He was emotionally confused and disturbed and he was headed for a great deal more trouble in a few years. If Colin had continued as he was, he would enter this next realm of statistics.

Higher Education

For every 100 women enrolled in college in the U.S., there are 78 men enrolled.

For every 100 American women who earn an associate's degree, 61 American men earn the same degree.

For every 100 American women who earn a bachelor's degree, 75 American men earn a bachelor's degree.

For every 100 American women who earn a master's degree, 66 American men earn the same degree.

For every 100 American women who earn a doctoral degree, 91 American men earn the same degree.

For every 100 women ages 25 to 29 years who have at least a professional degree, 84 men have at least a professional degree.

For every 100 women ages 25 to 29 years who have a doctoral degree, 80 men have a doctorate.

When Mr. Mortenson gave me permission to use these statistics, he said, "The situation is far worse than people think. These statistics are the tip of the iceberg." He acknowledged that many people in our culture believe males may be under-performing in school but are nonetheless dominating the workplace. This is not true either, he noted.

"Since World War II the American economy generally and the work force in particular has gone through substantial changes. Since 1948 employment in the United States has grown from 45 million to 131 million by 2009. Meanwhile, since the end of WWII the share of this employment in goods-producing industries has declined from 47.9% in 1948 to 15.5% by 2009. The share of total employment in manufacturing industries declined from 27.2% in 1948 to 8.9% by 2009. Employment in agriculture has gone from 14.5% of the total to 1.6% during this same period of time."

Mr. Mortenson continued, "These are all jobs that have employed males predominantly, thus, males are the largest share of employees in the industries facing the greatest declines: construction, mining, manufacturing, and agriculture. Males also tend to be the smallest shares of industrial employment in those industries growing the fastest: education and health care, leisure and hospitality." Tom has gone further to note that the exodus of American jobs overseas has severely hampered the ability of our males to find employment at home.

Wayward Sons, by Drs. Autor and Wasserman at MIT, echoes the Pell Institute and Mortenson findings. Drs. Elaine C. Kamarck and Jonathan Cowan, who commissioned the Autor/Wasserman study for the think tank, Third Way, confirmed just how dire the situation is getting.

"The growing disparity between men and women is easy to overlook given the fact that at the very top of our society, power and money is still overwhelmingly held by men. And yet, when we move to the realm of more ordinary people we see a tectonic shift. Over the last three decades, the labor market trajectory of males in the U.S. has turned downward along four dimensions: skills acquisition; employment rates; occupational stature; and real wage levels….These emerging gender gaps suggest reason for concern.

"First, because education has become an increasingly important determinant of lifetime income over the last three decades—and, more concretely, because earnings and employment prospects for less-educated U.S. workers have sharply deteriorated—the stagnation of male educational attainment bodes ill for the well-being of recent cohorts of U.S. males, particularly minorities and those from low-income households. Recent cohorts of males are likely to face diminished employment and earnings opportunities and other attendant maladies, including poorer health, higher probability of incarceration, and generally lower life satisfaction.

"Of equal concern are the implications that diminished male labor market opportunities hold for the well-being of others—children and potential mates in particular." This final point is one I will make throughout this book, from many different angles. Confronting our boy crisis is necessary for helping girls and women—not confronting it means greater suffering for girls and women throughout their life-spans. While a lot of good things have happened in the last five decades, especially in the erasure of gender role restrictions, male and female lives are interdependent—tens of millions of under-nurtured boys and men can erase many of our gains for women and girls, as well as place all of us in potentially grave danger.

Question: Are boys more fragile than girls?

Answer: Yes, in many ways, they are.

New research shows that a disadvantaged life affects the average boy in many profound ways more dangerously than it does the average girl—both in danger to himself and in danger to others. A study from the Northwestern University School of Education, headed by economist David Figlio and including Autor and Wasserman from MIT, analyzed brothers and sisters in 150,000 households in order to acquire comparative data.

Figlio and his team discovered that boys fared worse than girls who were raised in disadvantaged households. "Disadvantaged" was defined as possessing fewer physical, nurturing, and educational resources—for example, less food than an average home, or less discipline, or education, or less maternal or paternal attention. Boys ended up failing more completely than their sisters raised in exactly the same environments in all the markers of disadvantage, no matter their race or socio-economic level

Specifically, the males suffered more severe psychological issues, more mental illness, more dropping out, less college attendance, more getting into trouble and being imprisoned and, as a result of all of these, unable to get or sustain a job. The researchers concluded: "Boys are more sensitive than girls to disadvantage. Any disadvantage, like growing up in poverty, in a bad neighborhood, or without a father, takes more of a toll on boys than their sisters."

Economists Marianne Bertrand and Jessica Pan at the University of Chicago have studied the gender gap in child development extensively and echo the Northwestern findings. "Boys fare worse than girls in disadvantaged homes, and are more responsive than girls to parental time and resources... families that invest more in children are protective for boys."

Because of this new research, the suspicion that many of us have had anecdotally from our therapy practices has now been confirmed: boys do not have the neural and developmental fail-safes for social-emotional and cognitive development that girls have, on average, both in the female brain and in female development support systems to flourish when they are disadvantaged.

Not only are boys now behind girls in America in most

developmental and social success markers, but they are also more greatly disadvantaged in a society that does not recognize how troubled boys are and, thus, does not support the government, colleges, media, and families in focusing national resources on raising healthy sons.

To understand that boys are often more severely harmed by social disadvantage than girls is not to take away from the pain and suffering our daughters face, but making this point is crucial to seeing our invisible boys. While terrorists have killed approximately 5,000 adults and children in America in the last fifteen years, we've lost millions of boys in that same time to suicide, murder, despair, self-destruction, addiction, and immersion in lives and activities that lead them and others into harm's way. Millions of our sons are living with little or no purpose, failing to launch. Our troubled sons seek a mission in life but somehow end up in a basement without a job, few friends, and little skill to show for the privilege of being alive. These are the men becoming increasingly underemployed, driven away from college and higher education, escaping into drugs, alcohol, and pornography.

Boys aren't born this way. They don't start out in preschool saying, "I want to fail." They begin their lives wanting to become healthy men who care for their loved ones and serve their world. When we watch their toddler play we can see their innate beauty. Boys begin this life with an immense internal energy; they rush into the world to pursue life-goals of heroic character. They want to grow up ready to place their own meager resources into realms controlled by forces greater than themselves. These boys, brilliant creatures of human nature, begin their lives in love with life itself.

But our culture systematically neglects them. This was illustrated at a recent Helping Boys Thrive Summit® in Seattle. A school counselor, who is also the mom of two daughters, 14 and 11, and a son, 8, spoke out during the workshop. "Every system I turn to for boys—whether it is to help my own son or the boys in my school—seems equally lost. Someone puts a finger in a dam and puts off the flood for a day but then tomorrow another ten boys are suspended from school, another boy commits suicide, another one kills people, and countless others just seem to disappear into the woodwork."

I asked her if her school, configured as it is now, could help these boys.

"I hope so but we need more parents to rise up and create this revolution you're talking about because, frankly, there are a lot of social politics at play here. Last month I talked to my principal about 'the boy problem' and the principal was receptive, but then she said, 'Remember if we spend money on males in our school we'll get in trouble for not paying attention to gender equity. There's a lot more pressure now from Title IX and the Department of Education. We have to be very careful.'

"I said to her, 'Come on! We've done a gazillion things for girls since I've been at this school (fifteen years). It's not the girls who are failing, it's the boys!'

"She said, 'I know, I know.'

"That was it. I got no further. I think we're all stuck in an old way of thinking: that boys have it all and girls are victims. But just watch the news, just look at our school's data, just walk down the street. Our boys are in serious trouble."

Hundreds of people in that room—parents and professionals who care for both boys and girls—applauded and agreed. Nearly everyone working with boys raised their hands with stories of distress and none of these stories negated girls' sufferings and privations.

In thirty years of advocating for children, I am seeing a growing groundswell of these kinds of comments in the last decade. This is an important groundswell I hope to help you tap into with this book.

What You Can Do Right Now

With just this chapter in hand, you can now provide data and debate to people around you who do not see what is really happening with boys. You can join with friends and colleagues to invite speakers via your PTA; push your local media to do stories on male distress; respond to people accurately when they say simplistic things like, "It's girls who need our help, our boys have far too much already." I hope you will form "Helping Boys Thrive" teams of parents and community members that advocate for boys-friendly family life, schooling, counseling, and social programs.

I recently spoke at a university and met a courageous black woman, Dr. Felicia Washington, a psychologist and school administrator who said to the whole group during the Q & A: "Until you showed these statistics today I bought into the ideological concept that males are fine, females are worse off, and that if males are suffering it's only boys of color, not white males. But clearly, all boys aren't doing that well, and, to me, there's something else about that I think we have to face up to. If we keep using paradigms that say all white boys except a few misfits are doing well, it won't match what white people are experiencing, so we'll keep getting more of the extreme white male backlash. I even wonder if some of the new wave of racial hatred between whites and African Americans is rooted in this."

She was referring to a recent shooting of black males by white males in Missouri. "I mean, look, if you keep telling a group of males like white males that they're doing great but, in fact, their kids are not doing well, they can't get jobs, their marriages are falling apart…if you keep lying to a group, it's just human nature, their rage will grow. Sitting here today, I know it's weird to say, because it will require a whole shift in our national thinking, but I think we have to expand our ideology and our paradigms if we're going to really be called progressives, liberals, or even conservatives."

This is one of those comments in communities that feels revolutionary to me because it reveals our common ground—our children. They give us reason to build political bridges. Dr. Washington saw that we have not just *female issues* to solve but *a boy problem*, and not just a specific issue for *one* group of boys, but for *all boys*. She understood: once we push through political polarities, there is commonality.

Another person in the audience challenged Dr. Washington's assertion that white boys weren't doing so well. This audience member asserted, "How can you as a black woman say this? Caucasians are dominant. White cops are killing black males. Are you sure you want to come out on the side of the oppressor class and the dominant race and gender?"

Dr. Washington responded, "I think you might want to look at the Princeton study Dr. Gurian mentioned. I looked it up while he was talking. It is by economists Ann Case and Angus Deaton and published in November 2015 in the *Proceedings of the National Academy of Sciences*. It shows how careful we have to be from now on." Many people in the audience had access to the internet and so we all re-engaged with the study which shows that white males are now one of the fastest dying populations in our country. White American males are now experiencing depression, suicide and early death at rates startling to the researchers. In their commentary on the study, Dartmouth economists Jonathan Skinner and Ellen Meara wrote, "it is difficult to find modern settings with survival losses of this magnitude."

As we discussed this research we came to realize how important it is to go deep into all the nuances of what is happening to our males. Dr. Washington talked about how she, as a school administrator in a school in a predominantly white district, was seeing mainly failing white males in the principal's office. She concurred that boys and girls of color also failed, but that the great surprise for her over the last decade was the increase in white males in severe distress. The boy crisis involves race but also goes beyond race. It involves socio-economic status and also goes beyond money and power. It is a culture-wide denigration of hearts and souls of not just one group of males, whether black or white, poor or rich, but a denigration of males throughout a culture. This calamity needs a paradigm shift from those of us commissioned with caring for children, and I believe our country is ready for that shift. It is a shift we can actualize in large gatherings in our communities, and also one boy at a time. As I write this, the Trump Administration has just been inaugurated and joins a Republican controlled Senate and Congress at the top of our government. I plead with all of these federal policy makers and state governments to address the significant panoply of issues facing our boys and young men.

When Colin came into my office, I knew I had to help him move his life forward as a young male. He was an introverted, introspective, relatively silent adolescent American boy, well masked behind pain and armor. He was multi-ethnic, with a Hispanic mother from Mexico and a white father of Irish and Dutch descent. Some of the help I could give him would relate to his ethnic and racial origin; some would relate to his family's economic and social-emotional assets and situation. The common denominator in all of it would be, though, his gender.

Keeping his sex and gender in mind would be something I could do "*right now*" for this boy. From the moment I met him I made sure he knew I *saw* him as a *boy*. I related to him in ways that tend to work with *males*. Our time together, ultimately, helped him to become less invisible as a boy. He is now working in the high-tech field and has, in his mother's words, "turned out very well." This happened, I believe, because all of us—his family, his mentors, and Colin himself—set aside limited gender and cultural paradigms to save this son.

Because Colin wasn't very adept at using words to explain his deep distress—especially using words while sitting with his parents at their dinner table or sitting with a therapist in a chair in an office—I had to help him show his distress and develop his core self not just in words-for-feelings, but through innovations in actions, games, video clips, debates about current events and through his own storytelling. To this end I suggested he make videos of his daily life. I asked him to talk into video cameras (usually, his phone) to explain things to me and his parents at times of privacy when he felt safe, not overwhelmed at the dinner table or in my office.

His use of video was a new methodology by which to help him be *seen* as a boy and young man. And in no portion of therapy with him did I attack his need to develop his armor, his male self, or his masculinity. I helped him put them in context, but I supported them in him because they were a key to his future growth and health. This latter point is one of the nuanced points Dr. Washington was also trying to make.

Nearly everything we say about males today is more complicated than might be portrayed in some of our dominant cultural paradigms. For instance, our culture is highly focused on "removing masculinity" from male lives. Some of that is helpful, but much of our cultural obsession with focusing on "masculinity" as a theme rather than focusing on boys' deep needs across the lifespan, distracts us from really seeing what ails our American boys.

Something we can all do right now for our sons is to see through our cultural obsessions. To do this we'll have to confront our own masks, our own armor, and the Dominant Gender Paradigm that blinds us to a great deal of what boys and men really experience and who they really are.

Chapter 2

The Causes of Male Violence:
Confronting the Dominant Gender Paradigm

"Unsuspectedly from the bottom of the fountain... something bitter rises up: a touch of nausea, a falling dead of the delight, a whiff of melancholy, things that sound a knell, for fugitive as they may be, they bring a feeling of coming from a deeper region and often have an appalling convincingness."
—William James, Varieties of Religious Experience

AT THE END OF HER KEYNOTE AT the Women and Power Conference in 2014 the actor and activist Jane Fonda was asked by an interviewer to give a final comment to the audience. "I know we are going to talk about girls and women at this conference, but I have a grandson and I want to talk for a couple minutes about boys," Ms. Fonda said. Boys are having troubles, she noted, because they are being taught to disconnect feelings from their thinking (she pointed to her heart and then her head). They are told that feelings and emotions are for sissies. This masculine culture and masculine norming is destroying all of us, she warned, especially our vulnerable young boys "who can never be who they are because they live in fear of being shamed for having real feelings."

I watched Ms. Fonda with admiration. Bringing up the subject of boys at a women's conference was courageous but also quite appropriate, since women care as deeply about males as males do. And no one can dispute the fact that males often put on masculine masks, put other males down, don't express their emotions verbally as much as many girls do, that some boys are called sissies or wimps when they cry, and that a boy's feelings can get hurt. Fonda's implication that boys are more fragile than people may think was also very welcome.

I admired Ms. Fonda's comments, but watching the interview and hearing its content, my heart also sank. The sadness "from the bottom of the fountain" came up in me not from the protective and generous point made by Ms. Fonda but in the fact that this same point is generally the only major point about boys made by celebrities, government officials, and academics. Indeed, in that interchange and at that women's conference, it was the only point made, in phrases such as, "masculine culture represses boys' feelings," or "masculine norms and gender stereotypes harm boys and girls." The sadness rose up in me because this theme is the primary and sometimes only major theme explored in our academic institutions, governmental and legislative agencies, and media when "causes of male violence" or cause of other male distress is explored, studied, and reported. Even the loss of the American father, a loss our culture has just begun to awaken to, has its roots in our cultural obsession with needing to remove "masculinity" from the lives of children.

We will need to confront this "masculine stereotypes" obsession—what I call our Dominant Gender Paradigm—in the Big Three and in our own communities if we are to save our sons.

Confronting the Dominant Gender Paradigm: The Second Action-Step of Social Revolution

In a debate in a conference of male development leaders in Stockbridge, Massachusetts, in 1999 I first began to really see what I would later call "the Dominant Gender Paradigm" or DGP. This vision came when the feminist Carol Gilligan and I found ourselves equally compassionate for both genders, but not in sync with what is needed to help America's sons. In both my agreements and disagreements with Dr. Gilligan I felt resonance with the biologist E.O. Wilson who said, "I have been blessed by brilliant enemies." While I don't see anyone who cares about children—like Gilligan clearly does—as an enemy the Wilson phrase is important in gender issues. To be revolutionary, I must respect the differences, and the people who don't look at things the way I do, all the while seeing things for what they are.

My difference with Dr. Gilligan at that conference grew from her own, like Ms. Fonda's, adherence to this idea: "Our society is patriarchal, it is male dominant, its gender roles and masculine cultural norms 1) oppress girls and women by robbing them of equal power, and 2) rob boys of authentic and empathic life by giving them unearned privilege and repressing their emotions."

"So the culprit is masculinity," I asked her.

"Yes," she said emphatically. "Masculinity is a dangerous learned behavior that can't help but become toxic because it is based in unreasonable and dangerous gender stereotypes and patriarchal-masculine ideals of maleness. Because every parent, teacher, worker, and every boy and girl learns it, it is the root of our gender issues and must be deconstructed if we are going to empower our girls and help our boys mature into the men we want them to be."

Having been raised by feminist parents and educated in this paradigm, I understood it and saw its merit. I had been one of the sensitive boys, for whom the paradigm was, at times, protective. Talking with Gilligan and the others in the Stockbridge conference, I felt comfortable agreeing that there is definitely such a thing as "toxic masculinity" that can correlate with certain distresses in people and culture, including male violence.

But in my clinical practice and in my research and consulting I did not see *causation*. As I listened to my colleagues argue causation, I felt what William James talked about, a stirring from beneath the words.

Identifying the Dominant Gender Paradigm

I feel it even more now than I did then. Since 1999, the trend of linking male violence and nearly all male distress to "masculinity" has become entrenched in academic studies, government policies, and the media. Between 2005 and 2015, I conducted a 10 year meta-analysis of more than 4,000 current academic studies, governmental policy rationale, and media reports on male development. The majority—approximately two-thirds—presented causation in "the masculine role" or some form of the "masculinity" argument. Most analyses of other male failures besides violence, whether at work, at home, in school, and in society, reduced them to: "males are holding on to masculine privilege," or "male gender norms and gender roles create a climate or environment for…" This is an adherence to the Dominant Gender Paradigm that pretends to reveal causation for distress but cannot do so.

A powerful example of the DGP at work in academic study appears in Hanna Rosin's *The End of Men* (2013) in which the demise of men—loss of employment, parental alienation, loss of children in divorce, lack of maturation and motivation, fewer financial and personal assets, high suicide, and increased violence—is caused, in her view, by the fact that males are doggedly holding on to "masculine privilege." She offers no scientific proof for these assumptions but does find a number of like-minded experts to provide the same opinion. The result is a book that hopes to help men but does, for the most part, just the opposite—it presents boys, men, fathers, grandfathers, male workers, male bosses, and most males of our present era as inherently defective.

This kind of view, though applied more subtly, permeated a United Nations panel I served on in 2014. Experts were called together to discuss How to Prevent Male Violence Globally, especially violence against women. Every panel member from various developed countries, myself included, presented statistics on male violence rates in our countries—in each country, male violence had risen in the last five decades. When the issue of causation arose, most of the panelists implied or said outright that masculine norms and masculine systems caused the violence, especially in that these masculine norms inculcated violence against women by men, both in homes and in communities.

As you can imagine, I was the outlier in this conversation. I said, "I will only speak for the U.S., but as I interpret our statistics, during the last fifty years in which we've broken down most of our masculine social roles, we have an increasing not a decreasing epidemic of male violence." I provided an alternative analysis as to why this is—the multiple-systems and epidemiological approach—which I will provide in this chapter. But I sat alone in this approach and made little headway. Despite my delight that audience members from many countries and governments focused on male violence publically—especially male violence against women—I left the meeting with that "whiff of melancholy, things that sound a knell, for fugitive as they may be, they bring a feeling of coming from a deeper region," described by William James. The academics on the panel were locked into a very limited DGP.

Not surprisingly, very little tangible change that I am aware of came from that meeting. Political and ideological factions were satisfied that we had sufficiently targeted and condemned males and masculinity, but I believe little came from this U.N. meeting because its approach was not revolutionary. It was ruefully incomplete. Meanwhile, violence rates rise.

Another example of the DGP appeared in a recent *New York Times* article that quoted a public school counselor. The reporter asked the counselor, "Why do school boys fail in controlling their impulsiveness in comparison to girls?" The counselor did not present any scientific research or evidence; instead he quoted the paradigm that he has heard in his academic training: "Boys get a message from a very young age to be a man, and to be a man means you're strong and you don't cry and you don't show your emotions. I see boys suffering because of that, and a lot of that comes out in aggressive behaviors." Male impulsiveness, in this theory, is not caused by male body and brain (which are, as we'll explore in Chapter 3, naturally set up for more impulsiveness than girls) but instead is caused by boys being taught to become men.

A similar interaction often occurs when I'm contacted by the media. Very well-meaning and insightful reporters seeking expert research on why boys are violent bring up "gender norms," "codes of masculinity" or "toxic masculinity" as the cause of the male violence. I typically respond with something many reporters find either incendiary or impossible: "Yes, masculinity can become toxic, but masculinity training, gender roles, masculine norms, and gender norms play almost no role in causing the boys to kill innocent people."

There's often a gasp of disbelief as I continue. "We can't discuss causation, at least from my research, unless we discuss the holistic interconnection between *nature, nurture, and culture*. The 'masculine norms' paradigm is a culture-based paradigm that doesn't fully cover any of these other areas of causation and so we don't solve these problems."

Now a healthy debate begins. The reporter points out that "the violent boy or man who plants bombs in the Boston marathon, commits acts of terrorism on 9/11, shoots up a school or nightclub, or hits his wife is connected to some form of masculinity training, whether to a patriarchal religion (Jihadi Islam) that may prompt him in Boston, San Bernardino, or Orlando; or he is subject to the culturally-implanted idea that men are allowed to hit women in domestic violence cases; or as one academic put it to me recently: 'The pervasiveness of masculinity training in boys' lives in general causes boys to repress their feelings until those feelings, unexpressed and not understood, become violent.'"

I begin my response by agreeing, again, that some boys repress feelings in unhealthy ways. "In my own clinical practice," I say, "I've seen boys who cannot access their feelings except in anger or, in extreme cases, rage. But I'm saying that from a *causation* standpoint, the fact that a boy does not cry as much as a girl does not *cause* him to kill someone. The fact that he learned codes of masculinity from video games, media, or cultural icons doesn't *cause* him to develop a brain system that destroys his society."

Now I challenge: "Can you give me any proof that boys kill innocent people because they are taught a masculine role, or proof that masculine heroes, icons, and ideas cause boys to destroy the world and/or keep themselves immature, make themselves failures in the world, and cause them to harm the people they love?"

"Yes," a reporter often says, somewhat exasperated with me, "I've talked to a lot of experts who say exactly that." She continues, "Look, what the experts tell me is that it's similar to girls having eating disorders like anorexia and bulimia because of the constant bombardment by images of thin women in the media. In the same way, masculine roles and culturally pervasive images cause our boys to repress empathy and healthy development and this causes them to become immature, unmotivated, lost, and ultimately violent just like girls become sick because they aspire to be too thin."

I respond: "The comparison you've made isn't proof—in fact, just the opposite. Anorexia and bulimia are brain disorders caused by the interplay of genetics, trauma, neurotoxins, under-nurturance, and attachment stressors. While images of thin women are definitely not healthy for an anorexic to look at, looking at images of thin women does not *cause* a brain disorder. It's like alcoholism: the presence of alcohol in a room does not cause an addict to be addicted—addiction is genetically caused by DNA then physically caused by drinking itself. Social roles and fantasy images don't cause the brain disorder that leads to drinking or violence. One's masculine or feminine or other gender role—its pink or blue imagery, crying or not crying, heroes and villains don't cause violence."

In all these interactions, there is merit to all viewpoints and I remain respectful of the DGP used by my "enemy" but the whole paradigm, to some extent, feels to me like the story of the emperor with new clothes. The theory thinks it is wearing clothes of real causation but is actually, quite nakedly, empty of that necessary element of good theory. And while this theory of "masculine culture as the cause of male (and female) distress" can lead to good research and innovation, now, in a post-modern America, I believe we must come to grips with the fact that our dogmatic adherence to the DGP in the Big Three—academic writing, government and school funding, and media reporting—is actually harming our boys.

Why?

Because the theory has lulled us into thinking we have identified the single important cause of male distress when, in fact, our social issues go far deeper than "masculine norms," "gender roles," or "if boys and men cried more and talked about their feelings more we would have the American culture we want."

The Real Causes of Male Violence

To check my own research, data, and theory, I went from meta-analysis of academic studies and media reports to surveying parents, teachers, and mental-health professionals. I asked: "What do you believe are the causes of increased violence in the last two decades among American males?" I repeated the question a number of times via my own lecture audiences, and our Gurian Institute email lists and social media. I have received more than 8,000 responses that divide into 25 deep issues facing American boys:

- lack of available and active male and masculine role models in communities, especially to help single mothers raise their sons;
- lack of character and moral development for boys in our society;
- lack of an active, loving father in a boy's life, especially after a divorce/family court;
- physical abuse and child abuse and/or witnessing domestic violence;
- dysfunction in mother-son attachment or other early childhood distress;
- males returning from the Middle East wars severely damaged but getting little help from the health system;
- millions of males in the criminal justice system, especially minority males, without treatment, who come out violent when many did not go in that way;
- male rage at significant employment concerns, including the fact that even many of the most well-adjusted boys will not get jobs in the future, and will not be able to provide for families;
- racial tensions;
- significant economic and inner city/rural social issues, including gangs, poverty, and income inequality deepening between have and have-nots;
- lack of motivation and purpose among all socio-economic groups of boys "building up pressure in males" that turns to rage;
- increases in depression and other mental illness rates for males in the last three decades;

29

- decline in male school achievement, including the mismatch of schools with boys' learning styles; high suspension/expulsion of boys; high dropout and failure rates in pre-K through 12 and low college attendance; school-to-prison pipelines in inner cities;
- male chauvinism, sexism, misogyny, especially in domestic violence and rape against women where toxic masculinity and patriarchal gender-role pressure affect male/female relationships;
- increasing rates of ADHD diagnoses, autism spectrum issues, and other brain disorders, especially in the U.S., including the new AMA diagnosis of "violence" as a disease;
- substance abuse, drug use, gambling and sex addictions, alcoholism, alcohol use, binge drinking;
- gay and transgender boys constantly targeted for their difference by homophobic males;
- sexual abuse of males, especially by trusted family members and clergy, driving males to become sexually violent and/or commit suicide;
- general increase in male violence in the last decades reported by media and used as modeling by boys;
- masculine gender stereotypes, masculine norms, the masculine role that trains males to be dominant against others and repress their own feelings and empathy;
- bullying trauma, cyberbullying;
- lack of healthy rites of passage experiences for adolescent boys;
- exodus of boys and men from faith communities, thus less values training of boys by social systems;
- boys' natural aggression being villainized and pathologized in cultural institutions;
- the effects of technology in boys' lives, including violent gaming and the increased time spent in front of screens of all types.

This survey pointed out an even wider disconnection than I expected between the DGP in the Big Three and people's theories in the grassroots. Only two of the causes described by parents, teachers, and others in the grassroots are a direct fit with the DGP. Three can be stretched to fit, but most of the list deal with other causation than "toxic masculinity."

The paucity of connection between the grassroots experiences of our communities and what many people in our media, academics, and government tend to focus on, should alert us to something important. It is part and parcel of the institutional and society-wide blindness we discussed in Chapter 1. Most of the real suffering of our boys is invisible to us in part because we blind ourselves to the real lives of boys via an incomplete, flawed, yet constantly repeated gender paradigm.

The Provable Causes of Male Violence

Here is an alternative approach I hope you will use in your interactions with your children, your families, and the Big Three in your world. This is the "systems biology paradigm" that has come to be known by some people as Gurian theory or "nature-based theory" because it argues that nature, nurture, and culture are all crucial factors in gender development, with nature being foundational. This is a science-based approach to gender that is protective of both boys and girls. While its usefulness in broader contexts than aggression and violence will become clear in Chapter 3, here in Chapter 2 I'll focus on male violence as an extreme form of general male distress that has *three causes and one correlation* in the nature, nurture, and culture triumvirate. Into these causes and correlation, various sub-causes and correlations, such as the 25 mentioned in our Gurian Institute surveys, are bundled.

First Cause: *Genetic factors, including environmental neurotoxins attacking our genes.* These factors are found in both genetics and environmental toxicology research. Neurotoxins such as lead and aluminum in homes, BPH in plastics, artificial sweeteners, red dye, and monosodium glutamate in food, and endocrine disruptors in fertilizer, have been negatively affecting male gene expression over the last fifty years. This direct cause of male violence remains relatively under-studied or expressed in our Big Three social literature yet is wreaking havoc on male development and, thus, on our society as a whole. I will explore it with you in detail throughout this book.

Second Cause: *Nurture-trauma received in neurotoxic amounts by boys between birth and young adulthood.* These traumas include physical and sexual abuse, poverty, repeatedly witnessing violence, repetitive and dangerous bullying, head injury and repeated concussions, and other continuing negative stressors in social-emotional development. To become violent, generally, males will have experienced significant and repeated trauma to brain development at some point in their first decade and a half of life.

Third Cause: *Under-nurture of essential components of male development by nuclear, extended, and communal families.* Lacking a science-based understanding of males—but abhorring past patriarchal paradigms—we have systematically broken down neurodevelopmental scaffolding for males, including robbing them of fathers. Without fully realizing how profoundly this multi-faceted under-nurturance cripples male maturity and psychological health, our families and child-supportive institutions dramatically under-nurture males, causing many of our sons to be depressed and become violent.

Correlation: *Cultural stereotypes and gender norms.* This normative correlation requires other causes in tow and cuts two ways: 1) supporting the DGP (masculine cultural norms and gender stereotypes) idea for some males to whom masculine training is anathema; and 2) providing a newer anti-male stereotype (e.g. "men aren't needed," "males are defective," as in Rosin) that, either way, creates an anti-male climate. This climate shows up in misandry—"the hatred or dislike of males"—and andro-phobia—"the exaggerated fear of males." While the gender stereotypes in both of these normative correlations can indeed touch every male is some way, they are not causal of male violence without interconnection to one or more of the other three causes.

Because these four elements are biologically and socially interconnected, we can't solve male violence with the DGP. We can only solve it with *multiple systems thinking* that deals with all four elements together. In other words, we can no longer push one single theory (e.g. "masculine norms cause males to be violent"). We must deploy more scientific rigor and more provable scientific evidence, which makes the revolutionary gender challenge before us a challenge of deep importance to every boy. When we hear DGP adherents like Ms. Fonda or Dr. Gilligan or the school counselor or reporter claim that the DGP explains boys—and even when we hear them say, "Wait a minute, the DGP is in fact systems thinking because the masculine system permeates every system"—we can notice the merit of the correlation but also point out the flaw in causation.

Throughout the rest of this book, we will make the correction toward a systems-biology and multiple systems approach. We will use this new thinking in the nitty gritty of raising, educating, and mentoring boys.

Simultaneously, I will help you marshal its multiple assets in ways you can use to gradually convince academics, our government and schools, and our media to go deeper into real male life. This combined effort will give us more political clout for programming and funding to help males in the same way we have been able to marshal those forces to aid us in championing female development: It was only when we took multi-systems approaches to girls and women—setting aside old patriarchal stereotypes and gender norms—that we came fully to the aid of female equality and our girls and women.

Question: How do I become a citizen scientist?

Answer: Develop your own in-house research.

Almost fifty years ago, Albert Einstein said, "Science should not be left to scientists." He was not denying the genius of a scientist—rather, he posited that science should not remain in the laboratory. Even people who are not scientists can model from scientific study to create studies and experiments of their own. So that you can confront the Dominant Gender Paradigm in your world, help end male violence, and help your sons thrive, I encourage you to become a "Citizen Scientist." Because you're a parent or mentor of children, you have access to "a laboratory" for multiple-systems thinking and you have a plethora of "laboratory subjects." You can volunteer at your children's school and study the children there. You can observe your children's play time, car pool conversation time, chores and work time, media time, bedtime, study time. You can see how your kids interact on the playground with each other as four-year-olds then move some of their social life to interactive video games as fourteen-year-olds. You can study how their hormones make them seem somewhat "crazy" in adolescence while their growing brains make them almost mature for glorious moments before they revert again to childhood. Wherever you travel, in whatever you do, there are boys and girls, and women and men—all can be your test subjects.

To become a citizen scientist of gender—males, females, and the whole gender spectrum—you need a keen eye, a yellow pad or new document in your computer, and access to the Internet. You can use the three causes and one correlation as your own starting point for analyzing males—not only why they become violent, but nearly every other aspect of male distress, as we will do in Chapter 3. All the while, citizen science among your own children is a very rewarding bonding experience. When your kids are asleep or out of your care, it continues beyond observation. Because of the Internet, citizens like you can even do "personal meta-studies" of hundreds of scholarly and clinical studies in your own living rooms.

I have personally participated in citizen science for three decades. Over a period of a year, for instance, while my first daughter, Gabrielle, was between 2 and 4 years old and I was writing various sections of *The Wonder of Boys*, I replicated the now famous "dolls and trucks" experiment in our father-daughter playtime. On one occasion I vividly remember, I sat on the floor with her and asked, "What if we bring this truck over here, Gabrielle?" moving a yellow truck from the floor over to my right into the array of dolls between us. This truck, three inches long, was part of a set of two Mack trucks and two Mustang cars I had bought for two purposes: first, to encourage Gabrielle (then Davita) to play with trucks and, thus, avoid gender stereotypes that might keep girls out of professions; second, to test my nature-based gender theory.

After she said, "Sure," I moved the truck while asking her what we should do with it. She pondered the question with a crinkling forehead then offered me a trade, lifting a curly haired Ainsley out of the nest of dolls to give to me with her left hand while she took the truck in her right. "I think I'll name the truck Larry," she said as she put a doll, Sarah, into the truck bed. Happy with the fit, she smoothed Sarah's dress neatly into place. I combed Ainsley's hair and watched Gabrielle drive the doll-laden truck toward the pile of Legos to her left.

"Where's Sarah going?" I asked.

"To school, Larry's taking her."

"That's great. I bet she'll really like school," I smiled.

Now came the next part of the experiment. Setting Ainsley down to my right, I picked Winnie the Pooh and Chewbacca out of the array of dolls. As Sarah arrived at school and Gabrielle lifted her carefully out of the truck, I swatted Winnie and Chewbacca together with my hands.

"Daddy, don't!" Gabrielle cried as the two dolls made a kind of muffled slapping sound.

I continued smashing the dolls together as if I hadn't heard my daughter's plea.

"You'll hurt them!" Gabrielle grabbed at the dolls, getting them away from the misguided father.

Having had a brother two years older, Phil, and remembering our own playtime with dolls and trucks, you can imagine my personal comparison of playtime between brothers and between sisters (or fathers and sons and fathers and daughters) with these play objects. For a male growing up in the sixties and seventies, GI Joe, Superman, Batman, and Fantastic Four figures were as sacred to me and my brother as my daughters' dolls were to them. But we loved these toys a bit differently. Phil and I spent more of our object-bonding time swatting action figures and dolls together, throwing them at one another or up in the air, pulling them apart to peer inside them, battling them against (and, thus, with) one another, and then leaving them strewn on the floor to be battered and experimented on the next day. The hair of most of our dolls did not exist to be quietly combed but to be caked with mud.

Even more mysteriously to me in my years as a young philosopher and father, I remembered that wherever we traveled in the world as boys, whether to Hawaii, Minnesota, India, Wisconsin, Wyoming, Colorado, New York, Washington, Israel, or Turkey, girls we met did what I later saw Gabrielle and Davita doing: they spent more time talking relationally with their objects of play. Despite the fact that Phil and I were raised and socialized by our parents and their community to be more like girls in our doll play than many boys were (our parents, a sociologist and anthropologist, were first wave feminists who guided us to "nurture" dolls as much as possible because they wanted their boys to be gentle and talkative about feelings), and despite the fact that Phil and I gained a great deal of good from this effort—still, even as little boys in India we did not put as many verbalized feelings into our doll play as girls did.

Over the last thirty years, I've asked tens of thousands of parents and teachers to replicate these and many other experiments and thus provide "data" on their children, their students, and their communities. In the field of gender study, parents and professionals like you, in the trenches, can help academics, governmental officials, and the media push through encrusted and ideological gender theories by developing your own version of this citizen science that is called, in academic circles, "wisdom of practice" research.

Without realizing it, you have already begun doing this wisdom of practice research in our first chapter. When you looked at national and international statistics and then compared your son and the boys around you to those statistics, you began your own "meta-analysis" of American boyhood. Take it further, now, as you read the rest of this chapter and this book. Analyze children around you to see what is really happening in their lives—and if they are in distress, what exactly is causing their distress.

The Epigenetics of Male Aggression and Male Violence

Regarding male violence in particular, your citizen science and wisdom of practice research will prove that for males to become violent there must be an epigenetic attack on their brains, both from within (their cells, genes, hormones, and neurochemistry) and from without (via brain injury, neurotoxins, abuse, trauma, or under-nurture of the brain). One of these attacks, alone, may not create a violent male, but two or more will raise the likelihood, and three or four combined raises the likelihood significantly.

A great deal of this understanding—and the multiple systems thinking we must use to fully accomplish it—we have gained via research in neuroscience and genome mapping that post-dates the inception of the Dominant Gender Paradigm. Scientific research in brain development has entered our public consciousness most powerfully in the last twenty years and genome mapping in the last ten. The field of genetics and, recently, epigenetics (the study of changes in organisms caused by modification of gene expression rather than alteration of the genetic code itself) is only just now available for citizen science.

But it *is* now available and the rest of this chapter will explore its impact on your son with you, especially as regards aggression and, if he is experiencing it, violence. It is important to note that fifty years ago, without understanding the genome or the human brain, it was logical to construct a Dominant Gender Paradigm in which "male" is a social construct and "nature" meant "reproductive organs and physical body." We did not yet understand the complexity of who, specifically, males and females are. We could not yet be sure that masculine stereotypes cannot cause male violence, nor that multiple causes were needed for a boy to become psychotic and shoot up a school or murder his family or other community members. Now we do know this and your citizen science can prove it.

Environmental Toxicology and the First Cause

As you study all of this in your neighborhood and community, a startling and fundamental place to begin is with environmental toxicology. I will first mention this field in this chapter on aggression and violence but it will come back up throughout the rest of this book. It holds significant answers to a number of questions we all have about what is happening with males in the new millennium.

Environmental toxicology is a burgeoning field of multi-systems scientific research connected to the field of genetics. Since 2003, it has become increasingly possible for parents and professionals to participate in this field and thus gain insight into their own families. With my own counseling clients and to my lecture audiences I implore families facing any kind of difficulty with a child's development to send away for genetic tests in order to become a scientist of your child's (and your own) genome because many aspects of the genome have been mapped and many complex portions—those that apply to the workings of the human brain—are being mapped as you read this book. We know now that while our genes are not our destiny, they possess an initial template for that destiny if they can be safely expressed in their families and environments.

You've seen it already in your children: one of your children is innately good at math and another not so good, one started reading at four and loves books while another started at six and may prefer a more physical life; one is naturally empathic and emotional while another is not as emotionally generous. Talent, personality, temperament, gender…there is a basis for each or them in our children's genes and most parents see it in their children.

Question: How does the social movement that says gender is all a matter of how we think about it—not binary or fixed between "male" and "female"—affect what we're saying about genetics and gender?

Answer: How individuals feel about their gender is an emotional and personal assessment of their gender identity while sex (male and female) exists in both body and brain—this is even the case, as we'll explore further in Chapter 3, with transgender individuals who have a body/brain disconnection (a more female brain in a male body, or more male brain in a female body).

In the context of the Bruce/Caitlin Jenner gender transformation, many of our Gen Z kids and their parents are experimenting with ideas like "there is no gender" or "we're all transgender in some way" or "gender identity is a free choice, not innate, so it would be just gender stereotyping to have toys for girls and toys for boys." These sorts of experiments are very valuable, actually. Even though they comprise a social trend rather than a full scientific reality, they reveal the gender spectrum—everyone can feel as they feel about where they fit in "male" and "female." These feelings matter and the right to feel these feelings must be protected in our children and adults.

Meanwhile, tens of thousands of clinical, neural, and genetic studies have proven that the male and female brain do differ profoundly, as we'll explore further in Chapter 3. As a citizen scientist, you can study your children (and spouse and friends) to see what you think about "male" and "female." As toy companies experiment with not having gendered toys, you may well end up saying, as I have, "Give it a few years. When the Gen Z kids grow up and have kids of their own, they'll look for the toys their boys and girls want, but all the while, how interesting and valuable our human freedom is."

Each of your child's genes—their DNA—comingles adenine, cytosine, guanine and thymine in combinations that repeat one or two or thousands of times. The repetitions are largely responsible for the talent sets, personalities, temperaments, and gender of the child (even including exceptions to "gender rules" noted in the Box). The exact repetition of these chromosomal elements also causes specific diseases via both a pre-destined genetic cause and/or an interaction of the gene combinations with the child's or adult's environment and intimate, daily world.

For example, one of your children but not the other may have certain combinations of the adenine and the other three elements that ground a genetic predisposition to a physiological illness such as cancer, heart disease, obesity, or hemochromatosis, or brain disorders like ADD/ADHD, schizophrenia, bi-polar, and others. Meanwhile, in many cases, even in the child with that DNA combination, that combination may not lead to the actual illness or at least not until your child is an aging person, because despite the genetic predisposition, the genetic markers in your child didn't get triggered in the child's biological, personal, and social environment. This is epigenetics at work—many of our genes and gene combinations remain dormant unless triggered. But sometimes, no matter what we do to protect the child, the markers get triggered. Autism is one of the best researched examples of this form of gene expression. Scientists have identified more than 65 genes such as the MECP2 gene that can play a part in an autism spectrum disorder (ASD). Because of this gene expression and these genetic mutations, it's highly likely that, no matter what his parents do when this child is a baby, he'll show some form of ASD.

Why?

In 2007, biologist Michael Wigler of Cold Spring Harbor Laboratory and geneticist Jonathan Sebat of UC – San Diego discovered, "*De novo* mutations linked to ASD in the form of copy-number variants—

alterations in chromosomes that involve the deletion or duplication of whole chunks of DNA—that can affect multiple genes." These *de novo* mutations on the genes give the ASD brain low density social-emotional pathway development—the hallmark of ASD—via mutations triggered pre-birth by as little as a single-nucleotide variant on the child's DNA, which can raise the child's risk of ASD by 20 to 80 times. Dr. Wigler and his colleagues know of no children with these variants who don't have ASD.

Practical Value of Genetics Research to Your Children

As regards boys' behaviors in particular, looking at the genetics, epigenetics, and environmental toxicology (study of gene-affecting toxins in the boys' environment) can be life-saving. A parent of a boy in my clinical practice could tell, as I could, that talk therapy was not working. In talking with the boy and his family I began to suspect epigenetic involvement and environmental toxicology. Her son, no matter what we said or what new family practices were instituted, further acted out, became increasingly and excessively angry, even more aggressive than a year before, and on one occasion, violent—hitting a sibling in rage. The boy was seeing a psychiatrist and was on medication but I also guided the family to seek epigenetic wisdom from a naturopath or other similar professional.

This mom and dad went online to study epigenetics and environmental toxicology as citizen scientists. They also scheduled a series of visits for the boy with a naturopath who helped the family—through trial and error with eating habits—to discover a "gut-brain" connection (this is a popular term for the chemical and cellular reactions that transpire between digestion and neurochemistry). This connection was distorted in this boy via foods and food allergies, throwing off all of his neurochemistry.

Once this discovery was finally made, a lightbulb went off in this mom's mind. She remembered someone else in the boy's genetic line, his great uncle, who had needed significant diet and nutrition changes when he was in his twenties. She called the uncle who told her he had cut out sugar and artificial sweeteners and it changed his life back in the 1990s. This inspired her to help her son keep from eating these foods because they comprised neurotoxins—poison to the cells and the brain of the boy. "He is a different person now," she told me with tears in her eyes.

"He isn't angry all the time and he's doing better in school. He's such a good boy now."

Your son's male journey is his own male journey—his genes and brain are unique. If your son is facing any kind of rage, depression, anxiety, school failure, hyper-aggression, or social isolation, talk-therapy may not be enough. In helping parents of boys who have become angry, withdrawn, hyper-aggressive, or violent, my first question is, "Has there been physical or sexual abuse or other repeated trauma?" Then my next questions involve the study of environmental toxicology.

Here are a few of them.

- What do you know about his genome, genetics, gene mapping, and epigenetics?
- Have you looked at the effects of neurotoxins on his brain before?
- Has your son ingested alcohol or drugs before becoming aggressive or violent?
- Have you looked at the possible presence of food allergies?
- Does he drink a lot of pop, eat a lot of junk food and artificial sweeteners, and/or eat a lot of refined sugar?
- Does he eat a lot of white flour (gluten)?
- When does he eat, how much protein, how much diet balance in the various food groups?

Especially if he has become aggressive or violent I also question whether he has had an automobile or other accident or played sports, like soccer or football, in which he experienced any kind of head or concussive injury.

This whole battery of genetic and neuroanalysis as well as environmental toxicology inquiry is citizen science that comprises, to me, a "new plan" for raising both boys and girls. While it does not answer all questions, to avoid doing this for our boys, especially if they have become violent or hyper-aggressive, is to deny them the assets of new science, assets that can directly speak to the first and second causes of violence and hyper-aggression which involve the neurochemical and epigenetic relationship between a boy's testosterone-based, genetic biology and his potentially traumatic or toxic environment.

Why is Violence a Predominantly Male Disease?

Both boys and girls can suffer head injuries, be otherwise traumatized in their upbringing, and ingest neurotoxins, so why are most physically *violent* people males?

In some part the answer lies in the Y/male genetic template in which aggression is normal for gene expression. "Male testosterone goes to the brain in late prenatal life," Melvin Konner of the Department of Neuroscience and Behavioral Biology at Emory University has noted, "and prepares the hypothalamus and amygdala for a tendency to physical aggression."

Genetically formed testosterone expression is so clearly "male" that transgender identification for Olympic athletes is tied to testosterone levels. For a male-to-female person to be identified as female in the Olympic protocols she must prove that her testosterone levels are below a "male" level. Testosterone doesn't cause male violence but it is the ground of male and female aggression.

One reason we do not say testosterone, an aggression neurochemical, *causes* violence is this: while violence can correlate with naturally or artificially high testosterone in one of the males you know, it can also be linked to low testosterone levels in another male—especially one who is depressed, socially anxious, or psychopathological. For centuries, parents who've raised their two or more children in the same way have seen one child become more aggressive or, in some cases, more violent than the other.

Before going any further, let's define our terms. By "aggression," I mean the human activity of challenging and manipulating others and the environment; by "violence" I mean the human activity of attempting to kill others or cause severe harm to another person's body or core-self. Violence can be justified in wartime, for instance, but it's still primarily abnormal human behavior while aggression is generally within the range of normal human behavior.

Testosterone does cause male aggression levels to be higher than female, but it is not the "cause" of male violence, as we've noted earlier—there are three primary causes of that violence, but the amount of testosterone in males, coupled with other causes, will tend more males to violence than females, whose testosterone levels (thus their physical aggression baseline level) is generally lower than males.

The American government began to look carefully at male violence in 1983 when the Centers for Disease Control and Prevention mandated the study of violence in the U.S. as a potential epidemiologically caused disease. Three years later, the Violence Epidemiology Branch (VEB) was integrated into the Division of Injury Epidemiology and Control (DIEC). Now, following decades of research by these and other agencies, the American Medical Association in 2009 altered its protocols to name "violence" as an epidemiological disease—meaning, it is caused by both genetics and environment.

Their work and other studies have shown that ragged edges on the Y and other chromosomes can set some males up for violence. These males can be raised in the same family and same circumstances as siblings, yet they become violent and their siblings don't. New research, featured in *Nature Neuroscience* in 2014, found that "violent genes" can be passed down from generation to generation. Isabelle Mansuy of the University of Zurich along with her colleagues discovered that the offspring of male mice who were more violent than normal mice passed those genes to their children via micro-changes in RNA in the father's sperm.

This is a discovery with importance for every parent and every citizen. It tells us that we must absolutely deepen our understanding of male development—and alter the limited paradigms we use—right away. To keep saying that "masculinity" causes violence is to specifically not study epidemiological and toxicological causation for violence, and thus, perpetuate a cycle of violence and distress into the next generation.

The mom who discovered the gut-brain issue in her son became a citizen scientist who was able to marshal forces around her to learn the exact epidemiological cause of her son's anger, aggression, and violence. She, her family, and the professionals caring for her son most likely saved this boy's life and future. They may also have saved the lives and futures of others who, years later, this boy might have harmed.

Aaron and the Weight

How young is too young to start looking at boyhood aggression epigenetically? There is perhaps no age too young, as long as we look carefully—without seeing violence when it isn't there but also, simultaneously, seeing what is there.

Aaron was a six-year-old boy whose mother and father asked me to help them understand why he was so physically aggressive with his sister and other children. His parents worried that he was becoming a violent male because one of his teachers had complained about his "pushing and shoving," and a "tendency to hit and not say he was sorry." She had asked the parents to "alter the masculine stereotyping that he seems to be learning. It's making him violent," she said. As Aaron's mother told me about the teacher's view, she was clearly worried that the teacher was right about the toxic masculinity: "Is it possible he's picking up masculine norms from his dad who's so playful and masculine, and then they're making him so aggressive? What if he becomes a violent male? This scared me to death."

After determining that Aaron had not been abused or traumatized and was well-attached and well-nurtured, I suggested that I come to his home to look at his home environment to interact with him there rather than in my office. His parents readily agreed and I drove to his home on a warm day in late May. The flowers were out, a breeze played on green leaves, and my window was open as I enjoyed the sun. In a strange coincidence the classic rock radio station I listened to played "The Weight" by The Band. This song's chorus is: "Take the load off Annie, take the load for free, take the load off Annie, put the load right on me." As I drove, the song resonated because of what I knew about this boy, Aaron.

From talking with his parents in an office visit already, I knew I would meet a "high testosterone" boy with lots of energy. He was too young to be surging with actual testosterone (puberty would bring that) but higher than normal testosterone surges in utero most likely wired him for some of the behavior his community was now seeing. This behavior included his parents' comments that he was "so physical," "so energetic," and "so aggressive." Other wonderful parts of Aaron's self were also at work. His parents said, he was "the sweetest kid," "very compassionate, when he wants to be," and "very loving." So I sensed I would meet a boy filled with aggressive "boy energy." If I was right, it would show up in ways that confused parents and teachers and, yet, it would also ground this future man's ability, later in life, to take the load off others and put the load on himself. Many high energy, high testosterone males are some of the most self-sacrificing men around—for example, our soldiers in wartime. It did not surprise me to learn that the boy's father had been a soldier.

In this context I went to the house ready for anything—including a different kind of boy than I expected. When I arrived, I saw a 6-year-old male who was 15 pounds heavier than normal for his age, and 3 to 5 inches taller than average. That he was a big boy wasn't surprising since his father was 220 and 6'2" and his mother, 5'11", both having been college athletes. Aaron shook my hand and smiled very politely as I sat down with him and his parents in the living room.

A few seconds into the adult conversation, Aaron began to walk, pace, and jump up on the couch. His mother, embarrassed, told him to stop and sit down and apologized to me for his behavior. I said it was no problem. In fact, I was glad it happened because of its instructiveness. We were all engaged in citizen science in those moments though we never said it. For instance, when his father said in a firm voice, "You're just trying to get attention, sit down!" Aaron did so, but a minute later he was up and moving again so I decided to take the science into his bedroom by asking him to show me his room. I saw all his bouncing as attention-getting but without malice—it was his own aggressive (and very functional) way of saying to us adults: "I'm the one you're talking about, so please let me into this discussion!" While he didn't have the consciousness at his age to say this in words, he was saying it nonverbally in a kind of physical and kinesthetic communication males tend to be masters at, even when we, who prefer words, just feel like the boy is driving us nuts.

Glad to be moving around, he led me down a hallway to a small bedroom, around 10 by 15 with a twin bed, shelves, a small desk, a television, and a maroon I-pad on the bed. Action figures, stuffed animals, dolls, and games were stacked along walls and in colored plastic boxes. His mom or dad had clearly instructed him to clean things up for my visit, but within moments of our play on the floor, the room became a disaster area again. And while I let Aaron lead me in playtime, he bumped into me many times, stepped on my hand accidentally, and nearly hit me in the eye with a plastic Spiderman figure.

Using the superhero play as a foil, I asked him questions and received, sometimes, full answers. Other times, I received silence.

I asked: "So, Aaron, your parents told me you bump into people a lot at school…is that right?"

He paused for a moment of silence which I took for embarrassment. "Yes, I guess so."

"Do you do it because you're angry at the other kids?"

"No." He frowned as if I was a bit stupid to think so.

"Do you do it because other boys or men do it?"

This complex question got only a frown (which would be normal for a 6-year-old).

"Do you do it because Superman does it?"

"I don't know."

"Do you think there's something wrong with you when you bump into people and jump on them so much?"

"I guess so."

"Why do you think you do it?"

Silence.

"Is it like your dad said, to get attention?"

Silence.

"Do you know what that means?"

"Sure. So people will look at me."

"Right. Very good. Is that why?"

"No."

"Then why?"

"I don't know."

"It just happens," I suggested.

"Yeah. It's no big deal."

"But it's a big deal to the other kids. I heard you've made a few kids cry when you push them."

"Yeah." His face showed regret.

After about a half hour into our interaction, I felt sure that there was nothing at all wrong with this boy in a social-emotional sense nor that his aggression was caused by a cultural factor, like masculine norms. I suspected that he was a boy who was hard-wired by genetics and biochemistry to need a different kind of assistance—one based further within, at a cellular level—than his present social institutions gave him.

"Your folks told me you don't like to say you're sorry when you knock into people. Is that right?"

Silence.

"Why not?"

Silence.

"Does it make you sad to say you're sorry?"

"Yeah."

"Why?"

"I don't know."

"Is it because you don't think you've done anything wrong?"

"Yeah. Yeah."

"But pushing another kid to the ground is wrong, isn't it?"

"But we're just playing!"

"So it's not wrong."

"It's wrong if I hurt him but I don't hurt people."

"What about your sister? You made her cry the other day."

Pause. Silence. "Yeah, that was wrong."

"So it's wrong sometimes to push someone to the ground."

"Yeah. But I don't hurt people most of the time."

We continued playing and talking then I thanked him for his time. He remained in the room and I returned to meet with his parents. They asked me for my thoughts. I assured them there was nothing wrong with their son but also asked that they get emails from the teachers on what specific things Aaron did and what time of day they happened. I explained that I needed both the parents and the teachers to become "scientists" of Aaron's behavior; I also asked the parents if they would look at having Aaron do some genetic and blood tests. I said, "I think you'll discover some very interesting things."

Over the next week they researched genetic testing through a local psychologist who utilizes the blood-based studies of the Walsh Institute in Chicago, as well as other genetic assets. The tests revealed genetic vulnerabilities in the way Aaron processed gluten and sugar. Emails back from teachers about the times of day when Aaron seemed "especially aggressive" were also instructive. Sugar, it turned out, was an environmental toxin for this boy, just as it had been for Colin. It poisoned him by making him even more impulsive and aggressive at two ends of a spectrum: when his sugar level was high, right after eating sugared cereal in the morning, for instance, then going to school and pushing and shoving and when he "crashed" (as the sugar left his bloodstream) making it much more difficult for his brain to control his impulses and learn cognitive lessons, which in turn frustrated him and led to more physical aggression.

His parents took him off sugar. They also took him off foods with artificial sweeteners and red dye in them. Within a month of instituting these environmental and nutritional changes, Aaron's parents and teachers agreed that his behavior was significantly improved. Aaron himself could feel the difference in his own happiness.

Meanwhile, I had also asked the parents to try some environmental changes. Because Aaron was prone to more physical aggression than many other boys, he needed more physical space around him than some other boys might, so I asked his parents if they would consider moving him to a larger room. They loved the idea. I also asked them to concentrate on sending him outside to play more than they had before. They saw the logic of this. Joining with this strategy, I suggested his parents remove the TV from his room and curtail his screen time in general.

As the family made changes to both what he took into his body/brain and where he lived his life, I wrote an email to Aaron's teacher that the parents forwarded. In that email I requested that recess specifically not be taken away from Aaron when he did something in the teacher's mind that would qualify as "misbehavior." I explained that he needed physical space, the outdoors, the "spatial time" (playing with balls and other physical objects) to move his energy through his body and his brain. Sitting inside during class time and then getting no physical time because of recess-deprivation made things worse for Aaron and for his teacher and school. And I reassured his teacher and his parents that there was no proof for the causal assumption that Aaron was in danger of becoming a violent child because of masculine norming.

When I went back to his house two months later Aaron reported, "I told my sister I was sorry." He remembered our conversation and was working internally to self-manage, to learn, to grow, and to do the right thing.

Aaron is 12 now and not violent. He is still more aggressive than many of his peers but his parents now understand where he fits on the genetic spectrum, and how much of that is hard-wired into him.

"He's still a big awkward kid," his mother reported to me recently, "but his teachers love him. We have really focused on making sure he is with teachers who understand his 'boy energy.' I feel sort of weird that I let myself label him back then as some kind of bad boy or bad masculine guy. I can see now that we just didn't understand him."

Like so many boys who are not understood and whose male energy doesn't fit a DGP school paradigm, Aaron and his aggression were being labeled defective with vague causation that had little to do with his life. Because the caring people in Aaron's nurturing systems didn't see him from the inside out, they could only see him as defective, and label him a bad, too-masculine, pre-violent guy.

In reality, however, this big awkward boy possessed, like all children, an internal "map"—his nature—that required his environment to see, understand, and subtly shift to *nurture that nature*. Once his nurturing environment made those shifts, the "weight" of incompetence and failure he felt as a little boy was lifted off Aaron, his family, and his school. He now has the best chance to grow into one of those men who will gladly make the sacrifice of carrying the weight of others on himself as a father, husband, partner, friend, and employee or leader.

Epidemiology vs. Ideology

If our first step of revolution is to vastly increase human awareness about the struggles of boys, our second step involves deepening our understanding of where that struggle begins—its real origins and deepest sources. To that end, I hope you will foment a revolution on behalf of boys by confronting ideological single-mindedness with your own call for more epidemiology, epigenetics, and environmental toxicology research.

And I hope you will get your own children tested as needed. You will need to do this with the help of psychiatrists, geneticists, naturopaths, physicians, or others professionals who can help connect you with businesses such as 23andMe, Alpha Genomix, and others. You can also discover these businesses online. As you and the professional interpret the genomic information, you will be using a powerful tool for understanding the nature-based map your son (or daughter) has brought into this world.

Overall, I hope you'll encourage others around you, including people who have power over your children's daily life, to expand their conversation much farther into male nature, toxicology, trauma science and the etiology of male and masculine under-nurturance than our ideological approaches to male aggression/violence have allowed. In advocating for a new plan for understanding boys, we will need to seek ways to convince violent males to allow scientists to study them. School shooters, for instance, generally fit a profile but we still have little or no biological data to help us understand the genetic, epigenetic, and toxicological backdrop of that profile.

I first learned this over a five-year period, 1999 to 2004, when I was asked to assess the profiles of school shooters. One of the reporters who provided profiles to me nuanced her request this way: "We're unfortunately very accustomed to inner city and minority males killing one another but these are now white males committing the violence, so we may need a different paradigm than hyper-masculine gangs in inner cities. Is it trauma like bullying that makes these white guys so violent? Is it the loss of the father? Is it violent video games? What is it?"

I learned from the psychological profiles that many of the school shooters had experienced sex abuse trauma and bullying. At the same time, many had not.

Many had distant or absent relationships with father; however, many had normal father-son relationships.

Many had been under-nurtured in some way and some played a lot of video games, but some had not and did not.

Some had been raised with strong masculine norms but most had not and very few of the boys seemed to have been exposed to toxic masculinity.

And many of the shooters had siblings who had been raised in the same way with the same family and school but the siblings had not become violent.

While the profiles gave some clues to the "why" of male violence we are facing in our society—availability of automatic weapons, social isolation of the males, bullying and abuse trauma, among other factors— we will need to go much farther into studying this male disease from a genetic/mental illness standpoint than we have. This will require moving the Dominant Gender Paradigm aside and instituting a multi-system epidemiological approach. Private and public funding will need to emerge that facilitates this study, but we do not yet have enough groundswell of public pressure to support deeper analysis of boys and men.

However, I believe a passion for this study is growing. There are millions of Aarons out there whose parents are seeing their normal boys misdiagnosed as potentially violent and pathologized. These parents want more information and may be open to genetic analysis. Similarly, parents of the mentally ill, especially those who become violent, are impatient for greater insight into their sons' psyches than culture-causation provides.

Utilizing the Prison Laboratory

Some of that insight will come to us, I believe, from studying our prisoners, if they will let us. Here's why. When I visited a maximum security prison in the Midwest ten years ago during a consulting assignment, I met with a number of prisoners in group settings. I asked them for their opinions as to why they had become violent. Two of the ten said, "I think I was born that way." Others detailed child abuse, lack of father, substance abuse, poverty, and parental abandonment or neglect.

I also asked them what part they thought masculine stereotypes played in their behavior. One of them said, "You mean crying or not crying, that kind of thing?" That's a part of it, I agreed. This group of ten maximum security prisoners, each of whom had committed violent acts, said they had openly cried in group therapy and in chapel. When I talked with the group therapists there we discussed the inadequacy of the idea that "boys not crying is what causes them to be violent," or "boys not talking about feelings cause violence" or similar "masculine norms" stereotyping. We agreed as therapeutic professionals that talking about feelings and crying is a powerful therapeutic strategy, and that some men who lack these skills are violent, but it was clear to all the professionals in this prison that masculine norming promoting "lack of crying/feeling-talk" did not determine the violent outcomes of these men.

One of the therapists in that prison was an immigrant from Japan who had been in a lot of trouble as a juvenile, righted his ship, and became a therapist specializing in hard cases. He provided a fascinating take on the lack of proof for the idea that masculine norms create or cause violence. In Japan, he noted, masculine norming in video games and comic books include constant violent imagery of violent males at levels even more pervasive, in many cities, than in the U.S. There is also a great deal of traditional masculine/feminine role development in many parts of Japan, and many if not most Japanese boys and men are shamed for crying or talking about feelings. But Japan's murder rate, he accurately noted, is almost nonexistent while the American murder rate is the highest in the civilized world. Even the suicide rate is Japan, known worldwide, is lower than the American male suicide rate. A culture that involves far more masculine norming than the U.S. has created very few violent males. Our culture, which has mainly disavowed this masculine norming, creates tens of thousands of violent males per year. "Something more complex is going on," he observed, "than masculine norms."

While I am not personally equipped to take on a study of the magnitude I want to suggest here, I hope I can help set it up. The study would involve genomic analysis and brain scan data from every prisoner in the U.S. who would allow it. The study would also involve survey instruments in which abuse, trauma, abandonment, under-nurturance, and toxic masculine upbringing would be measured via existing measurements such as the CAS (Child Abuse Survey). As geneticists and psychiatrists look at all the data, we will finally have, I believe, some deep answers to the question, "Why are so many American males becoming so violent?"

Until we do compile and complete this study or others like it that involve epidemiological analysis of huge numbers of our violent males, we may well fall back publicly and privately on a single ideological theory, the Dominant Gender Paradigm, with its inadequate focus on patriarchal gender norms and masculine stereotypes.

The Path Before Us

While the Dominant Gender Paradigm has done and continues to do good, and while masculine norms can be debilitating for some people, I hope this chapter has helped you to feel safer in doing the important work of confronting the DGP when you read, see or hear it being used in ways that are too dominant in social, academic, or government dialogue, and too limiting of innovation. I hope our coupling of the DGP with the disease of male violence has provided evidence that we need to give our boys' lives and issues much more in-depth analysis than we give them.

The intellectual truth we must finally face is this: We have had five decades of the DGP penetrating our culture, five decades of its particular explanation for male behavior and violence, but the very disease of male violence we have hoped to remove from the male psyche is only getting worse—in San Bernardino, Minneapolis, Sandy Hook, Orlando, Dallas, Baton Rouge, and nearly everywhere else.

If you have access to corporate or non-profit funding for research and local program support, I hope you will use your clout to expand theory and practice for study of and practice with males around you. Hopefully, now, we can agree that it is time for a revolution in the way we think about males, a revolution that compels people at the most public levels of discourse—such as our governments and the U.N—to confront the DGP as too thin. This confrontation can be done in diplomatic ways that honor the good results the Dominant Gender Paradigm has produced over the decades, but it must be done right now and all around us if we are to save our sons from our own limited cultural conversation.

If nothing else persuades others to believe the need for this confrontation, male violence may, unfortunately, do so. Since there is no compelling proof for the idea that dressing boys in blue and girls in pink or telling boys to repress feelings while telling girls to express them actually rewires male brains and male epigenetics toward violence, we can issue this challenge to DGP adherents: "How much more rampant violence must we suffer in our communities before you will engage in a deeper view than this old ideology can provide?"

Chapter 3

Forward-to-Nature:
Embracing the New Science of Healthy Boyhood

> "The new sciences of human nature…expose the psychological unity of our species beneath the superficial differences of physical appearance and parochial culture. They make us appreciate the wondrous complexity of the human mind, which we are apt to take for granted…. They identify the moral intuitions that we can put to work in improving our lot. They promise a natural-ness in human relationships, encouraging us to treat people in terms of how they do feel rather than how some theory says they ought to feel."
>
> —Steven Pinker, Author of *The Blank Slate: The Modern Denial of Human Nature*

ASSISTANT PRINCIPAL KATEY MCPHERSON sat in her office talking with 13-year-old DaShon. He was a tall skinny kid from a poor mixed-race family dressed in a hoodie that hid his face and low-slung pants pulled down below his behind so they dragged on the floor. In charge of student counseling and discipline, Katey knew DaShon got low grades and often acted out in class. The present school year had only started a month ago, but this was DaShon's third visit to Mrs. McPherson. The first time this year he had pushed a younger kid against a locker; another time, he sent inappropriate photos to a girl. Constantly angry and defiant, he had now refused to take his earbuds out of his ears in math class to answer a math question.

"Kids like DaShon," Katey told me a few weeks later when we met, "try to intimidate me with their size or glare, especially because I'm so small in stature (5'1"), but I will not be intimidated!"

Katey recreated this conversation with DaShon for me.

"Why did you refuse to do like Mrs. Credwo asked you to do with the earbuds?"

Silence, frown, fidget in the chair.

"You need to answer me."

"I don't care about any of this shit."

"Watch your language. And I don't care if you care or not. Show me some respect and answer the question."

Silence.

Katey waits a beat, sits back, her chair creaks.

He slumps further in his chair, out-waits the silence.

"Do you know what respect is, DaShon?"

"I know what it is."

"Do you respect me?"

Silence, then: "I respec' you."

"I appreciate that. I like you—I think you could go somewhere—but I'm having trouble respecting you. I want to respect you."

"You do whatever you like, I don' care."

"What's the difference, DaShon, between respecting and liking someone? Do you know?"

"Course I know."

Katey opens her hands above her desk, inviting the answer.

"You like someone, you like 'em. You respec' 'em you lookin' up to them."

"Right. I like you because I see fire in you and I think you could take that fire somewhere good, but you do things that you just can't do at school, and I can't respect that."

DaShon shrugs.

"Thas' yer' probl'm."

"You want to be suspended, don't you?" Katey asks.

DaShon shrugs. "I tole you—I don' care."

Katey ended up having to suspend DaShon for three days even though she knew, "Our school wasn't set up to really help him. It's that way in every school district I've worked in. We have hundreds of kids our teachers, counselors and parents can't really handle. We're overwhelmed with these cases, and nearly all of them are boys."

Co-author of the book, *Why Teens Fail: What to Fix,* a book that explores cyber-bullying and other crucial topics of teen life, and a mother of four girls, Katey continued to express how sad she has become about what she called "the American schoolboy phenomenon."

"My whole life was about girls. I went into teaching and then moved up in administration with the idea that girls were behind boys. When I got into classroom teaching and then, especially, school administration, I saw the reality—90 percent of the kids sent to my office are boys. I started disaggregating the data not just in my school but my whole district. We had a big boy problem. Then I looked at the data from other districts around me and saw even more trouble. Then I started looking nationwide. The issues these boys face are absolutely glaring.

"This is how I found your work and it's what brought me to your Gurian Institute training. Until you showed the PET and SPECT scans in your keynote, I had never seen the science of boys' and girls' brains. But this science and the nature-based theory makes sense. It fits what's going on in our schools and in the trenches. Now that I'm beginning to study the neuroscience of males and females I want to rewrite parts of the book—I want to add the neuroscience and the developmental science. Parents and teachers may learn a bit about the science from media but we need to learn so much more about it to serve these kids! We just don't know what we don't know."

I asked Katey if she knew of any graduate school of education around her that taught a one-semester course in teacher training on gender and the learning brain. She didn't.

"As an adjunct instructor at Arizona State University," she said, "I need to talk with the department about this. At first I was shocked to hear you say that 99.9 percent of graduate schools of education don't teach a class in male/female brain material to teachers, but I know, the politics are very tough. Your concept of a Dominant Gender Paradigm is very true in every school of education I know."

"What's the end result of these gender politics, in your view?" I asked her.

"Most of us are women and so we go into our classrooms as young teachers pretty good at understanding the girls but unable to understand a lot of the boys. And most of us have been indoctrinated to think boys fail because they're too masculine while girls, when they have trouble, have trouble because of the oppressive 'system.' It's so simplistic, but it's what we learn. I remember a boy, Travis..."

Travis, a white boy, 12-years-old, came to her school in a bad mood and unable to focus, Katey recalled. His race and his natural temperament were different from DaShon's. He was better dressed, more eager to please. His family's economic status, Katey knew, put him in a higher income family than DaShon's. Katey also knew his parents were in the process of divorcing. She had been told by two of his teachers that they wondered if Travis might have ADD so Katey had suggested an evaluation to Travis's mother and asked for a parental visit to the school. That visit had not happened, but Travis had been put on Adderall by his pediatrician and the Adderall showed promise—Travis was less distracted now than a couple weeks ago.

Yet, still, here he sat across the desk from the assistant principal.

"What's wrong?" she asked. "What's going on, Travis?"

Travis finally confessed. "I can't stand it at home. I have to get out." He opened up about his parents' distress, his own fears and anxieties, how angry he was.

Katey saw behind his anger to his sense of inadequacy: this boy desperately wanted to help his parents to heal their rift, stay together, he wanted to "save" his mother and father, and his brothers and sisters. He felt ashamed for not being able to save all of them, for being so powerless.

"Are you being hard on yourself?" Katey asked. "Do you blame yourself for the breakup?"

"No," he said immediately, "but if I wasn't such a screw up, you know, like with my bad grades and not handing in my homework, if I could just be, like, a better student, it would be better. Everything's so f—, I mean, so messed up. *I'm* so messed up. Thanks for talking to me, Mrs. McPherson. Thank you."

Travis's left eye brimmed with a tear and his voice cracked.

"The reason I'm telling you about him," Katey said to me, "is because of what you said about how we aren't looking past some of the myths and simplistic ideas we have about boys and why they fail. These two guys couldn't be more different or come from more different parts of society. DaShon would never let you see him cry but Travis is fine with it. Travis talks a blue streak about how he's feeling and DaShon doesn't. Travis is on medication and DaShon isn't. Their race and ethnicity is different. DaShon's biological father is in prison and Travis's is home, an active father—I know him, he's a good guy.

"The point is these two boys are like all the boys I try to help: different culturally but they all need far more help then we know how to give them as *boys*."

Katey and I first met at the Gurian Institute's summer trainer certification. Two years later, Katey retired from her job in the schools and became the Gurian Institute's new Executive Director. "I have to do this," she said when she took over GI, "because this nature-based approach to understanding boys and girls is the most effective way of helping our children, not just our boys but our girls. I say that as a mom of four daughters—this nature-based approach to boys and girls is the future I want for my daughters."

Embracing Nature-Based Gender Theory: The Third Action Step of Revolution

I first developed nature-based theory in the early 1990s, just before publishing *The Wonder of Boys*. My research in my counseling practice, in schools, and in communities—coupled with scholarly research in neuroscience—showed me the importance of the natural sciences in understanding both females and males. In early drafts of *The Wonder of Boys,* in 1994, I wrote:

> "Society has the choice of whether to fight our natural and inherited abilities or channel them effectively. When we use the common sense of nature in our upbringing of boys, we work with boys not against them, and give them the love, structure, discipline, and wisdom they, as boys, need. When we accomplish this, we don't create more random violence, we ensure less of it; we don't make boys into men who victimize women, we ensure less victimization of women. In our lives as parents, mentors, and educators, we stop feeling as if we're fighting against boys and masculinity; we start realizing how to work with boys and maleness. Consequently, our homes, schools, streets, and bedrooms start looking very different."

Katey and many others have, over the years, joined with me in the process of discovering that American boys are growing up in lifestyles and institutions that are unnatural to them. As a result, boys often find themselves in the vice principal's office, in prisons, over-medicated, unmotivated, and in depressed psychological states where they can survive only by becoming brutal or withdrawn. As Katey and I and many others have learned more about the natural sciences and "the natural boy," we have discovered a focus for social and systemic change that can lead to positive growth and health for boys, girls, and everyone on the gender spectrum.

In particular, Katey *saw* boys like DaShon and Travis differently than she had before she began using nature-based theory. She asked the parents of Travis and DaShon to work with professionals to do genetic and blood-based nutritional tests to determine the way the boys processed their own neuro-chemistry (as we did with Aaron in Chapter 2). Even though these boys were not acting out violently, for the most part, they were under distress, and a first cause analysis of any male distress (epigenetics) is almost always useful.

DaShon's mother wasn't able to engage in this research but Travis's parents agreed to work under a psychiatrist's supervision to have Travis do the genetic testing. Through those tests they learned that Travis was a person who "under-methalated folate, most likely because of mutations in the MTHFR gene." This meant he didn't metabolize or absorb folate, one of the body's essential B vitamins, in an adequate way. This genetic folate-processing issue led to a great deal of mood difficulty for Travis. The psychiatrist suggested a prescription formula for folic acid, including Deplin® capsules, as one way to address the folate issues, and Travis's mood, behavior, and everyday life improved. Simultaneously, Katey helped the family look at issues in nurture and culture (we'll look more closely at these in a moment).

Certain corporations and workplaces are now offering genetic testing to their employees, but even if you don't work for such a company, these tests are getting easier to do every year—some kinds of genetic tests use spit or swab (a Q tip inside the mouth) and other related tests, such as the Walsh Institute tests for nutritional deficits in the body using blood tests. You or a medical professional can order these tests for your son, but this should be done with a professional who knows how to interpret the tests.

I suggest these tests for any boy who is under any kind of duress or, simply, "worries you"—under-motivated, unable to focus as well as he should, lethargic, becoming obese, anxious, sad, depressed, moody, isolating himself, feeling lost. Costs are generally not prohibitive, and should continue to come down if we lobby health insurers to fund them. The tests can reveal developmental vulnerabilities and difficulties in our boys and girls that we can address through removal of neurotoxins, nutrition changes, coaching, counseling, lifestyle change, and biomedical support.

One area of nature-based theory that has become generally accessible in the last decade is the genetic study of obesity. Travis was overweight by about 30 pounds. When his genetic tests came back, the psychiatrist, his family, and Travis himself could see that he was prone to process what he ate and drank in ways that could harm him because of vulnerabilities on three genes: DRD2 (an "eating behavior" gene), MC4R (an "appetite" gene), and FTO (a "body fat" gene). This information was given, by his parents, to a physician who, working with the psychiatrist, suggested dietary changes—no more pop, smaller meals with less unhealthy carbohydrates, no more refined sugar and flour, no more artificial sweeteners, much more exercise. As with the interplay of genes and environment in your son's life, Travis's interplay was complex. The obesity genetics and his folate and mood regulation genetics actually worked in tandem, increasing negative outcomes for Travis because of their interconnectivity.

Pursuing the New Plan

As I introduced in Chapter 2 using the Three Causes/One Correlation model, nature-based gender theory involves the study of nature, nurture, and culture but it is "nature-based" because it *starts* with discovering everything we can about the actual *nature* of the child. I ask parents and professionals to take this tack so they as individuals and all of us together in our human community will "nurture the nature" of each child. Life will be much safer for all of us once we do. It is the nature of each individual child that carries the greatest wisdom for development of a strong core-self and a positive future.

While we gather foundational information about who our child is (much of which is instinctive to us as parents and mentors but some of which is hidden until we discover it through scientific means), we can also make changes in nurture and culture to fit the natural systems our children need. With your own son, you can receive the results of the tests, go over each chart with a physician, psychologist, or other expert and then develop a nature-based plan for altering the nurture and culture around your son's health and well-being.

This approach is a new plan for child development because it could not exist in this exact way until very recently. While parental instincts, psychological wisdom, and empirical data from centuries of child-rearing have existed for some time, this exact nature-based approach, which shows great promise for the raising of healthy children, is made possible by the explosion of neuroscience, the natural sciences, and the science of genetics in the last four decades.

To help illustrate this new plan at work, Katey and I discussed the cases of DaShon and Travis. We did so using the nature-based tool of Three Causes/One Correlation from Chapter 2. I am disclosing the results of our discussion here (with names changed and confidentiality assured) so that you can apply this kind of multi-systems, nature-based analysis to boys in your home, school, or other system.

First Cause. In both DaShon and Travis we saw genes at work; while we couldn't get genetic tests for DaShon, we could for Travis. Once Travis's internal issues were resolved with intervention—prescription folic acid and other supplements—behavioral improvement occurred. Then, altering his diet helped him lose weight. Also, we needed to help him with natural motivation strategies (the subject of Chapter 6). As we applied these strategies, his situation improved further.

Second Cause. DaShon and Travis's brains were also affected by the second cause, trauma. Travis's trauma was situational to the divorce—a source of higher cortisol stress hormone levels in the preceding year. DaShon's brain trauma had gone on longer: since early boyhood, he had witnessed domestic violence—both his father hitting his mother in the months before going to prison and repeated street violence. Unfortunately, the trauma in which he was raised kept his cortisol levels abnormally high for most of his life, which gradually affected the development of social-emotional and cognitive centers (processes) in the brain.

When cortisol levels are chronically high in the male brain they can raise and lower testosterone levels, both, as we noted in Chapter 2. Chronically high cortisol can throw off testosterone levels in cells, blood, and brain as to be so unhealthy for brain development that the boy experiences volatility, lability, and depression—manifesting as anti-social anger, numbing sadness, and/or barely-restrained rage. Many disadvantaged boys are raised in constant trauma and so they have some degree of this epigenetic cortisol/testosterone issue in adolescence and adulthood. As the nature-based approach to raising healthy children gains traction in the next era of American life, I believe we will be able to assist communities in inner cities by medically affecting cortisol and testosterone levels (something our youth are already trying to do biochemically through excessive alcohol and drug use).

Third Cause. Dashon and Travis also shared the under-nurture/neglect causation, though to different degrees. Dashon, raised almost completely without a father and without compensating male role models, and Travis through a contentious divorce, lost or were losing the paternal asset—Dashon's father was gone and Travis's father received infrequent visits and a general demise of the father-son bond at a crucial time in the boy's life. This was dangerous to each boy's development.

One of the primary ways the natural aggression in testosterone is directed, integrated, and "trained" (i.e. mentored in appropriate functioning) is through *father-attachment*: the ongoing contact with and training of youth by dads, trusted elder males, and male role models. *Fathers/father figures are the best-proven relational asset testosterone and male adolescence has.* Every time we remove a father from an adolescent boy's life—or the father removes himself—we potentially negatively affect the boy's brain chemistry, thus his behavior, motivation, and emotional development. We will explore this issue in even more depth in Chapter 5.

One Correlation. DaShon fit the first side of the culture coin—becoming, of necessity in his culture, macho/masked/invulnerable in order to protect himself (and later, his family) in a social system around him that did not know to do much more than suspend/expel him (later in his adolescence he would go to prison). Travis lived on the other side of the culture-spectrum. His school system had received no training in the male brain or male developmental science, making Travis a casualty of male brain neglect and the DGP in that school. The easy answer under the DGP approach to maleness was to medicate him to effect improvement.

As you can see, throughout this process, interventions on behalf of these boys were more accessible for Travis, whose family had resources and belief in the process of intervention than for DaShon, whose family was significantly disadvantaged in terms of personal and social resources, and who had little faith in any system of intervention.

Question: But is there *really* a "natural boy" who is different from a "natural girl?" In other words, are male and female brains really different?

Answer: Yes, they are quite different and integrating their differences into child-rearing, marriage, and workplace interactions is crucial to saving our sons.

University of San Francisco neuro-scientist Dr. Louann Brizendine, author of *The Female Brain* and *The Male Brain*, has said, "The male and female brain are different in the ways they handle stress, communicate, learn, grow, and love. The male brain is understudied for various reasons, some of them overtly political. We suffer the consequences of our ignorance every day as men do things we don't understand."

In the Notes and Resources section, you'll find research by the National Institute of Mental Health, the National Institute of Health, the Amen Clinics, Dr. Camilla Benbow at Johns Hopkins University who has revealed the male brain by studying brain and gender differences in more than one million children, and Dr. Tracey Shors at Rutgers University, who has proven the cross-species applicability of male brain research. You'll also find one of the most comprehensive studies on male/female brain difference, Halpern, D.F., Benbow, C. P., Geary, D.C., Gur, R.C., Shibley Hyde, J., and Gernsbacher, M.A., "The Science of Sex Differences in Science and Mathematics,"which comprises the August 2007 issue of *Psychological Science in the Public Interest. (*Volume 8:1).

I hope you will read this study and the work of these others to arm yourself with deep knowledge of the male and female brains. To access approximately 1,000 more studies and resources of this kind, you can go to the Research Reference List on www.michaelgurian.com. Familiarizing yourself with at least a few of these original studies can empower you to help the "natural boys" around you. As you deepen your reading and research into the work of these scientists, you'll find that there are few if any parts of "male and female" that don't include differences in the male and female brain. You'll also find that the gender-different brains appear in all races, on all continents, in all countries and cultures, because boys—no matter where they are from—have a Y chromosome (with all the effects of that Y) and girls do not. The Y chromosome triggers testosterone surges in utero that format the male brain differently than the female. By the time children are born, their brains are already formatted differently. Here are a few examples.

The Male Brain	The Female Brain
Up to 7 times more gray matter activity	Up to 10 times more white matter activity
Verbal centers on the left side of the brain	Verbal centers on both sides of the brain
Less connectivity of verbal centers to emotive	Many more verbal-emotive connections
More spatial-visual centers in the brain	Fewer spatial-visual centers in the brain
Lower words-to-feelings ratio	Higher words-to-feelings ratio
More cerebellum activity/ larger cerebellum	More cingulate gyrus activity (up to 4 times)
Slower developmental/ maturation tempo	Faster developmental/ maturation tempo
Slower limbic to frontal development	Faster limbic to frontal lobe adolescent development
Higher testosterone/ lower oxytocin	Higher oxytocin/lower testosterone
Testosterone (aggression) rises when under stress	Oxytocin (bonding) rises when under stress

These and other brain differences affect:
- How trauma influences the behavior of boys and girls;
- The way boys and girls learn well and don't learn well;
- The way boys and girls grow, physically and social-emotionally;
- How environmental toxins affect boys and girls;
- How males and females approach sexuality, love, and commitment;
- Differences in communication, discipline, self-discipline, motivation, conflict resolution;
- Different approaches to bonding, attachment, and relationships with peers and adults.

An important note: the male and female brains occur on a gender spectrum. Some males and females are more "extreme male" or "extreme female" and some male/female brains, when scanned, look somewhat more like the other gender's brain—I call these "bridge brains" because they bridge the genders. Some of those bridge brains are transgender. Meanwhile, because of this vast gender spectrum "boy" and "girl" will not show up in real life as one single replicable "boy" or "girl" (a stereotype) but instead "boy behavior" and "male brain" and "girl behavior" and "female brain." Your son(s) will fit somewhere on the gender spectrum, and each of their brains will be a male brain fitting somewhere on the male brain spectrum.

To me, to build a society that does not base its nurturance of males and females on brain science is unconscionable. Fifty years ago we didn't have this science and so we had to create paradigms, like the Dominant Gender Paradigm, to explain males and females almost exclusively from a culture perspective in which "nurture" served "cultural and masculine norms regarding gender." For fifty years we have pretended nature did not exist in the realm of gender but now we have the science of gender available to us. We can now enter a new era in gender development.

The Usual Antidotes to the Male Brain

When a society like ours doesn't understand the male brain, male nature, and the natural boy, we are going to make huge systemic mistakes. Without realizing it, we are going to develop "antidotes" to behaviors created by a brain system that we have under-nurtured or just plain do not get. Travis and DaShon provide examples. Up until the time of intervention, they had been subjects of two of the usual "antidotes" to maleness itself and to distress among American boys: school-to-prison pipelines, and medication.

When boys like Dashon are lost in social systems, their maleness is sent to the assistant principal then moves towards suspension and expulsion. They don't get the kind of help that can immediately deal with some of their neurochemical issues and so they are further traumatized and go down a rabbit hole of distress and, like Dashon, can end up in the school to prison pipeline. Neuro-psychiatrist Daniel Amen told me, "Without the right diagnosis and medication, tens of thousands of these disadvantaged boys just keep getting worse." Forensic psychologist Neil Berman has worked in our nation's prison systems for three decades; he told me, "If a male wasn't already a criminal, sending a boy to prison will almost certainly teach him how to become one. Prison is the worst place to put most of the boys and young men we are trying to save."

For DaShon, a Three Cause/One Correlation approach might have led to diagnoses and medications, such as ADD/ADHD medication, as well as other interventions he as a young male needed to stay in school, stay out of prison and survive past age 30. He needed these medications and male-specific interventions to support his own vulnerable and best nature, and he couldn't get them. Funding and opportunity—whether through corporate assistance to impoverished schools or government mental health programming—did not exist to help DaShon and other boys like him. In Chapter 4 we will explore the dangerous negative politics behind our particularly American dislike of investing in the holistic mental health of boys.

But meanwhile, medications for boys are also a double-edged sword. For a boy like Travis, the medication is the wrong "antidote" to natural maleness. Our Gurian Institute data shows that approximately 40 percent of boys diagnosed with ADD/ADHD don't have it. Pediatricians and others are "diagnosing" boys as having the disorder based on a few minutes spent with parents who report difficulties at school for their son. Teachers, parents, and pediatricians mean well, but they are blaming the boy for their own lack of training about and for male nature.

Dr. Leonard Sax, a physician who practices science-based gender theory himself, pointed out in *Boys Adrift* the problem with so many boys on Ritalin and Adderal: these medications, used by parents and others to help boys become more focused and more motivated, can affect male neurochemistry so severely as to *lower* motivation in some boys. Concurring with this research, Dr. Amen told me, "The misdiagnosis of ADD for many boys who don't have ADD harms our young people in numerous ways. They may seem to 'get better' but can end up worse in the long run, and meanwhile, we keep neglecting to deal with the real issues in the systems that raise our sons and perpetuate a very negative cycle for our culture."

Medication and punishment are often our general American antidotes to being a boy. If you are pondering medication for your son or daughter or yourself, I hope you'll explore the kinds of genetics and blood tests I've mentioned in this chapter. At the very least if you are considering medication, the genetic tests can help your care provider and help you to see which medications may work best (and which may work worst) with the genome being medicated.

Caleb and Josh, Michael and Phil

Cases such as those of Travis, Colin, and Aaron prove to me that a nature-based approach can lead to best results. To further plumb that approach, let's look at something central to it—understanding the nature of resilience in our boys.

In a family I worked with in the early 1990s there were two boys, Caleb and Josh, who mirrored, somewhat, myself and my brother Phil. Phil was two years older than me and the two boys in the family I worked with were two years apart. Both the father and mother of Caleb and Josh, like my own parents, wanted the boys to grow up well and, to a great extent, treated both boys the same way—criticizing the boys, showing dissatisfaction when the boys underperformed, loving the boys deeply. They were what we tend to call, without really knowing how to define it, "a normal family." There was no abuse, neglect, or huge drama in the family unit.

The family came to see me because the younger boy, Caleb, 11, seemed depressed. The older boy, Josh, 13, was not depressed—he was flourishing. From family reports and from meeting Josh, I understood him to be more athletic and extroverted than his younger brother. Caleb, for his part, was more of a "bridge brain," more introverted, and did not seem as naturally resilient as his brother.

At 11, Caleb found his parents' critiques of him especially troubling, specifically his mother's criticism. He was a highly sensitive boy, but the parents didn't realize it. An epiphany happened in a parent counseling session (without the kids) when the father said in genuine exacerbation, "Why isn't Caleb more like Josh?"

That was a very good question. These two boys—like my brother and me—were brought up in exactly the same way by the same parents in an intact home. The boys had different interests. Josh liked large group sports, so his parents helped him find them. Caleb liked the violin so his parents helped him flourish in music. The parents supported the boys by matching their environment with opportunities in their talent sets.

In the early 1990s, when I met this family, we didn't have genome mapping yet, but I was writing *The Wonder of Boys* based on the available PET and biochemical and neurochemical research. These boys both clearly had male brains, but there was still much more to them—personality differences and other genetic differences.

My brother and I were like them: we were boys who were different from one another, too. As with Josh and Caleb, the mom was the more critical parent in our home. Our mother criticized both of us mercilessly. Our father, like the father in Josh and Caleb's family, was more passive, but did support the critiques of our mother. And like Josh and Caleb, my brother and I responded to the criticism differently. It turned out that, because of my own family, I had a lens into Caleb that I might not have had without my history.

By the time I met that family I had been in therapy for my own childhood trauma. As a boy, I had been physically abused by my mother over a prolonged period and sexually molested at ten-years-old for a six-month period by a psychiatrist to whom I'd been sent for having trouble in school. These childhood traumas took me most of my twenties to unravel in therapy.

During some of my therapy sessions, my therapist and I discussed the fact that while Phil was not sexually abused he was raised with the same often brutal mother and passive father but Phil turned out differently than I did. He has lived an isolated life, hasn't held a job for more than a few months at any time in his life, and has never married. He is a wonderful uncle to my daughters and a good man, but he and I clearly didn't respond to our similar upbringing the same way. I suffered more abuse than Phil, but the more traumatized son had more success later in life while the other son had less. Why did this happen? My brain and psyche were clearly more resilient than Phil's, but why?

The answer lay in our genetic palette for resilience—but I didn't have concrete evidence of this before genome mapping. Since 2003 and genome mapping, we can better understand how this can happen to two brothers from similar circumstances.

Researchers at Duke University have discovered that some children have more activity in the OPRMI gene and others have less, causing some children to be more naturally resilient and others less. I have the OPRMI genetics that favor natural resilience. My brother's genetics are built differently.

Researchers at Emory University have studied the GABA (Gamma-aminobutyric acid) neurotransmitter, as well as polymorphism in the GABA alpha-2 receptor gene. This Emory team found that people with a genotype for G-protein signaling 2 (RGS2), a protein that decreases G protein-coupled receptor signaling in the brain, and also experienced repeated trauma, were more likely to experience a lifetime of damaging behavior, especially if they don't receive therapy or other support. Those without this genotype were less likely to do so.

I have the better GABA receptors for surviving, even flourishing, despite abuse. In this, my "resiliency" genetics are very good.

Another important element in all this is fewer single-nucleotide polymorphisms (SNPS) in the FK506 binding protein 5 (FKBP5). This binding protein emboldens significant negative outcomes from trauma, but I have fewer of the low-resilience polymorphisms. Thus, my childhood trauma did not affect me as it did my brother who appears to have more polymorphisms and, thus, fewer genetic fail-safes for surviving and thriving after trauma.

And in tandem with this difference between us, I have received one long and one short allele on my 5-HTT serotonin transporter gene, a circumstance associated with more optimism and more resilience.

Without knowing yet about these genetic specifics, I tried to help the parents of Josh and Caleb answer the question, "Why isn't one brother like the other?" with what I knew from early brain research and my own experience. By the early 1990s, we did know that genes for specific personality traits came with the child. We also knew that certain talent sets came genetically. We further knew that the male brain was a complex genetic system working on a gender spectrum. From my own experience I knew there must be some genetics related to resilience. So, I approached the parents and family with what I knew and confessed to them what I "assumed."

Caleb, I suggested, had different genetics than his brother for resilience and thus was a more "sensitive boy" on the gender spectrum of male brains. As a growing child, he was experiencing trauma—not physical abuse, but emotional distress—directly from his mother's harsh and unabated criticisms. As a boy he was feeling under-nurtured by his father, as well. To Caleb, his father felt like a betrayer when he let Mom verbally attack him as she did. In this analysis, I tried to work with the Three Causes of male distress in a systematic way for this family.

The One Correlation also fit in our discussion, in two ways. This mom had in her mind a stereotype of a "tough guy" who could withstand her angers or, even better, flourish because of them. One of her boys, Josh, fit her stereotype. Caleb didn't. The larger culture and community, too, had not provided these parents with any knowledge of the male brain and its diversity. Caleb's physical education teachers and coaches were being much harder on him than the boy needed, just like his mom was doing, as they expressed disappointment in his inability to flourish in larger group sports.

Discussing "the natural boys" with these parents, I asked them to make a chart, together, of who they thought each boy was—his nature— and bring those charts in. Here are some results of their collaboration.

Caleb, 11	**Josh, 13**
More sensitive	More resilient
More artistic	More athletic
Just a few friends	Everyone likes him
More serious	A jokester
Competes one-on-one	Competes more and all the time
Cries more	Cries less
Gets bullied more	Doesn't get bullied
Scared of aggression	Not scared of aggression

I asked for qualities the boys shared.

Can't sit still	Can't sit still
Talks pretty well about feelings	Talks okay about feelings
Is empathic	Is empathic
Likes to wrestle with brother/dad	Likes to wrestle with brother/dad
Pretty good in school work	Okay in school work
Does not do enough homework	Does not do enough homework

The picture we now had was of two boys along a male brain-gender spectrum. Based on these charts, I asked each parent to tell me "who" each boy was in the context of the two parents' genetics (of course, everyone had to guess about this, then).

They answered with "he's like his dad in…"

"he's like me in…"

"he's like mom in…"

"he's like me in…"

I asked the parents to go even further afield.

"In what ways is Caleb like his grandparents or any aunts or uncles?" Now we moved further into genetic inheritance than just the two parents. This led to a number of "ahas" as the parents "saw" their boys in new, multi-faceted ways.

"He loves math like his grandpa does."

"He's really empathic like his grandmother is."

This exercise helped the parents gain a deeper picture of the natural boys in their care, which was crucial work because the parents had come to my office with the monolithic cultural idea in mind that nature meant very little, and "kids will turn out the way parents make them turn out." In one session an "aha" moment occurred when I asked the parents about all the criticism they colluded together to put Caleb through. "Do you, as parents, *trust Caleb's nature?*" I asked. The answers showed me that Dad trusted this boy's nature more than Mom. For Dad, "things would work out, we don't have to be so hard on him or correct him so much." For Mom, though, "we have to be vigilant." Here is some of our conversation.

Me: Perhaps there is a middle ground you can stand on that both trusts Caleb more and nurtures him more tactically.

Mom: What do you mean?

Dad: Tactical?

Me: You asked why Caleb isn't more like Josh. From talking with you both I can tell that you know, instinctively, that Caleb and Josh are different people, but I'm not sure you may be noticing the unique nature in each boy. You are trying to form Caleb to be like Josh.

Mom: No we're not.

Me: But isn't that what's behind your question about Caleb and Josh? Life would be easier if Caleb were more like Josh?

Mom: It's Caleb who's having trouble, not Josh, so we are correcting Caleb more—he needs it and we just want the best for him.

Me: Which is why you're so hard on him.

Mom: Don't make me the bad guy here. You're saying I'm not helping Caleb like I'm helping Josh.

Dad: He's not saying that, honey.

Mom: He is. He's saying I'm wrong about Caleb being weaker than Josh. He doesn't realize how much I'm trying to help him—to make him stronger. And you're not doing much, either. Everything falls on me. How the kids turn out—that's going to be put on *me.*

Dad: It's not, no way.

Me: Angie, you're right about Caleb. He *is* built differently than Josh. You are calling that difference "weaker" but I would call it something else. Let me tell you a story.

Now I talked about myself and my brother.

"My mother was hard on her kids, like you are on yours. My father was more like Tony—he influenced us as men but without being as hands on as Mom, nor as critical. In my case, unlike in yours, my mother not only criticized us constantly but also beat us with belts, wooden spoons, and coat hangers. Some of this kind of discipline fit the era and places we were raised in, but some of it was extreme—a result of my mother's mental illness.

"During this trauma my mother didn't realize how fragile my brother's brain system was in comparison to mine. She criticized us equally and, initially, hit us equally. My brother pulled back from any attempts at confronting her. He did whatever she wanted, and from then on, got much less punishment than me or my sister. I was built differently. I confronted her more and more and got hit more and more.

"You are not hitting your son, so he is not in as much trauma as my brother and I were, and you're not mentally ill like my mother, but you don't trust Caleb's own nature and so you are highly critical of it. If you don't decide to better understand Caleb's nature, you could do damage."

This direct line of counseling created tension, and after some more conversation, this mom stood up and left the room. Her husband apologized and followed her. For many days after the confrontation, I assumed I had lost the possibility of helping this family. That night and many nights afterward I played the therapy through my mind, thinking of how I could have worded things differently.

Two weeks later Tony called to set up another appointment for him and Angie. Here is a part of that conversation.

Mom: I was mad at you and I still am. You made me out to be like a child abuser.

Me: I can see why you think that but I didn't mean to.

Mom: I don't hit my children. When they were little they got spanked a few times but not more than a swat on the butt now and then, nothing abusive.

Me: I know that from talking with all of you. My comparison wasn't about abuse—it was about the nature-based approach.

Mom: Well, you did get me thinking. I didn't know you had talked about your mom in your books so I didn't know about it. It surprised me.

Me: Yes. I refer to myself and my siblings to use my trauma as a teaching tool, about nature and neuro-biology.

Mom: I get it. You're afraid Caleb's a very sensitive boy by nature and you're saying I'll do damage to him by criticizing him so much.

Me: Do you think it's possible you will?

She was silent.

Dad said: We're worried about that. I'm worried that I'm not being strong enough, either.

Me: Are you being strong enough to help Caleb?

Dad: I don't know. I'm the kind of guy who just lets a kid be. You have to tell me if I should do more.

Me: Yes, I think you can, especially now that these boys are entering adolescence. They need Dad in new ways now.

Mom: We both need to make some changes. I want your help to figure out how to criticize Caleb better, and Tony promised me he'll spend more time with the kids, especially Caleb.

Mom (to Tony): You promised, right?

Dad: I promise.

From there, the conversation moved toward making a plan.

Thankfully, direct confrontation with these parents had moved therapy forward rather than ending it two weeks before. As that therapy continued, these parents altered the way they cared for these very natural and different boys. In doing so, they saved at least one of these boys from male anhedonia, a condition of upbringing detached from male nature that is derailing increasing numbers of our American sons.

Male Anhedonia: The Depressed American Boy

Caleb came to my office with a mild depression, an internal numbness he could barely understand. He would report in our sessions "just kind of feeling like nothing's really going right." "Sometimes I just don't want to do anything." "I just wish she'd get off my back so I can breathe." Evaluated by a psychiatrist before the family came to me, Caleb wasn't depressed in the clinical and diagnostic sense, but he was clearly suffering some kind of low grade sadness that had increased enough to alarm his parents. The teaching tools and action plan we used to help his family alter the trajectory of his upbringing also helped treat his background condition—what I call "male anhedonia."

In the 1990s, a number of us were reporting mild depression among males in increasing numbers. Dr. William Pollock at Harvard University's McLean School of Medicine has written about his cases in *Real Boys*. Harvard psychologist Daniel Kindlon and Boston psychologist Michael Thompson have explored the same phenomenon in *Raising Cain*. I believe nearly everyone working with males in the 1990s sensed some increase in male depressive symptoms. I certainly sensed it in boys like Caleb. Unfortunately, now, two decades later, this condition is increasing, with approximately twice the number of boys depressed now than there were then, yet many males are still not quite "depressed enough" to fit a DSM official diagnosis. So I've used the clinical diagnosis of sexual anhedonia—especially in its relationship with testosterone functioning—as a baseline for naming this new boy phenomenon, "male anhedonia."

Sexual anhedonia, clinically diagnosed in more than a million males per year as of 2016, is a condition of non-arousal from sexual activity. A male with this disorder feels little or no pleasure from sex and is relatively unmotivated to pursue sexual activity. Philip Garwood, M.D., a pioneer in the study of sexual anhedonia, points out the neurobiology in *Clinical Neuroscience*. "The severity of anhedonia is associated with a deficit of activity of the *ventral striatum,* including the *nucleus accumbens,* and an excess of activity of ventral region of the prefrontal cortex, including the ventromedial *prefrontal cortex* and the *orbitofrontal cortex*, with a pivotal, but not exclusive connection to the role of *dopamine*."

These areas of the brain are interconnected and combine, in the normal brain, to create reward, pleasure, joy, and motivation. Their healthy connectivity to dopamine provides a healthy baseline for adolescent growth. When there is "deficit of activity" in these areas, there is less active reward chemistry in the brain, and thus, in the case of sexual functioning, anhedonia.

The same brain biology can apply to a young male who is unmotivated or seems constantly, mildly depressed—the boy suffering from male anhedonia. Caleb came into the world with certain genetics in place that gave him less natural resilience than his brother. He had an edge of melancholy about him—not associated with sexual activity (he was too young) but displaying the lack of a sense of personal role or mission, constantly comparing himself negatively to a sibling or social environment, experiencing extreme stress from the socializing critiques that were mistakenly meant to help him be stronger. His parents had started to worry about him because he'd begun to isolate himself in his room. This bewildered his parents and teachers because, they reported, "He's a boy who has everything he needs, he's well taken care of, nothing should be wrong with him." Yet something was wrong.

And it is getting worse for our males. Renowned psychologist Gregory Jantz, coauthor of *Raising Boys by Design* and Founder of The Center: A Place of Hope in Edmonds, Washington, recently told me: "We are seeing significantly increased numbers of males in our clinics, especially in the last five to ten years. More and more males start out with something like mild depression then the situation worsens gradually into young adulthood. As adults, the situation gets worse. The numbers of these men keep rising."

Indeed, was Caleb my client today, I believe he would be much worse off, as many of my own clients now are, fitting some or all of this profile:

- getting Cs and Ds or Fs;
- media and technology addicted, the kind of boy we will explore in Chapter 7;
- (when puberty hits) porn addicted or "porn preferring" (preferring porn to actual relationships);
- somewhat or very isolated from family members;
- cyber-attached rather than person-attached ;
- experimenting with (or addicted to) prescription drugs, alcohol, and other substances; and/or;
- unmotivated, "failing to launch," an "underperformer."

I fear that Caleb would now be an adolescent boy who can't fully *feel* without the hyper-sensorial, hyper-aggressive, and hyper-spatial video games/visual porn to give him the "dopamine rush" and "ventral striatum" and "nucleus accumbens" activity his more socially adjusted brother or sister would experience naturally from normal (less extreme) human interactions and activities. For some of these males, medication is very useful, but not for all. Until the "male anhedonia" diagnosis exists in our diagnostic manuals, and until we focus deeply on this condition, I believe we will lose more and more males to it. While we can't track exact numbers because we don't have a diagnosis for it yet, hopefully the "male anhedonia" category will help researchers and caregivers help males who live just this side of an abyss, and fill up with fear and, potentially, rage.

Question: Could the attraction of Jihadism and other fascist groups to some "normal" American boys be related to male anhedonia?

Answer: Yes, a portion of it could be.

A startling way we may be watching male anhedonia grow in our world is extreme doctrinal Jihadism and other similar, extreme fascism in other religious denominations. Some of the young men attracted to these doctrines are severely mentally ill and were ill before they became terrorists, but some are "normal boys" reported by their parents as listless and undirected (purpose-less) before they became extreme in their views.

This shouldn't surprise us.

While extreme Muslim rage against the West grows from a number of geopolitical factors and personal traumas, it also requires the human brain, especially the male brain, to "need" the internal rewards of violent and extreme doctrine. For the reward centers and prefrontal cortex of the brain to become fascistically violent, that brain will likely have experienced many earlier adolescent years already in low-grade numbness and mild depression (anhedonia). That brain may possess "addiction" genetics and the boy's parents may have noticed that the boy battled with addictions and/or seemed to become obsessed by other subjects before the religious extremism took hold. Some anhedonic boys and men may self-generate significant anger and rage in order to "feel alive." Religious or other similar intellectual systems and mentors can tap into that rage by cycling it through the brain as a stimulant. Soon, the brain may not develop or feel internal reward/dopamine chemistry through normal developmental channels but may well seek out even more violence that promises constant stimulation, constant aggression, and ultimate reward.

As we deepen our understanding of male anhedonia in males between 10 and 30 years old in the next decades, we'll need to look carefully at all its manifestations, including its violent outcomes. As parents notice their sons withdrawing or becoming listless, we will need to have trained professionals available to help these males—not just "angry children" but *boys.*

It is my profound hope that every graduate school of psychology will, within ten years, give a Master's degree in Male Studies so that we can generate enough professionals to help with this subtle and difficult phenomenon among our boys. At this time, only a handful of universities have been able to confront the Dominant Gender Paradigm well enough to teach holistic and informed classes in male development. I'll further explore this lack of academic attention to boys with you in the next chapter.

Fixing Unnatural Education

Male anhedonia is felt at home and also, increasingly, in American schools. Teachers and parents report "the loss of our males in education," and "males checking out of school." A school principal wrote me with her sense of calamity at the situation boys face in school: "Our teachers are bright and very competent people who care deeply about their students, but it has become clear to us over the last ten years that American education, in general, is doing much better for girls than boys. Please don't print my name, but I do think most school principals feel the same way I do, even if they can't say it publicly. Boys just seem so much more lost and listless in school than girls."

I hear this constantly from educators. American schooling has become a profoundly important example of what goes wrong when we neglect the natural boy. Our schools provide, also, a beautiful example of how things *can* get better for both boys and girls when nature-based theory is applied to the systems. All our schools are filled with heroic teachers and staff, but they have been systemically set up over the last fifty years in a way that is anathema to millions of males, hence the statistics we noticed in Chapter 1.

- Two-thirds of the Ds and Fs in our schools are received by boys.
- The majority of high school dropouts are boys.
- Boys are suspended and expelled at five times the rate of girls.
- Boys are behind in standardized tests throughout the country and developed world.
- The largest gender gap is the literacy gap, not the math/science gap—boys are three times worse off in literacy than girls are in science.
- More than 80 percent of discipline referrals are boys.
- The male failure rate in schools afflicts all the industrialized countries, even the ones we think of as "patriarchal."

From a nature-based ("natural boy") lens, the reasons for male failure in schools are three pronged, involving nature, nurture, and culture.

1. Boys are coming to school with epidemiological issues from neurotoxins and emotional trauma-responses in families and communities. They bring their fragility to classrooms but academics and educators don't learn about the male brain in training, so they don't realize our males have fewer learning fail-safes than our females, and often need boy-specific learning settings and tactics for males to compete as well as females in present day classrooms and schools.

2. The problems are compounded by the dual move our industrial and post-industrial classrooms have made a) toward a mainly verbal literacy learning platform (which highly favors the female brain) and b) away from the nature-based and spatial-

kinesthetic learning platform that helped males learn for centuries. School, thus, becomes a new traumatic environment in which a boy's fragility and failure compounds and accumulates. As developmental standards for each grade level generally fit female neurobiology better than male, trauma to boys grows into over-medication, learning failure, anhedonia, and in some boys, school violence.

3. Over the last fifty years, the American educational system has followed the Dominant Gender Paradigm's assessment of where the genders are, which put all its eggs in the "culture" basket rather than in a nature-nurture-culture alliance. Because nearly all teacher training in academic environments leans toward DGP training when males are studied, our educational system generally leans towards the idea that "gender equality requires gender sameness." Despite being disproven more than two decades ago, the paradigm forces educational leaders to avoid teaching teachers that boys and girls learn differently for fear of political backlash.

As you experiment with and observe boys around you, study your children's schools. See if they are party to significant educational mistakes in male nature, nurture, and culture. If they are, blaming the teachers is generally the wrong course—it's better to study the system as a whole, including the teacher-training systems related to gender training, and then offer nature-based theory and training to update the teachers on the science of male and female brains.

Because teachers themselves are generally hungry for more training on the male and female brain, if you can finance or organize that training for them and for the parent community, you may well find your local schoolteachers and administrators very grateful to you. It only takes a few of you whose boys are falling behind to go to the principal and say, "Here's what we are willing to invest to help our boys. We will certainly do it with your permission and in ways that do not harm but instead help girls, as well."

Signs of Male Abandonment in Schools

Here are some of the specific errors regarding the natural boy that our Gurian Institute team has noticed in the thousands of schools we have worked with. You can track these easily in your conversations with other parents, teachers and other professionals.

Sign 1: Look for developmentally inappropriate behavior policies in schools, including zero tolerance policies that punish boys for having male brains. For example: are boys punished for drawing gory images or using physical aggression to show affection and bond with others? If so, your sons will know instinctively that this school is irrelevant to, or a mismatch with, their nature, and may begin to act out or withdraw—stop doing homework, get in trouble, skip class.

Sign 2: Look for an inequitable developmental educational platform that favors girls' brains and disfavors boys'. This hyper-verbal-emotive platform may manifest in teachers constantly saying "Use your words" without using other strategies equally. It may involve teachers assigning a plethora of irrelevant worksheets and "make-work" homework. It may also show up as an early childhood learning platform that doesn't fit male brain development, like requiring all students to read at 4 or 5, when many boys don't read as early as girls because of differences in developmental tempo for literacy and language in the male and female brains.

While you'll certainly notice that some boys read early and well and many boys can do fine in any learning environment, millions of boys will need a more experiential, physical, natural, and project-based learning platform than our schools might offer. As you notice all of this, remember that children who fail at something in their tender years rarely associate that environment with reward chemistry and motivation. If boys begin failing school in early years, traditional education may become anathema to them by the time they reach middle school.

Sign 3: See if people in your school community are arguing that protecting self-esteem in children requires the erasure of competitive learning, competition, and "losing" or "doing badly." That gospel has emerged in the Big Three over the last thirty years, but doesn't fit with actual brain science. Competitive learning and competitive play—including winning, losing, and hurt feelings—are actually essential for the healthy development of both boys and girls. They increase the development of emotional resilience and social skills. Boys often cannot mature into healthy students or adults without the self-motivation that games, debates, and other competitive education formats provide.

Sign 4: Study the use of medication. If your son's fourth grade classroom has one-quarter of the children on medications, the classroom is most likely dysfunctional. The national rate of actual ADD/ADHD appears to hover around 11 percent so the number of students on attention medications ought not be 25 percent. Teachers, parents, and physicians who become convinced to use medications without doing actual genetic and blood tests or male brain assessments indicate an educational system that's under-nurturing and neglecting the male brain.

We must remember: revolution happens because of friction between what is and what must be. You can both support the schools and teachers around you who are indeed doing amazing work in a system that is often stacked against even a teacher's natural instincts while, if needed, creating friction on behalf of boys who are not being served in your community. The Gurian Institute and many others around the country have been creating and deploying training and gender initiatives in schools that create some friction with what was or was not previously learned by teachers and parents about boys and gender. On www.gurianinstitute.com you can learn much more about schools and communities that have succeeded in closing achievement and gender gaps through this kind of work. It really works because it is respectful and supportive of teachers, families, and the children and students themselves. This kind of healthy and supportive friction is essential for saving our sons.

Educational Innovations on Behalf of Boys

Social revolution is always a systemic expansion of human love that requires both new passion and new restraint. As we excite in ourselves and our communities the passion to change a misguided and blind academic/educational system, let us also practice restraint against blame. The Big Three comprises a system of social education that has betrayed many of our sons, but the individuals in these systems care for our sons and are not malicious—they are doing their best within a system that constantly robs them of needed knowledge, information, and tools regarding boys and males.

The German poet, Rainer Maria Rilke wrote, "If we surrendered to earth's intelligence we could rise up rooted, like trees, but instead we entangle ourselves in knots of our own making, alone and confused." To a great extent the natural boy is confused today in our schools. He and his family feel alone in our social systems. This loneliness, social isolation, and hidden anhedonia sit at the center of what must activate our revolutionary passion, and here are examples in the grassroots of revolutionary passion to educate and love the natural boy.

Samantha Iverson responded to her son's anhedonia with a unique solution in the face of her fourteen-year-old Alex, in her words, "having trouble in school for the last three years, not learning well, not doing homework, getting bad grades, acting out, going to the vice principal's office, getting suspended."

"When his father and I were still together," she wrote, "we tried everything, then in this last year, alone, I've tried everything. Finally, I decided to take Alex out of school and let him learn online while we take a one-year trip around the world. I'm lucky: as an educator, I can get a teaching job on a ship. Now I can rescue him from what he is becoming at school, so sad and angry, so hard on himself and others, and me.

"He was such a compassionate boy when he was younger. He was affectionate and kind. I'm very verbal and so are most of his teachers but he's not very verbal. He thinks more with his hands, his heart, and I can't let that part of him, that beautiful natural boyishness, die. We'll go around the world on a ship together and he'll learn school work the way he was meant to learn, with adventures.

"I think I'll get my son back. I sure hope so."

Other parents are trying other non-traditional innovations. For example, the Homeschool movement is a fascinating approach that allows for smaller classrooms, more one-on-one time, more outdoor and natural learning, more physical movement and more apprenticeship; it will only grow, I believe, over the next decade. While it has, like any system, its drawbacks, one thing is clear to me in the movement— devoted parents are trying to save their sons and daughters by protecting boy-friendly and girl-friendly education.

In Tampa, Florida, the Hillsboro County Public School District is innovating within traditional frameworks. That District is using a science-based approach in some of their schools, especially schools that serve tough populations. Carla Sparks, Supervisor of Magnet and Choice Programs, and a large team of educators working with her, have been instrumental in the development of Franklin Boys Preparatory Academy and Farrell Girls Preparatory Academy. In these schools, all teachers are provided the training that helps them fully "see" the brains and needs of boys and girls. To look at the qualitative and quantitative success these educators and students are having, please click www.gurianinstitute. com/success.

In response to success with a science-based perspective at Central Catholic High School in San Antonio, Texas, the school and local stakeholders have recently developed the Center for Excellence in Educating Boys and Girls. Our Gurian Institute team has been honored to assist in this effort. School President Paul Garro told me: "At Central Catholic we see gender as an important part of who boys and girls are, and we know from decades of experience that good teaching happens when every part of the child is understood and educated. This new Center will help our own and other educators use good science to re-invent education in ways that fit the needs of the learning child's brain."

The Army and Navy Academy (ANA) in Carlsbad, California, has been educating boys for more than a century. In 2014 the Academy became a Gurian Model School in order to launch a strategic campaign to utilize brain science to refine and enhance teaching and learning across campus. My team and I have worked closely with Dr. Lisa Basista, General Art Bartell, and many others on staff to study the efficacy of the military model for educating boys. ANA is not a military preparatory school, but it does use a boy-friendly model borrowed from military structure.

A parent whose son's life was changed by the school's approach shared this story.

Jessie did well in school until he reached about 12 or 13 years of age, which is when he started changing. We switched schools several times, but it seemed that those schools lacked the structure that Jessie needed to succeed. His teachers said that he was very smart, but that they simply couldn't get him to do anything. He was getting Ds and Fs and he was disengaged in school. To us he seemed depressed and withdrawn. By the end of the 9th grade, we began to fear that he might not finish high school.

I researched the Army and Navy Academy and decided to drive down and take a look. We took a tour of the school, which was extremely impressive. Although we were met with some obstructions from the admissions department because of Jessie's now low GPA, the admissions officer believed in him, took a chance, and allowed him to apply. After the Board interviewed him personally and gauged whether he had the potential to succeed at ANA, he was accepted on a conditional contract—he was given one semester to bring up his grades.

It was tough going at first, but after about six weeks, we began getting reports back from teachers saying that he was getting involved. He joined the surf team, and a few other teams, and had good roommates that he really liked. He started to get C's, which was not his usual thing, and from there on in he just kept going higher, and striving for more. Jessie has been at the Academy for two years now and has a 3.89 GPA. At the end of last semester, he was on the Honor Roll and Dean's List.

I attribute his success to the way the school works. The school has taken him from this little boy that didn't care about anything, to a young man who is striving to go higher, do better, and get to a better place in life. People could always see that potential within him, but the Army and Navy Academy, with its male-friendly programming and structure, has brought it out of him. The school and its staff could really SEE him and what he needed, and we as parents are eternally grateful.

McCallie School in Chattanooga, Tennessee has also educated boys for more than 100 years. At McCallie, the National Center for the Development of Boys has just been launched; it's goal is to help others in the U.S. and internationally to understand and practice what works best with boys. My GI team and I are honored to be working in partnership with Troy Kemp, Executive Director of the Center, and the Board to get the word out and facilitate this kind of grassroots educational reform.

One Board member, Kenny Sholl, also the assistant headmaster of the McCallie, shared with me the evolution of McCallie's science-based programming. "We looked carefully at our approach to boys in the late 1990s after reading *The Wonder of Boys*. As educators of boys we felt we already knew a lot about how to do this very well and we did, but adding the science to our understanding has been very powerful. It helped us understand what really makes boys tick."

One McCallie innovation involves making sure every student has a purposeful afternoon activity in which the boy commits to something larger than himself—whether in forensics, academic competitions, music groups, athletic teams, group research projects, outdoor program teams, or many others. "The key," Kenny told me, "is for the boys to be in a position where others have to count on them. This makes their work meaningful."

Kenny emailed me this example of how this worked for a boy in football.

Recently, I was talking to one of our students who had just completed a difficult football season. He hadn't played well in a very visible position, he was injured, and had come to dislike the sport very much and couldn't bear the thought of going through another season. He was struggling with the decision to walk away from the game and to focus on other activities.

As we talked through the process he was going through to make this gut-wrenching choice, I asked him to make a list of pros and cons to help facilitate his decision. His list of cons (leaving the team) far outnumbered the pros (staying on the team). In fact, he listed only one "pro" on the page: he did not want to abandon his teammates.

"Coach", he said, "I just can't do that. I have to stay out there no matter how tough it is and how miserable it makes me at times... Those guys are counting on me."

As Kenny discussed this boy with me, he brought up the idea of "task specific empathy," how boys develop empathic bonds by doing something together in which they compete, prove themselves, and in tandem try to accomplish something of value not only for themselves but for the team, and for others around the team.

Understanding this kind of male-friendly empathy-development, McCallie makes sure to tap into it as a baseline innovation and tool for male success. This means making sure to help boys compete together "in service." "This kind of approach is often lost in education today," Kenny said, "because educators are generally not taught how to integrate competition into curricula. But a lot of boys need that kind of attachment and bonding in order to learn successfully."

These schools and people, along with charter school founders and staff, are just a few of the innovators who have decided to alter the downward spiral of boyhood in education. For more educational settings like these, and to look at bringing innovation to your schools and homes, please visit the Gurian Institute website as well as www.michaelgurian.com/articles.

A Strong Part of the World

Katey McPherson told me recently, "Boys are such great kids not necessarily because they will do whatever we say or try to please us no matter what—they are great because of who they are—so direct, so compassionate, so full of energy and wonder, if we can just see it and love it. It's that nature inside them I want to nurture as a woman and a professional. To nurture it, though, especially as one of four sisters and a mother of four girls, I had to commit consciously to seeing male nature as a strong part of this world that needs my help to be and remain strong. This took some stretching on my part because the systems I work in don't see the same beauty in boys that I and others like me see."

What a beautiful phrase for the nature of boyhood: a strong part of the world. Male nature, like female, is strong at its core, solid, active inside boys and men, ready to be nurtured and tapped for goodness and love. This male nature, sometimes so confusing to us, is an important part of the ground of human being. Yet, "it is difficult to say to anybody that you should become acquainted with your natural self," Carl Jung wrote in his first *Visions Seminar in Human Psychology* in the 1930s. "People think this means you will open up a sort of lunatic asylum. They think the animal is only the part of us that is jumping over walls and raising trouble all over town, while, actually, the animal is pious, it follows its natural paths with great regularity…only Man is extravagant." To Jung, we know there is "nature" in us, but some people come to fear that nature as "too animal," and these people seek the luxury of calling all nature "animal" and then disavowing that nature.

This is what our civilization has been doing with males—positing that male nature either does not exist ("gender sameness not gender difference is the male/female baseline") or that maleness is the "lunatic animal" ("masculinity is dangerous"). In this paradigm, we have created families, schools, communities, and social systems that consciously or inadvertently denigrate or do not support the nature of boys. Without our realizing it, our society has decided to live in the false luxury of pretending that human life should be more a matter of ideological culture than natural growth.

Jung's "only Man is extravagant" holds gravitas we must deal with in this anti-natural approach to child development and gender studies. It can provide a basis for revolution because Jung challenges us to find and ground our new path for nature in science, and in rigorous attention to the natural boy who is, right now, knotted up in America. As we redefine rigor and passion for boys' health in our social systems, we will nurture a strong part of the world in ever new ways. From the passion and knowledge inherent in our amazing new sciences, we will nurture strength and resilience in our schools, neighborhoods, and homes.

Our attention to nature itself, and within that fold, our attention to the new sciences of male and female nature, will constitute an enormous act of love.

Chapter 4

Protecting Our Sons:
Ending Three Dangerous Attacks on Boyhood

"All of us in administrative positions in higher education know about the boy problem but, frankly, we lack the courage and resources to open up this dangerous topic to full accounting on college campuses. Certain political groups control the conversation. Males are privileged and females are oppressed: that's the narrative we have to stick with if we want to survive in academe."
—"Carrie Franklin," university administrator who asked to remain anonymous

CARRIE INVITED ME TO HER CORNER OFFICE in the large brick administration building on a grassy and green-treed college campus. I arrived there because she had come up to me at my lecture the evening before and asked me to come see her the next day. "I want to explore with you the idea of looking at the 'boy problem' we have here, on campus," she had whispered to me. She further told me that males not only make up the minority of students on her campus (60 percent female and 40 percent male), but also comprise the minority of "actively involved students." I didn't know what she meant by "actively involved," but I had a suspicion, based on other college visits, and promised to visit her office.

Now I sat down in a leather chair across an oak desk from a woman around 6 feet tall with an athletic build, black hair back in a rubber band behind her head, and gray-blue eyes. She wore a blue jacket, white shirt, and gray slacks and I was dressed similarly—blue jacket, light blue button-down shirt, khaki slacks. We were two caring professionals in our late fifties, both academically trained, who felt nervous about taking on an issue we could get flack for. I knew, too, that I'd fly home tomorrow, while she would stay here, in this office.

"But I want to do something—I really do," she insisted, "not just for my own campus but because I have three sons—I know how tough

89

life has become for boys, and how angrily they are being attacked everywhere."

I asked her what she meant by "minority of actively involved students." She told me that the average male on campus gets involved in fewer clubs, activities, journalistic investigations, and classroom dialogues than the women. Compared to the females, who get very involved, the males are "here, I guess, I mean, they're present in their dwindling numbers but even their presence is somewhat disengaged. We're looking at ending the fraternity system here, so now we face even more loss of males." She explained that the new college sexual assault statements coming out of the White House and the U.S. Department of Education were doing some good but were such a vast overreach of "anti-male insanity and infantilizing of our youth" (her words) they were causing a great deal of difficulty on campus.

"Ultimately," she continued, "I don't know what's chicken or egg, but the guys already get lower grades on average, they matriculate less than the women, and they have less success when they leave our campus in the fields we've trained them in. The only exception to this would be in engineering. Otherwise, our young women are flourishing, but our boys and young men just seem…lost. That, in a nutshell, is our boy problem."

"Why do you think this boy problem exists here, on this campus?" I asked.

She sat back, leaving her arms extended and her hands folded on the edge of her desk. "I think it's a lot of things, of course, many causes, but the thing that worries me the most is the question of whether we can really do anything. I listened to you speak last night, and I love how diplomatic you are about the gender politics. I know you're trying to build bridges, but I'm not sure how we would get through the gender traps in our college. The powers-that-be are entrenched and have control over the social dialogue here."

"What do you mean?"

She leaned forward. "You didn't hear it from me but the 'Dominant Gender Paradigm' you outlined absolutely rules our campus. It's an easy paradigm politically, it fits the oppression model, it creates sympathy for young women, it has a villain—young men—so it allows us to feel righteous about punishing males for bad things a small group of males do or for just plain neglecting males. We also have the 'racism/women's issues' you talked about, so even though our young women have been doing better than our young men for years, 'gender' is a minefield and the result is: 'gender equity' is about females. With this minefield in place, we can't stop the loss of the guys who are, truthfully, the people on our campus who most need equity."

The "racism/women's issues" phrase referred to language we've used over the last fifty years regarding "women and minorities." In the lecture the evening before, I had made the point that while linking women's oppression with oppression of minorities in the colonialist and patriarchal past was an important connection, and while it still fits the situation of women in many countries in the less developed world, it is difficult now to show quantitative or qualitative data that supports that link in America, Europe, or elsewhere in the developed world.

Women as a group are doing better in many ways than men as a group. And within minority groups, many women are better off than the men. African Americans women are healthier and doing better than African American men, for instance, as are Latino women vs. Latino men, and Native American women vs. Native American men. This holds true throughout the minority group demographics, as we noted in Chapter 2.

"I mean, you saw what happened last night," she said, referring to an angry group of students heckling me, then standing up and walking out of the lecture when I made this exact point.

"Yes," I nodded, "but I'm guessing the people who stayed—which was most of the audience—in some way agreed with the point."

"Maybe," she said, frowning, "I hope so, but still, there's a lot of one way of thinking on our campus. And I've thought for a long time about the immature, entitled kids staying children by trying to get overprotected on campuses. I think this immaturity is hiding behind a mask of righteous indignation against males. To me it's immaturity emboldened by ideology. We haven't had this on our campus yet, but I read about the trend in some colleges, where young women are saying any speaker who uses the word 'rape' is actually abusing women and should be fired. This is just immaturity cloaked in 'women's issues.'"

"I agree. So," I asked, "is that theme a way you could talk about the gender politics here on your campus? By using that maturation and developmental framework in psychology classes, for instance?"

"No. If we call it immaturity, we come off as 'female-oppressive culture.'"

I had hoped for a different answer, but in the last twenty years, I have spoken at numerous campuses with these exact issues in place.

At the grassroots level there is some understanding of the disappearing boy, but as this administrator noted, the academic narrative of "male privilege" can often seem different from the reality.

"This is definitely not where I thought my feminism would go when I was the age of these young women," Carrie sighed.

At the end of the conversation, I offered my help in studying with her and an executive team what was happening to the boys and young men on campus. She said she'd be glad to look at that possibility. That evening I left town and a week later heard back from her by phone.

"Okay," she said, "I've talked to some of our folks here and we've decided we would like to start this assessment and consulting process with you doing a blog for our website on the boy problem on American campuses. We'll make it the cover blog on our website and we'll fill in a sidebar on how it specifically exists on *our* campus."

"I would be glad to begin this blog and can begin writing it immediately," I responded.

A week later, she called again.

"Well, listen, we've had a setback. We still want you to talk about your nature-based theory and the gender lens in a blog, but the blog can't be the lead article, and it can't be about just males. It has to be about females equally. Also, you can't go into the boy problem at all."

I paused for breath. "Did I hear you correctly? Wasn't the whole reason we got together to at least give a little bit of voice to boys issue?"

"Well," she sighed sadly, "our administrative team really wanted to go forward with this, but when it got up to our academic vice-president there was a meeting with the president, and they decided this was too risky. Talking about boys might invite Title IX and gender equity issues, and our president was also worried that alums learning about a boy problem would affect donations. I think she's worried that to now say we have male issues along with all the women's issues that are made public every day would confuse the narrative and make it seem that both genders on campus are doing badly. Like I said last week, this is a minefield."

I agreed to write the smaller blog the higher-ups wanted but months later, when only three sentences about boys' issues on college campuses—and in America—made it through the editorial process, I realized there was little good in my writing that blog, so I declined. The administrator and I talked more and she agreed with my choice. She felt unable to budge any of the powers-that-be into looking at boys and men's issues on campus, and the 'boy problem' on that campus just keeps getting worse.

The Academic Minefield

If you've spent any time in an academic environment lately, and if you've tried to discuss gender issues with depth there, you will no doubt have noticed "the minefield." Larry Summers, Harvard University President, walked into the minefield when he mentioned that American universities should look at *all* aspects of gender, including spatial differences in the male and female brain, to study gender gaps in STEM fields.

He lost his job soon after this comment.

Warren Farrell, Chairman of the Commission to Create a White House Council on Boys and Men and lead author of the meta-study discussed earlier, also ran into the minefield at his lecture on the boy crisis and men's rights on a college campus. During the lecture he was physically and verbally threatened for talking about these issues, and campus police had to help him safely away from his lecture hall. "It was frightening," he told me, "not just because of my feeling of lack of personal safety, but also, intellectually, where is free speech? Where is the civil exchange of ideas? Political correctness is destroying the gender dialogue on these campuses."

Academic institutions have substantial control over our culture's future. Governmental agencies rarely pursue a program or course of action without substantial academic support. Therefore, if academic environments only pay attention to one gender, the other gender will increasingly fail. Funding from both the public and private sector will go solely to the gender that the academy studies.

Similarly, the media is trained in academic ideas. Once reporters and producers move into their workplace, they quote academics who provide them with the political and paradigmatic ideas they learned in college or graduate school. The "chicken or the egg," as Dr. Franklin noted, is indeed difficult to track. Did this problem begin with government and the media asking academic environments to study gender from a Dominant Gender Paradigm perspective, or did academic environments decide on this perspective in the middle of the last century because of past gender inequities? Does academe now stick to that early choice, leaving government and media with barely any other perspective to investigate or utilize?

Whatever the source of the dilemma, we who care about boys must confront and heal the cultural schism between tragic male development issues in the grassroots and the academic world's myopia about gender. This is the fourth step in our revolution.

The Fourth Action-Step of Revolution: Ending Academic Attacks on Our Sons

Here are the three attacks on boys and young men we must counter and end if we are to save our sons.

1. The Female Victimization Hyperbole and Neglect of Male Mental Health
2. Devaluation and Denial of Male Emotional Intelligence
3. Unequal and Incomplete Paradigms of Gender Equity

We've mentioned the first attack in earlier chapters and will focus on it even more fully in this chapter. We will explore attack 2 in Chapter 5 and attack 3 in Chapter 8. Two further aspects of male mental health— lack of motivation and use of technology—will be explored in Chapters 6 and 7.

The Female Victimization Hyperbole in the Big Three

Women and girls have suffered brutality and inequity for millennia. They have been treated as chattel, raped, abducted, and murdered. Even in enlightened democracies like the U.S.A. they didn't have the basic right to vote until August 26, 1920 with the passage of the 19th Amendment. The foundation of that amendment was a response to the struggle of women who claimed they were being treated like second-class citizens in a patriarchal society—and they were right.

But something has happened to the integrity of that central principle over the last five decades. As feminist Sheryl Sandberg pointed out in *Lean In,* the vast majority of American women today do not call themselves feminists. Young women, she argues, don't realize how much they are losing by not being feminists. She hopes to call women back to the cause.

I found her book very empowering to young women like my daughters, but I wondered if she fully understood why so few women, especially young women, self-identify as feminists. Mothers and fathers, grandmothers and grandfathers won millennial and Gen X/Y young women the right not to be victims and not to see themselves as victims.

I think Sandberg and others often miss this fact. Today's young people in general not only embrace their empowerment but feel entitled to it. They feel that most men in America and most present-day cultural systems are no longer set up to be victimizers of women. These young women and men lean into their computers and social media and see vast parts of the developing world that fit the males-as-victimizers paradigm, but they also see that most of the developed world, including the United States, doesn't.

Camille Paglia is a feminist who argues for a new kind of women's rights advocacy, one that doesn't depend on broadcasting men's victimization of females.

"A peevish, grudging rancor against men," she wrote in *Time* in December of 2013, "has been one of the most unpalatable and unjust features of second and third wave feminism. Men's faults, failings and foibles have been seized on and magnified into gruesome bills of indictment—including by ideologues at our leading universities." She continues, "When an educated culture routinely denigrates masculinity and manhood, women will be perpetually stuck with boys. And without strong men as models to either embrace or resist, women will never attain a centered and profound sense of themselves as women."

Academic environments have not leaned into reality in the same way that the majority of young women in America have. The kind of academic institution described by Dr. Franklin still functions in an unreasonable attack mode that ends up keeping young women immature and young men increasingly absent from campus or anhedonic on it. Ironically, the patriarchal ideological corruption that kept women second-class citizens has shifted to DGP ideological corruption. Even lying about real victimhood is now allowed if men can be cast as villains and women as victims.

A Case Study:
The "Rape Culture" on American Campuses

One of the clearest examples of this corruption is a Big Three attack on our sons that began in 2011 with governmental misuse of a misleading academic survey inside the "Sexual Assault Survey" at the Department of Justice/Centers for Disease Control.

They held a press conference in which President Obama told the press and the nation that one in five college women were sexually assaulted every year. He was outraged by this and called for Title IX mechanisms, attention from the U.S. Department of Education, and other solutions.

When he and his staffers were questioned about "proof," the University of Wisconsin "Sexual Assault Survey" was referenced. This culture-wide attack on our young women must not continue, he said, in an impassioned plea. Along with many other fathers of daughters, I was incensed. I nodded vehemently, feeling kinship with a president who was also the father of two daughters and applauding his courage in calling attention to these crimes.

But the next day, I sat back to think about this. Did it really make sense that around one in five young college men were rapists? Even if one figured that some young men multiply raped young women, the promulgated statistic would still imply many millions of raping young men.

There are reprehensible sexual assaults of both females and males in American culture and on college campuses, but this "rape crisis on college campuses" had no actual scientific research base. I immediately joined experts like Dr. Farrell and Dr. Sommers to examine "the study."

We discovered that the University of Wisconsin researchers had conducted short surveys that took just a few minutes to fill out. The surveys included "having sex while intoxicated" as sexual assault and "being sexually touched after having a drink" was defined as sexual assault. No wonder the public number became one in five women raped or sexually assaulted (both of which are felonies). Despite the fallaciousness of the statistic, it was repeated constantly by candidates and leaders in both parties because our national zeitgeist of male development is already inclined toward "an oppressive masculine system that protects males and denigrates females." The zeitgeist creates solid background for nearly any accusation against men. Even when we suspect an attack on males is false or at least a massive hyperbole, our nation tends to buy in.

Soon, a small number of actual examples of college assaults presented in the media became proof of the rape *crisis* on American college campuses. *Rolling Stone Magazine* published a cover story accusing a group of young men at a fraternity house at the University of Virginia of gang raping a girl who, it turned out, was not assaulted at all. By the time *Rolling Stone* had to retract the story, lives had been ruined. Meanwhile, the "rape crisis" phrase grew in such proportion that it became the norm for academic conversation, governmental interventions, and media reports.

As Dr. Farrell, Dr. Sommers, myself and many others disagreed publicly with this kind of deceptiveness, I saw just how deeply the female victimization hyperbole had corrupted politics. I had voted for President Obama in both races and still believe he is a transformative and successful figure in American politics, but my respect for him fell when I saw how corrupt this whole "rape crisis" debate became. In a blog I wrote a month later I asked him to reconsider his position, begging him to look at statistically correct and science-based positions on gender issues. Then and now I believe politically correct and inaccurate positions will ultimately backfire on our daughters.

You can be a citizen scientist in this debate. You can find the real statistics from the Bureau of Justice if you spend about an hour going through their website's many pages—make sure to go back before 2011 in the archives. From my research, the number for women 12 and over who experience sexual assault (a lifespan number) appears to be between 14 and 15 in 1,000. This is not 200 out of every 1,000 young women. However, it is possible that numbers of college women assaulted would be higher than the lifelong average, and researcher Wendy McElroy developed a model for tracking the exact numbers under that rubric. She discovered 1 in 53 as the correct figure, which would translate to 20 in 1,000 college age women sexually assaulted. This number is higher than 15 in 1,000 but clearly lower and more realistic than 200 in 1,000.

As you ponder the real numbers, remember, if the "one in five college women" statistic were actually true, our courts would be overwhelmed with sexual assault cases in the millions, because if the statistic were accurate, millions of American male college students are felons. For more than four decades, various people in the Big Three have pushed a figure of 1 in 4 or even 1 in 3 women sexually assaulted in their lifetime. As McElroy points out in her new book, *Rape Culture Hysteria,* this kind of statistic manipulation is not new, and now it involves nearly outright lying.

Harvard Law Professor Jacob Gersen recently pointed out the subtle sleight of hand that accompanies corruptions like the rape culture hyperbole. He discovered that the Department of Education is forcing colleges like Harvard to alter policies via Title IX but bypassing the Administrative Procedure Acts guidelines that are legally binding. Basically, DOE threatens lawsuits that force colleges to do what the government wants even though the government's statistics and processes have not been vetted and are, in fact, corruptive in their political motivation. In the wake of this kind of pressure, state laws are changing in California, New York, and elsewhere to compel "affirmative consent" which takes away legal defense from males.

While these laws are likely to be overturned in the long run as unconstitutional, they are going to harm millions of lives in the meantime—not just your sons, but your daughters as well. "This is a tidal wave of bad theory, bad practice, and bad law that will cost American taxpayers billions of dollars, to say nothing of ruined lives of both young women and men, all based on a political feeding frenzy of ideological academic 'science'," Ron Henry, Founder of the Men's Health Network in Washington, D.C and senior attorney at Kaye Scholer told me. "When we realize that this is yet another ideological attack on males not based in fact, we'll have to spend billions undoing the damage."

And things just keep getting worse. Confronted with the bad science, a new "study" was commissioned in 2014-2015 by the Administration. This one, conducted by the think tank RTI International, increased the bad science by only looking at nine colleges and made sure to still include "unwanted touch" and "unwanted touch after drinking" as sexual assault. Not surprisingly, this miniscule survey found varying degrees of sexual assault in these campuses—some, as high as 38 percent, a figure that is, of course, impossible (if it were true, there would be rapes every day). While this study further codified the bad science, it was, unfortunately, co-funded by the Bureau of Justice Statistics so that, now, the federal "average" for sexual assault on American campuses is based in nine schools with survey formats that are not scientific enough to reflect real life, but do cover the government by backing up the "one in five" statistic.

I have daughters and I'm angry about the academic corruption behind victimology like this. I can only imagine how parents of sons feel as they send their son to a campus that buys into female victim/ male villain hyperbole. For this parent and this son, the "rape crisis on campus" is now yet another academic "fact" that gets traction because it villainizes males. While people across the country raise sons who may get drunk and may do stupid things, very few are villains capable of raping young women in college.

And perhaps most subtly damaging to our children is the fact that the vast majority of sexual issues of consent or non-consent that arise among young people in college arise because of alcohol use by both genders. Most instances are issues of sexual confusion and, at times, misconduct, that need to be dealt with at their source: abuse of the substance and confusion about how to handle sexual intent while intoxicated. They are not a result of systemic male oppression and victimizations of females. To focus punitive governmental resources on everything except the real problem is to once again abandon our children for political gain. As Dr. Franklin told me, "We are in a gender minefield and we try to accommodate it but it gets worse as boys drift farther away from the very kinds of environments, like college, where we want and need them to be."

The Female Victimization Hypothesis works in our national consciousness because some girls and women are indeed victims of boys and men and that pain taps into our primal fear of bad men (androphobia). Every one of us except the most sociopathic or misogynistic is naturally constructed to protect females. This protectiveness is the ground of our evolutionary success—males are relatively disposable but females, who bear children, are not. The Dominant Gender Paradigm, in which females are victims and males and masculinity are villains, taps into this protectiveness. In academics, government, and media, men can get accused of nearly anything because of androphobia, which to me constitutes a covert form of gender profiling in which males are profiled as dangerous or defective because of their gender.

Question: What about gay boys—isn't homosexuality unnatural, and so, shouldn't we try to change these boys?

Answer: Homosexuality is as natural as heterosexuality. Approximately five percent of human beings identify themselves as gay and we don't know how many more gay people are still in the closet for many reasons of their own.

We have nothing to fear from gay boys or men, or for that matter, from gay girls or women.

Gender profiling cuts a equally painfully when LGBT individuals are also attacked from androphobic ground. They are profiled because of sexual orientation as dangerous and defective. Among the gay males who are so profiled, androphobia is operative at a deep level: homophobia is, in these cases, androphobia writ very large.

Fortunately, as in all areas of gender study, the natural sciences can bring balance. Genetic and neuroscience research over the last forty years have proven that same-gender sexual orientation (homosexuality) is natural for approximately 5 to 10 percent of females and males. This sexual orientation is set before birth in the sexually dimorphic nucleus of the anterior hypothalamus of either gender just like heterosexuality, via chromosome markers such as the Xq28 marker, and in utero hormonal surges during gestation. Approximately 5 percent of dolphins, whales, gorillas, and lions are also wired this way. You can access the research about this by Googling "the gay gene" and I have included some of it in the Notes section of this book.

Despite the availability of this science, many people, especially in religious communities, ask me about LGBT and homosexual "choices." They argue the importance of LGBT conversion therapy and point to lines in the Bible and Qu'ran that they believe condemn homosexuality as unnatural, not created by God—an aberration to natural design. They accuse LGBT boys and men of causing AIDS and corrupting families.

I can't change a person's religious beliefs. My province is science. On that basis, I must challenge everyone who cares about children to look more deeply into the available science. I agree with Gov. Andrew Cuomo of New York and other governors and legislators who are acting against gay conversion therapy. Gay children and adults are who they are. LGBT women and men have provided essential services to humanity throughout history and still do, in nearly every walk of life. They are doctors, lawyers, artists, scientists, spouses, parents, and friends. They no more need to be forced to change their sexual orientation than a heterosexual person does. Many so-called gay conversion therapists, moreover, have been exposed as frauds who charge huge amounts of money for doing something they know is impossible.

To help ease the androphobia people feel toward these individuals, especially about gay boys and men, we may have to build bridges that might not show immediate fruition but provide a long-term conversation. This need for bridges is demonstrated to me by a friendship I have with a close colleague who is an evangelical Christian. Whenever we see one another, she hands me literature about her church. She tells me how worried she is for my soul and that she is praying for me. She tells me, without equivocation, that as a Jew who has not taken Jesus into my heart, I am condemned to eternal damnation.

Early in my career I reacted angrily to interchanges like this. I remembered being a seventh grade boy in Laramie, Wyoming where Christian boys grabbed me, pulled me behind trees, and used pliers on my nose to see if they could force my "Jew-nose" to become even longer. Having been beaten up more than once in Wyoming for being Jewish, I lived in reactivity that interpreted religious attitudes like my evangelical colleague's as anti-Semitic.

In the last two decades, I've spent much of my professional life working with individuals who are like this colleague— people from a deep religious background who don't see God and love the way I see God and love. Because I seek a social revolution on behalf of our boys, I make sure not to overreact to what I consider an idea untenable with the God I know and love. Using a scientific framework to build bridges with colleagues, I try to see if there is harm in my colleague's view. I don't see immediate harm, so when my colleague says what she says I thank her for the literature and meanwhile continue working closely with her on behalf of children.

Micro-Aggressions: Creating Immaturity in Academic, Government, and Corporate Culture

In the first part of this chapter we heard Dr. Franklin talk about immaturity encouraged by politically correct overprotectiveness. If the "rape crisis" or attacks on gay males are a stark example of androphobia among specific populations, the "micro-aggressions" movement, beginning in academic culture and spreading to corporate and government environments, is perhaps the most widespread use of androphobia in our time.

Here are examples of what we mean by "micro-aggressions."

- A boy is suspended from school in Kentucky for drawing pictures of guns. The guns and his behavior—making his finger into a gun—"constitute a dangerous set of micro-aggressions" that will, in the principal's opinion, "produce an unsafe school culture." The principal is responding to parental pressure and school board oversight. Like thousands of other school administrators, he's been told by his powers-that-be that these micro-aggressions must be removed from school culture, i.e., from *boys*.

- A man is warned that this comment at an office between two friends borders on sexual harassment: "I think Carlos is gay." A fellow-worker has overheard this and reported it to the Human Resources department. When Carlos was told by HR about the other man's comment he says, "It's well known that I'm gay. I don't hide it." But the man who said the words is reprimanded by the HR director for "a micro-aggression that could make Carlos or other gay individuals stand out and thus feel uncomfortable." The reprimand comes with the threat of being fired, if such a comment is ever said again.

- A domestic violence case worker at a local governmental agency is called an abuser because he brings up in a staff meeting that, according to a nine-year study conducted by the world-renowned couple therapist, Julie Gottman, 70 percent of domestic violence cases begin with a slap or punch by the woman. Other people in this meeting attack him for being misogynistic and anti-female. It turns out that none of the staff had read the study, nor did the man bring it up for any attacking reason. His intention was to say, "We have to look closely at how we intervene with couples. If all we do is blame men and classify all women as victims of these men, we won't solve domestic violence."

- Corporate counsel at a university campus instructs the university leadership that they must consider not teaching classics like Ovid's *Metamorphosis* because sexual assault is mentioned in it. Meanwhile, at other campuses, professors are told that if they do teach these ancient works, the professors should receive training in what to emphasize and not emphasize based on the probability that some female students will feel unsafe. When the professors respond with an incredulous, "Really? You want to censor how I teach because you worry that a micro-aggression will startle one college student?" the answer is, "Yes. We must make sure everyone is comfortable."

- A lecturer at a university is attacked for using the word "rape" in his lecture. That word, women's advocates on campus maintain, constitutes a micro-aggression that will increase the feeling of lack of safety of females in the audience who have been sexually assaulted. In some universities, women's advocates argue that universities must invest in creating a "safe room" for women who feel offended or hurt by keywords like "rape." Not doing so, they argue, is gender discrimination and should be prosecuted.

What do all these cases have in common? Many things, not the least of which is this one: "micro-aggressions" are almost exclusively "*male* aggressions*." When gender data on micro-aggressions is disaggregated by school, college, or corporation, there are very few "micro-aggressions" that result in female suspension, female expulsion or similar punishment of females. Despite a dominant culture paradigm that touts constant female oppression, in fact, it's difficult to find a university campus that actually oppresses women; there are very few if any "micro-aggressions" in our colleges, governmental agencies, or schools that require females to see themselves as constantly defective; few if any micro-aggressions in corporate environments bring the ax down on women.

The micro-aggressions movement works because it taps into androphobia. While protecting females from male violence is intrinsically important, none of the above cases rose to violence nor did they create a climate of violence. None should have been dealt with putatively. The thing most of them had in common was that a woman could argue she felt uncomfortable as a potential victim of masculinity. Yet feeling uncomfortable is not dangerous. "Feeling discomfort" is not hostile but in most cases, it is a positive challenge to the psyche, a method of self-appraisal, an invitation to civil argument, and a part of the maturation process of human beings.

Some people are beginning to speak out against the micro-aggressions androphobia. Dr. Everett Piper, president of Oklahoma Wesleyan University, publicly condemned it. "This is not a daycare. This is a university!" His reference to immaturity is critical. College students are already maturing slower today than ever before, and few things serve college women's maturation process less than to assume that a college administrator will rescue them even when they're not hurt. Similarly, few things subvert true gender equality in the workplace more than a micro-aggressions mentality that condemns normal male behavior and "rescues" a particular young woman even when she hasn't been harmed. Resentment follows among most males and even many females, and productivity declines.

Columnist Peggy Noonan has responded to the micro-aggressions movement with wise words for the "victimized."

"Life gives you potentials for freedom, creativity, achievement, love, and all sorts of beautiful things, but none of them are 'safe'. And you are especially not safe in an atmosphere of true freedom, like college. People will say and do things that are wrong, stupid, unkind, meant to injure. They'll bring up subjects you find upsetting. It's uncomfortable but isn't that the price we pay for freedom of speech?"

Question: Is soft science research (social science) the best research for creating social policy that affects male and female lives?

Answer: Because it relies heavily on ideological surveys and opinions, "social science" often lacks full scientific rigor.

We can't become fully revolutionary in our approach to gender and male life if we don't compel academic and governmental researchers to practice full scientific rigor. This is an ironic thing to say, perhaps, because academics and government researchers are the very people we would most expect to already use a medical or scientific model for research; however, there is an interesting undercurrent of backlash against science in the Dominant Gender Paradigm, as exemplified by the rape crisis "research."

Noretta Koertge, a philosopher of science at Indiana

University and an avid critic of "micro-aggressions il-logic," has pointed out that many people in many academic fields related to gender get away with providing ideological opinions rather than actual and rigorous science because "all manner of logic itself is patriarchal anyway—logic is, thus, suspect." For these people, hard science is not needed because, "Even to force the study of logic on female students is to aggressively support the patriarchy that devalues women."

The lack of hard scientific base for the micro-aggressions, rape culture, and other androphobic attacks on boys and men comes part-and-parcel with the deception that "everything is male anyway" and "male" already means oppression. What ends up arising from the shadow of these assumptions is commentary and opinion from small groups of women or men that support a certain position—what is called "anecdotal social science research."

While this kind of research can be useful and while all of us do use it on occasion, including myself, it is also specifically not meant to be used in isolation but, in fact, as a support to hard science. One reason for this in our gender field is the fact that the small sample sizes in soft social science research can be manipulated to form any opinion one wishes to promote. For a powerful example of almost pure soft science research, read the book by Hannah Rosin, *The End of Men,* mentioned earlier. The book is based on her "cultural observations" and a few interviews with people who said pretty much what she wanted to hear. Her conclusion was ideological—men and boys are failing and falling behind today because they refuse to give up masculine privilege.

Part of revolution must be new accountability so I hope you will become something of a critic of all anecdotal and soft science research, including your own. Given that the dangerous state of boyhood in America is in some part exacerbated by "research," let's all learn more about that research. Given that government agencies and legislative bodies rely on academic research, as do the media who propel images and ideas into our culture, each of us must now become well-versed in the kind of "research" by which a social policy regarding the genders will be made. When you read something in the media, when you see it on TV or online, and when you hear politicians talk about it, be revolutionary! Study the study by scrutinizing the expert opinion, political commentary, and research with an eye for *scientific rigor.*

This means:

* *Ask for and expect neuroscience of gender to be a part of the study.* Given that gender neuroscience is a massive field now, the conclusions of anyone writing about boys and girls, or women and men, without reference to neuroscience, should feel "off" to us. In Rosin's book, for instance, she mentions gender neuroscience in a few paragraphs in which she says we don't really have good data from neuroscience so let's disregard it. She had to do that because if she didn't, she couldn't write her book or express her opinions—neuroscience of gender ultimately denies much of the probability of her conclusion.

* *Scrutinize sample sizes.* Look at the number of people studied to make sure the writer or researcher has studied large sample sizes over a period of many years, not just a few boys or girls, or women and men in a few settings. Few means hundreds or less. Large means many thousands or even millions. Neuroscientist Camilla Benbow, for instance, has studied millions of children. What she and others like her in the field say about gender differences can be trusted.

* *Test the research instruments for objectivity.* See if the researcher(s) has used methodologies other than short surveys and questionnaires. There are thousands of studies done in the gender area by people asking questions and receiving answers. These can be useful, but they are most useful

for magazine articles about relationships or for ideological argumentation like the "rape culture" argument, rather than actual science. Surveys and questionnaires rise to rigorous science only when they're evidence-based and constantly replicated, like MMPI or Meyers/Briggs personality tests, or when they're neuro-psych batteries to determine brain disorders, such as ADD/ADHD. Outside of these circumstances, they have a high potential to mislead.

* *Assess the research subjects chosen by the researcher.* Important, also, is not just how many and how much replication but *who* has been chosen for the study. Are the people all of one type? Is it just a few males and females of nearly homogenous social groups? Is it mainly very verbal males and females? Is it males and females of only one age group? Generally, if the sample size and type is pretty limited, the findings are highly suspect in the area of gender study because gender conclusions should be drawn from heterogeneous demographic groups.

Here's an example of how soft science that utilizes only a few people of a certain group or type will draw conclusions that are false or misleading.

A study published in *Science* in 2013 provided results of automatic recording devices (ADRs) the researchers placed on 396 college students—345 Americans and 51 Mexicans, both male and female. These devices recorded the speakers every 12 1/2 minutes, which constituted 4 percent of a person's daily utterances. Using this method, the researchers "discovered" that the females talk a bit more than males but not much. Psychologists involved in the study, such as Matthias Mehl and James Pennebaker, concluded that the neuroscience evidence utilized by researchers like myself, Dr. Brizendine, Dr. Amen, and others that alleged that females use substantially more words than males was now suspect. Because of this study, headlines throughout the media followed Dr. Mehl's and Dr. Pennebaker's comments with similar conclusions. Ideas in the Big Three that gender is just a social construct without any real depth in human nature gained traction yet again. However, this research was flawed or misused in these ways:

1. Its sample was too small to make wide conclusions about gender groups (a few hundred people should never be used to make conclusions about 7.3 billion people).
2. Its cadre was college students among whom the males are already very verbal individuals (this was a too-small sample size of a particular and limited type of person).
3. Its test mechanism measured spoken words, not written words or words that are read on a page (more on this in a moment).
4. Its mechanism did not study gender differences in words-for-feelings ratios between women and men. This gender difference, not number of words used per day, is the most significant difference between male and female verbalizations.

Had the study used brain scan technology and large samples in the tens of thousands, had it measured many kinds of males, not just highly verbal ones, had it measured the number of words used in all three word-use modalities, including reading, writing, and speaking, and had it studied words-for-feelings ratios, the study would have shown what large-scale, longitudinal, brain-based studies show regarding males and females in all cultures, the kinds of neuroscience findings in the studies we mentioned in Chapter 3.

The study did not work with enough scientific rigor and so it perpetuated the myth that males and females should perform equally well in verbal formats—a myth that crushes our schoolboys whose brains do not process words in the same way the female brain does. The point I made earlier about the education system's direction over the last fifty years toward a "verbal literacy and cooperative learning platform" fits right in the middle of this kind of "research." Because of soft science "proof" that males and females are the same, education has moved toward less physical movement, less competitive learning, less spatial-kinesthetic learning, less natural learning, less apprenticeship of males to tasks, hyper-reliance on "use your words," misdiagnosis of male non-verbal behavior, and professional illiteracy about the profound (though often wordless) ways that males process emotion and cognition.

In this way most of the soft science research that comes out regarding gender ends up fulfilling the agenda of the Dominant Gender Paradigm but paying little heed to all three areas of importance in gender research: nature, nurture, and culture. A cultural assumption about males (that they are or should be as adept as females in verbal literacy) receives research-backing from a "study" and social policies are established in the Big Three—especially in academic and governmental agencies like Schools of Education on college campuses or Departments of Education at the state and federal levels—that perpetuate the boy crisis in schools and elsewhere, including in mental health care.

A Most Dangerous Outcome of the Minefield: Lack of Male Mental Health Research and Resources

Despite media statements that health care is skewed much more to males than females as a leftover of male dominance and the patriarchy, this is a soft-science myth. There are multiple agencies for Women's Health in the federal government, state governments, and hospitals and medical facilities, but few or none for Men's Health. Joy Moses, policy analyst for the Center for American Progress recently noted, "Funding for both government and nonprofit programs to help males has been scarce. A recent survey shows the top two ways that nonprofit service providers connect with males is through parole and child support enforcement programs. As a low-income man, you have to get in trouble to get help." This paucity of resources for distressed males was confirmed in 2014 by Jacquelyn Boggess, co-director of the Center for Family Policy and Practice, a Wisconsin-based think tank, who wrote, "The majority of United States anti-poverty programs almost exclusively serve women and children."

You can study all of this in your community. As you look at available programs, you will notice multiple programs locally and nationwide for girls' empowerment and raising healthy girls and few or none for raising healthy boys. If you have access to corporate funding and foundations, you will discover that corporate funding for women's health and girls' empowerment initiatives is in the billions now, with sponsorships of the Susan B. Komen March and other similar foundations, but corporations rarely fund men's health or boys' mental health initiatives.

An interesting exception occurred in President Obama's My Brother's Keeper initiative, which focused on helping boys of color. Gender politics made it unwieldy to try to get funding from the government for this initiative despite the fact that the government funded the White House Council on Women and Girls, so President Obama had to go to corporations to fund the initiative. Thankfully, they did so. Sadly, androphobia, the female victimization hyperbole, and general political correctness in the federal government made it difficult to try to get funding for this boys' development effort internally.

This significant imbalance in government care and assistance to males carries tragic consequences—male mental illness and lack of male mental health care is devastating our families, neighborhoods, and communities. Most of America's homeless are males, as are most substance abusers, criminals, incarcerated individuals, suicides, homicides, and violent people. Male mental health is equally as fragile as female but walking in the minefield, we avoid dealing with it. Meanwhile, we distract ourselves from our mistake by focusing on micro-aggressions and rape crisis hyperboles that fuel our protectiveness of females but ultimately backfire even on that protectiveness, as increasing numbers of women, children, and men are harmed in other sectors by mentally ill males.

From my work on the Commission to Create a White House Council on Boys and Men I've been able to learn some of the "mines" in the minefield that propel the government to avoid dealing with male health as vigorously as female health. These "mines" were spoken aloud by various stakeholders involved in the process of our trying, unsuccessfully, to convince the White House to catalyze a revolutionary new national commitment to boys' and men's health.

- Males are privileged and dominant in comparison to females and thus don't need help.
- Most of human history is about boys and men, so we don't need to focus on them.
- Supporting males will take resources away from females and it's females who need the resources, not males.
- It will cause governmental gender equity issues if we focus on male health and well-being when males already get more help in our culture than females.
- There are budgetary concerns about studying males—for instance, the White House Commission on Girls and Women is being funded by numerous governmental agencies and so there are no more funds for a male commission.
- Money, time, research, and resources are not needed for males because money and resources move toward helping males automatically through other sectors such as white men in high positions in government and corporate leadership.

It's true that a few men do have a lot of resources and many of them are white, but most men are in the same boat as women—living, struggling, trying to get ahead—and as Chapter 1 showed, there is no science-based or realistic way to argue any more that boys are ahead of girls in American health and well-being, yet the minefield and the DGP control the culture's conversation. As we see suicide, murder, school and community massacres, broken families, millions of boys and men in trauma, and general malaise and anhedonia among our young males— much of which bleeds over into harming females—how much longer will we succumb as a nation to the neglect of males?

Cleaning Out the Minefield

While the amount of money, focus, attention and resources provided to women is a wonderful thing, it is time to admit: We live in an era of ideological blindness that so controls us, when we do actually spend taxpayer money on males, it is not on studying and advancing boyhood as a living, breathing necessity of American life but, rather, on incarcerating males whom we perceive, from the get-go, to have already failed us. When I was consulting with a high-ranking official in the Department of Justice, he corroborated this in a way that still haunts me: "Actually, Mike, we do spend money on boys and men—once they get into our corrections system." He knew that massive incarceration was not a morally exemplary way to build a society, but he also knew the minefield.

Use Your Power to Influence Higher Education

If you are an alumnus of a university or college, study that environment as it is now managed to see if there is adequate understanding of male development in it. Meet with its directors and administrators and ask pointed questions:

- If there is a Women's Studies department, is there also a Male Studies department?
- Is the female victimization model mainly taught on campus when "gender" arises in classes or conversation?
- Does the administrator know that male mental health is just as damaged in the U.S. today as female mental health?
- Is scientific rigor guiding the gender studies produced by the university's scholars?
- Has the university culture become obsessed with political correctness and micro-aggressions?

As you ask these questions, challenge the university's personnel to expand its protocols to include systems biology viewpoints.

Challenge myths about gender that the university unwittingly perpetrates.

Point out the return-on-investment to university administrators if boys become a focus—more males will pay to go to that college when the college understands and assists males.

Use Your Power to Influence Governmental Focus

What you do for universities you can do for the government. Go online and study all the departments, divisions, and programs in your local, state, and federal governments that provide funds and services to constituents. When you see few or no programs and departments for boys' health or male mental health but many for girls and women, you can bring this up to division heads. You can further bring this up to legislators by voting for candidates who include male issues in their platforms. You can vote against those who are clearly androphobic in their platforms and purpose.

When you interact with government officials, probe them for knowledge of male mental health issues. If one of them talks about Eliot Rodgers, for instance, the shooter of six women and men in Isla Vista, California in 2014 and explains, as many officials did at the time, "he killed those women because he was a misogynist," you will hear his mental illness take second or last place in the conversation to a DGP principle. Yes, he was a misogynist, but that is not why he killed those people. Causation lay in male mental illness. Challenge this person of influence to see beyond single, popular themes.

Use Your Power to Influence Media Focus

Media literacy about male mental health is especially critical to a revolution on behalf of boys because the media mainly report the talking points given to them by academics and the government. About males, this is especially true, so as you read articles and blogs, study the "studies" reported in them as a citizen scientist on the frontlines of social change. When you see flaws such as those pointed out in this chapter, critique the study or media report in your community. Send the article/blog to your social media network with critiques attached. Simultaneously, write the reporter or blogger to correct them when they make mistakes.

And when you hear androphobic and inaccurate accusations leveled at males remind your friends, family, and social media networks that every time flawed gender research does this, every boy and girl will lose. When we amplify grotesque male practices beyond the few men who commit the criminal acts, we corrupt the very foundation of our democracy.

College administrators such as Carrie Franklin work in a minefield that they, as individuals, cannot remove. They need us, the parents of the college students and the young people themselves, to help them.

To move away from the DGP and toward a more appropriate and

fair millennial gender paradigm—science-based and equally focused on females and males—we will each need to individually affect the conversation in the Big Three around us.

Children's rights activist Marian Wright Edelman expressed what is at stake: "Investing in children is not a national luxury or a national choice. It's a national necessity. If the foundation of your house is crumbling, you don't say you can't afford to fix it while you're building astronomically expensive fences to protect it from outside enemies. The issue is not, are we going to pay; it's are we going to pay now, up front, or are we going to pay a whole lot more later on."

Not only "mental health" but "*male* mental health" must now rise above the minefield to full study by American academic and governmental institutions, and our investigative journalists. The effects of genetics, trauma, and neglect on "people" and "women" must be augmented by the study of their effects on "the male brain." Nature must join nurture and culture in our nation's visionary conversations. Any other course is a minefield in which boys and men, then the society around them, explodes.

Part II

Saving Our Sons

"I am assuming that you are man enough to be a man—not a mere machine of selfishness on the one hand or an anemic imitation of masculinity on the other hand. I am assuming that you think—and, what is more important, feel—that Nature knows what she is about; that 'God is not mocked'; and that therefore you propose to live in harmony with universal law. Therefore, I am assuming that you have established, or will establish, the new home in place of the old home. I am assuming that you will do this before there is a gray hair in your head or a wrinkle under your eye."

—Albert J. Beveridge, *The Young Man and the World*

Chapter 5

Male Nurturance: Supporting and Building Male Emotional Intelligence

> "Looking back, I saw that for my whole conscious life I had not understood either myself or my strivings…. But just as the waves of the sea knock the inexperienced swimmer off his feet and keep tossing him back onto the shore, so also was I painfully tossed back on dry land by the blows of misfortune. And it was only because of this ordeal that I was able to travel the path which I had always really wanted to travel."
> —Alexander Solzhenitsyn, *The Gulag Archipeligo*

A THERAPIST SENT ME this email.

I want to tell you a story about an athletic 15-year-old boy who was snowboarding with friends when he made a jump and fell and was unable to get up. He could not feel his legs. He was taken to the hospital and trauma surgeons removed bone fragments that were pressing on his spine and they fused his neck. He is now paralyzed from the nipple line down. He can move his arms somewhat but cannot use his fingers. He and his family became my therapy clients.

While undergoing rehabilitation therapy, his family surrounded him, including two brothers who returned from the war in Afghanistan to support him. His mom told me about watching them interact. In one incident that she described, the boy was able to feed himself with a special fork that fits over his hand. One day while feeding himself he put the fork down and said he was exhausted. He asked a visiting brother to feed him the rest.

His brother responded, "I'm not going to feed you when you can feed yourself."

The boy said, "But it's hard."

The brother said, "Hard? That's not hard. I'll show you pictures of hard. Do you want to see?"

117

The boy said, "Never mind," and fed himself the rest of the meal.

Another day the boy was unable to control his arms so he could not consistently reach his face. The brothers asked him to try to touch his face, and when his hand flopped on his chest or swooped by his face or hit other places, they all laughed, including the boy. The mom told me it's like that game when boys hold another's hands and hit that person with his own hand and say why are you hitting yourself? The laughing and humiliation worried the mom and she asked her sons to stop it.

Another day, the three brothers had grapes. The older brothers would ask the boy to open his mouth so the brothers could put grapes in his mouth. The middle brother took a step back to see if he could toss the grape in the boy's mouth. With each grape that went in the mouth he would take a step further back until he was across the room. Lots of the throws resulted in the brothers making fun of each other but each time the brother made a throw, all the brothers, included the 15-year-old, hooted and laughed, even if the 15-year-old couldn't catch the grape in his mouth.

As the mom watched these scenarios take place, she felt the urge to intervene in order to protect her youngest son, but gradually she decided to refrain from intervening because she saw the positive impact the brothers were having on the boy. He was joyful and adjusting well to his situation when they were around.

When I read this email aloud at my lectures there are always some gasps, especially when I imitate the disabled boy awkwardly trying to feed himself and slapping his own face. We all feel sympathy for this boy; we empathize with his mother's discomfort, sadness, pain, grief and protectiveness. We can almost hear her inner talk in our own minds: "What the heck are my older sons doing! They got leave from the war to help support their younger paralyzed brother. Instead, they're pushing unreasonable and grim expectations of independence on him. Instead of nurturing him, they hurt his feelings. Instead of helping him verbalize how he feels, they make him slap his own face. This is not empathy— this is torment."

We feel her pain and yet we also feel something else: hope. The mother ends up feeling it, too. Gradually she realizes that her paralyzed son gains from the discomfort, improves his state of mind because of the expectations, uplifts and rises from paralysis with new life almost imperceptible yet palpable in the goings-on of these young men. As the mother looks into her son's eyes, she alters her idea of torment—she sees nurturance, empowerment, and bravery born of this tough bond with these older males. Her stepping back—her grace of non-intervention—becomes a small act or revolution for her children.

I believe she had an epiphany in which she sensed (perhaps always knew but not until now knew it consciously) how different the nurturing methods of males can be, at times, from female. While it's her maternal instinct to protect her vulnerable young son from emotional pain at the older brothers' hands, she has raised these boys and lived with their father. She has sensed all through her life that these males have a life of the heart, an emotional intelligence, that is, at all times, similar to hers—of her blood and being, often deeply tender, quite honest, and directly empathic—and yet, also, because it is male, unique to these boys and men. As she steps back to watch the dispassionate compassion, the aggressive empathy, she allows boys and men to care for a hurt boy with male emotional intelligence.

"This mom could have stopped all this, and the guys would have stopped if she told them to, but she allowed it to go on," the therapist told me. Indeed, mothers and women in general have immense control over the empathic development of boys—arguably much more control now than ever before in human history because many boys are now raised almost exclusively by women. As fatherlessness grows and males are pushed out or recede of their own volition from the care of homes and neighborhoods, raising boys has become a new kind of challenge for moms and women. This is especially the case for single moms who raise multiple sons and daughters. They do much of the work of developing emotional intelligence in boys.

As they do so, they sense the difference in male and female physical impulsiveness and aggression, tolerance of pain and discomfort. These moms notice that their sons often seek out pain and discomfort and inflict it on one another as a form of love. What moms notice is crucial to human survival and helps all human beings thrive. It is a profound genetic and neural male and female difference in emotional intelligence that we must protect and nurture if we are to help our civilization, our streets, our schools, and our homes have a positive future for both our sons and daughters.

In protecting the use and success of male emotional intelligence, our fathers and our men will become as necessary as our mothers and women. When we see clearly the grace and necessity of both male and female emotional intelligence, we will feel a deep call to develop equal parts of both in the lives of children—a kind of gender symbiosis, an interrelationship that can help our children become whole. This equal respect for and utilization of male emotional intelligence constitutes our fifth step in social revolution in large part because understanding MEI will mean we understand the other half of empathy—the hidden male ways of empathy that root, to some extent, our androphobia. Understanding the deep intelligence of some of what we have been taught to fear at all costs creates significant empowerment for girls and women and frees our human relationships to progress forward into much greater mutual love.

Seven Traits of Male Emotional Intelligence (MEI)

"Emotional intelligence" is the general term for effective maturation, emotion-processing, empathic response, successful interaction and relationship, and general adaptability. The science of EI has perhaps been best popularized by Dr. Daniel Goleman's best-selling book *Emotional Intelligence* and other companion works. He defined EI as "the composite set of capabilities that enable a person to manage himself/herself and others." In this vein, an emotionally intelligent person generally has the emotional awareness, understanding, and expressiveness needed for good relations with others. This person can handle strong emotions from others and control his/her own strong emotions. He or she tends to solve personal and social problems with adeptness, and generally does so in a way that most or at least some others hope to emulate.

Given this definition, we could just say there is "human emotional intelligence" and leave it at that. Research from around the world begs us to go deeper, however, because cross-cultural EI research shows us that "emotionally intelligent" differs somewhat between cultures. In the U.S., for instance, there is greater emphasis on individuation away from family groups to assert emotional independence in young adulthood. Equally interesting, here in the States, it's considered emotionally intelligent to say "No!" more often than in, say, Japanese or Chinese culture, in which the emotionally intelligent individual is one who almost always says "Yes" while perhaps surreptitiously meaning, "No!"

Similarly, the male and female brain experience gender difference in emotional intelligence. "Males and females do their emotions somewhat differently," Daniel Amen has concluded after studying more than 100,000 male and female brain scans among patients of the Amen Clinics.

Here are some of the brain differences. You can test these with the most fidelity if you compare hundreds of boys and girls in your own school, neighborhood, play groups, and home. Remember, as with all brain differences, not every difference will apply to every child at every moment. Some girls and women at certain times might practice traits of male emotional intelligence in certain situations and boys and men similarly practice traits associated with FEI. Think in aggregates and in long-term studies (multiple observations of multiple children over a period of weeks and months).

Male Brain/Body	Female Brain/Body
Fewer nerve endings for feeling pain	More nerve endings for feeling pain
Fewer pain/pressure receptors in brain	More pain/pressure receptors
Less activity in insula (less direct empathy)	More insula activity (more direct empathy)
Quicker exit of blood flow from insula	Slower exit of blood flow from insula
Less rise in heart rate during conflict	Greater rise in heart rate during conflict
Blood-testosterone levels rise when under stress	More blood-oxytocin flooding under stress
Less cingulate gyrus (feeling-rumination) activity	More cingulate gyrus (feeling-rumination) activity
Fewer word centers connected to emotions	More word centers connected to emotions
Amygdala creates activity downward into body	More amygdala activity upward to words
More gray matter activity (singular focus)	White matter emphasis (multiple emotions)
More active cerebellum (physical/doing center)	Less active cerebellum during processing

These are just a few of more than one hundred areas of brain/biological difference that affect gender-differentiated emotional intelligence.

As I explore the Seven Traits in this chapter I will further explain what these are and their role in differentiating male and female emotional intelligence.

Trait 1: Male emotional intelligence is often more kinesthetic and more physical than female (gets into other people's physical space) and is often misunderstood or villainized.

A first trait of male emotional intelligence is the kinesthetic-physical. While females often tend to favor words-for-feelings, males often use more non-verbal physicality or physical-kinesthetic gestures associated with a few directive words. A mom might use and elicit words to care for her paralyzed son, while the two brothers might only use words that direct him to engage in physical actions and building toughness, even when these words are hard for him.

In the male, as a result of numerous brain differences including a larger and more active cerebellum (the part of the brain just above the brain stem), emotions move more quickly from the brain down into their physical bodies than in the female. Meanwhile, the female brain moves more of its instantaneous neurotransmission of emotion upward from the limbic system into the word centers on both sides of the top of the brain. If you notice that your son is more likely to hit a desk or punch a punching bag or stand up and pace and move around when he is in a highly charged feeling-state or even in a normal state of emotion, you'll see MEI at work. He is quite capable of using words when his brain connects emotions to words, but he's also more likely to produce physical-kinesthetic (and, often, pre-verbal) emotion-responses than his sister.

This is not necessarily a bad thing—it's just who boys generally are. In fact, males need to be impulsive to test their emotions and character experientially in the real world. They need this experiential learning curve of body/brain connection because they don't do as much of their emotional intelligence building through words as their sister does. This is why I teach "the three times rule" in my work with families and schools rather than zero tolerance policies.

The three times rule is: let's direct and correct the child each time he is too impulsive, but don't punish him until the third time. The exception to this rule is, of course, if he is being violent or dangerous. When people punish boys for their first impulse rather than guiding them into a three times format, they are generally penalizing males unfairly for utilizing MEI to learn who to be and who to become.

Adjusting our thinking to notice MEI will mean that our social systems must rethink what we do with male physicality and impulsiveness. As you and the people around you study MEI you will most likely notice that many of the "uncomfortable" hits, knocks, jabs, wedgies, and other physical gestures among males are forms of kinesthetic love—physical emotional intelligence building mechanisms. Boys will often feel not-loved or respected unless they get this physical love. Studies of father's play show that brain centers grow and mature for both boys and girls through the physical play and physical affection that our fathers, men, and boys give offspring and peers.

I've found this teaching very useful to help teachers and staff understand their own intuitions about boys and girls. These professionals already understand that male love is often more kinesthetic and female more verbal. But they haven't received scientific training in this before. As they came up the ranks they were told that the best way to do feelings was through words, so they've curtailed their natural instincts with males. As they go through training on MEI and FEI, they discover that they're working, in a sense, in two schools in one—a boys' and a girls' school—and within the boys' school, they have three sub-schools in one:

* approximately one-third of boys, e.g. sensitive boys like Caleb, learn better when schools become hyper-attuned to female learning styles, which tend to be less physical and more verbal, and significantly adjust classrooms toward the female brain.
* approximately one-third of boys are not affected negatively or positively by school adjustments toward the female brain. These boys would learn well in any environment.
* approximately one-third of boys are negatively affected both academically and behaviorally by the female-brain-centric classroom and the rampant misunderstanding and punishment of the male brain and MEI.

It's this third group of boys that schools tend to lose in the millions across the U.S. These boys, punished, medicated, or unloved for being boys starting back in pre-school, hate school by seventh grade and keep hating it all the way through high school. Thus, while all groups of boys and girls can benefit from a school teacher's deeper understanding of the male brain, the success of boys in the third group *depends* on families and school systems understanding MEI.

Trait 2: Male emotional intelligence does not avoid but seeks out pain and adversity.

This trait tends to be one of the most confusing MEI traits to moms and women. At the same time, understanding it as a part of the core of maleness can bring immense relief.

During the 2015 Tennessee rout of Northwestern in the Outback Bowl one commentator asked if it was fair that Tennessee, already ahead by 38 to 7, kept pressing for yet another long-ball touchdown. As Gail and I watched this game she pointed out that the Northwestern players looked pretty sad already from the thrashing.

"They're being way too hard on those poor guys," she said, as she left our couch somewhat appalled, and went to do other things. The first on-screen commentator agreed with her—he hinted that Tennessee should "mellow out." But the second commentator chuckled, "Listen, hey, don't play sports if you don't want your feelings hurt." The next touchdown was scored and the gap in points moved to a crushing 45 to 7. "This is sure painful," the commentators agreed, but they also agreed: painful and hurt feelings not only come with the territory of sports but are some of life's best teachers.

A grandmother of a 15-year-old girl told me a wonderful story in a similar vein as I was writing this chapter. "Cara has always been small, shy, and non-athletic. We've worried about her self-esteem for fourteen years. Right near her fifteenth birthday she finally gave in to her older brother, 16, who was always goading her into running track. 'You run like crazy when I'm chasing you. Just try it, for God's sake! Who cares if it's painful and you don't do well! Just do it!' She finally did sign up for track and she lost the first few races by such large margins that she cried, even sobbed in the car. But, you know, something happened to her; the losing inspired her.

"'I don't want to cry like that anymore,' she said to me. 'I want to do better.' She practiced and practiced and practiced and two months later she won her first race. Now she's 16 and loves track. She also loves winning. Her self-esteem is much higher. My worry about her being strong in the future has gone from about 8 out of 10 down to a 4."

This grandmother told me this story with tears welling up in her eyes. As we hugged one another I felt the leap in maturation her granddaughter experienced by being goaded by a brother and coached mercilessly by males to succeed through and with her pain. In her brother's goading, and in the ordeal of the sport, she encountered the second trait of MEI. While girls and women love sports and are great at them, sports are social institutions that grew out of the male love of "the ordeal." Males often tend to see life as a harsh quest in which a child must face ordeal after ordeal to build and show character, strength, and self-esteem—be an emotionally intelligent adult.

This male love of ordeal and "pain" is a part of nature—it involves male biochemistry, brain structure, and pain tolerance. In a recent study of 85,000 people, 45 percent of women experienced some form of chronic pain but only 31 percent of men did. McGill University pain geneticist Jeffrey Mogil has reviewed gender-pain research from all continents over the last 15 years and confirmed a significant gender difference in pain response—males tend to have a higher pain tolerance. This is part of why males on the average not only feel less pain than females, but actually go out and seek more pain than females. Factored into these averages is child-birth, an area where females obviously experience more pain than males, but on a daily basis males will take risks that create pain and then groan or cry but also laugh, wearing the pain or wound they receive proudly for all to see.

The source of male and female difference in pain thresholds is chromosomal: the XX female includes more chromosome markers for pain reception than the XY male. These markers compel females to develop more nerve endings for pain reception and more pain and pressure receptors for processing pain than males. Not surprisingly, then, it's easier for boys to wear physical pain as a badge of honor than girls. They feel less pain as they do at-risk things to test their limits. Their enthusiasm for superheroes and gory drawings in school is an expression of their sense of painful ordeal as stimulant of maturity. This isn't true for every boy at every stage of his life, but it is true for most boys in most stages of life—including adulthood. This differing pain-response provides a profound reason males often don't seem to empathize with others' pain in the same way females do.

"Neuroscientists tell us one key to empathy is a region of the brain called the insula," writes Daniel Goleman, "which senses signals from our whole body. When we're empathizing with someone, our brain mimics what that person feels, and the insula reads that pattern and tells us what that feeling is. Here's where women differ from men. If the other person is upset, or the emotions are disturbing, women's brains tend to stay with those feelings. But men's brains do something else: they sense the feelings for a moment, then tune out of the emotions and switch to other brain areas that try to solve the problem that's creating the disturbance. Thus women's complaint that men are tuned out emotionally, and men's that women are too emotional—it's a brain difference."

Pain-acceptance and problem solving link in the male brain. Not only are males more prone to go out and seek pain, they are more prone to put up with more pain as a tool of maturation. Meanwhile, they're also less prone to linger very long on "seeing their own or another's pain." When homes, schools, neighborhoods and our other social institutions have tried to delete "winning" and "losing," they have unconsciously directed human maturation away from Male Emotional Intelligence.

Over the last fifty years, they've accepted the DGP androphobia about males and thus tried to save everyone from feeling pain they asserted was created and administered mainly by males and male or masculine systems. In this paradigm, our culture has compromised or removed fathering and male nurturance from many of our systems, making communities and social institutions much more FEI-building than MEI.

From an evolutionary standpoint, this fifty-year shift has been positive in that it helped to re-value FEI in ways that patriarchal societies had deleted or diminished. Loss of FEI equality was not good for our families and communities. We need both kinds of intelligence. At the same time, the last fifty years have swung the pendulum too far away from MEI in schools, therapeutic treatment, organizations, and families so that now we have to rescue MEI in our time. The crucial point here is not that the female way is inferior but rather that it's not enough by itself, nor is the male way, alone, enough. Gender equality exists when we have equal parts FEI and MEI in all areas of child care and adult interaction.

As a citizen scientist, you can test your own sense of this second trait of MEI. The next time you're in a conflict experience or you observe a male/female conflict, track how long the male and the female "stay with the pain." Watch how much longer the female takes to talk about and process her pain. Notice how much more quickly the man moves to problem-solving or, even, to increasing the pain if it is physical in order to prove himself worthy. See how you feel about all this. Sit with it for a while. In popular culture, this male penchant for problem-solving—cutting off "empathy" and pushing for painful solutions—has come to be considered a flaw or fault in marital relationships. Popular magazines constantly scold men and try to improve males by telling them that, to become emotionally intelligent, they must "just listen to her, validate her, give her emotional feedback, then talk to her about what you're feeling."

This is fine advice, up to a point. Everyone can become a better listener and every relationship needs better listening. But the admonishments against problem solving are just like those against painful competition in schools—they push the definition of emotional intelligence almost exclusively towards FEI. A nature-based or neuroscience-focused approach, as Goleman himself has pointed out, will value the male way equally.

Healthy couples will become those that "meet in the middle"—discussing feelings for a while, then equally respecting not-talking-about-feelings and the attendant relief of problem solving. In child-raising, emotionally intelligent parents will become the ones who respect the healthy "ordeal" of males as much as the "use your words" and "feel your feelings" of females. The redemption of the father and of males in our culture will appear for the next generation as we come to understand the importance of all this to the survival and thriving of children.

Trait 3: Male Emotional Intelligence Nurtures and Builds Resilience Differently than Female.

The first two traits provide background for understanding the third trait. Male emotional intelligence tends more toward nurturing and empathy strategies that are aggressive and challenging of personal limitations. Female emotional intelligence is more directly empathic of the feelings felt by the person in distress. Both approaches to empathy teach resilience—overemphasis of one without the other can deplete the development of resilience in children and adults.

In your own citizen science, you can study these two kinds of empathy and nurturing this way: find a group of early adolescent girls and boys playing a sport together, for instance, flag football. Watch them until you notice a boy fall down. His knee is skinned, a bit bloody. While trying to hold tears he holds his knee and rocks back and forth in pain.

Watch a girl teammate come over immediately to touch his shoulder.

"Are you okay?" she asks in an empathic tone.

For her, the game stops—what's important now is the imperative of direct empathy—to give him personal aid for his feelings and consternation. She's stimulated by a rush of the human bonding chemical oxytocin that flashes through her brain and body as she sees the fallen child. Her insula activates immediately and remains very active as she creates mirror neurons for the boy's pain in her brain. She almost literally "feels his pain." Simultaneously, her cingulate gyrus (the attention/focus part of the brain) fills up with glucose metabolic flow that compels her to think out how to help this hurt child feel better as quickly as possible. If he can feel better, then she, who is now suffering with him in the mirror-insula, will also feel better. Her brain activates verbal/word centers in both hemispheres (asking him questions, verbally interacting) to help her give care to, return comfort to, and raise the self-esteem of this fallen child.

Simultaneously, watch what the other boys are doing. You may well notice a male teammate run past the fallen boy, conclude he's not badly hurt and yell at him, "Get up, get up, we need you!" In comparison to the direct empathy the girl is giving, where is this running boy's empathy for the fallen child? Even as the words leave his mouth he rushes away toward the football!

Let's look at what's happening inside his bloodstream and brain. Rather than oxytocin, surges of testosterone (an aggression chemical) heighten in his bloodstream and cells. Meanwhile, his mind is mainly driven by the competitive, aggressive, and purposeful "cause" of the game, a cause and purpose that doesn't "stop" in his mind like it does, momentarily, in the girl's brain. His mirror neurons barely change and brain moves blood flow away from the insula the instant he decides the fallen boy is not severely damaged. The aggression-success of game and goal—from which everyone, including the fallen boy, will get their high self-esteem—are far more important to him than this one bloody knee. This boy is just as empathic as the girl, but in a different way. While the girl helps the fallen boy feel better as soon as possible, the boy helps the fallen child feel stronger as soon as possible.

Study this difference in multiple settings—at home, at school, in your neighborhood, even in your workplace. You may notice that the boy and girl make unconscious decisions about what resilience is and how to nurture it in others. For the running boy, the fallen boy won't become resilient unless he continues to explore and find his strong part of the aggression and competition of the game. Self-esteem, he knows, is in large part a matter of being needed for the success of a group. Getting hurt is the normal sacrifice one makes for the greater good. Better, he believes, is to uplift the fallen boy by saying, "We need you! Come on!"

This testosterone-based third trait of MEI, just like its oxytocin-based counterpart in FEI, are often called "coercive nurturance" and "prosocial nurturance" in biological studies. While the Dominant Gender Paradigm has propelled an idealized socialization viewpoint as far away from "coercive nurturance" as possible, the growing field of brain-based educational psychology provides different wisdom, asking us to invigorate human nurturance "bi-strategically." Bi-strategic means using two strategies for resilience-building equally rather than using one predominantly (uni-strategically).

Patricia Hawley at Texas Tech University is a leader in this field and makes the case for "bi-strategy" powerfully in this way. First, she notes the lean of the DGP toward pro-social nurturance that has developed a view of "aggression as largely an outcome of a process of maladaptation to perturbations in a child's ecology—such as coercive parenting, economic disadvantage, or criminogenic urban ecology—that ultimately lead to dysfunction." In this prevailing contemporary model, aggression is generally not seen as prosocial or adaptive except to grab power or status, or to fight wars or predators. As Hawley notes, in the wake of this model, the vast majority of our children who fit our present American view of emotionally intelligent and "adaptive" children are female; the majority of children who fit our view of not-emotionally intelligent, dysfunctional or maladaptive children are male.

Yet as Hawley studied resilience and success of both boys and girls over a period of decades, following the children well into adulthood, she discovered that both boys and girls become more adaptive adults when they are raised in environments that include bi-strategic training throughout childhood and adolescence via both "prosocial (cooperative)" *and* "coercive (aggressive)" strategies. They are more resilient because they gain the assets of both strategies from their parents, teachers, and caregivers, and thus have both sets of assets for use as adults.

The "bi-strategists," Hawley notes, become the combination of male/female that lead to the most success in later life. Hawley explains: "Part of their success is due to the fact that they are high in aggression yet mitigate the costs of aggression by employing pro-sociality." She discovered that these children begin to show their greater success as early as fifth grade. Even more stunning, Dr. Hawley discovered that differences in maturation show up for preschoolers: the more bi-strategic preschoolers are, the more they "have an advanced understanding of moral expectations and the norms of the social group."

Hawley's findings and their corroboration among her colleagues beg us to reconsider our obsession with some popular constructs in child development, including our belief that aggression is inherently bad for preschoolers and schoolchildren (and, by extension, everyone else except sports figures or soldiers) and direct empathy, especially via verbal literacy in emotional expression (talking about feelings) is inherently better. In fact, aggression-nurturance and direct empathy-nurturance are both crucial to our children's success in life and love.

The Pro Bowl linebacker Sanders Shiver (Baltimore Colts/Miami Dolphins, 1976 - 1985), who now leads the Prince Georges County Early Start Child Education program in Maryland, told me recently: "I learned a lot about how to be a good *boy* from my mom, who taught me kindness and empathy, and I learned how to be a good *man* through the men who coached me in football and taught me how to stay strong through any adversity, even when I was in such pain I didn't know how I would go on. As a boy and a man I needed both ways of learning."

While in some circumstances MEI goes too far and in some circumstances FEI goes too far, it is generally MEI we try to squash in most of our child-rearing institutions today. As we systematically overreact to it, we try for a uni-strategic approach to empathy that ends up backfiring on the self-confidence and resilience-development of children. The loss of a strong father in a divorce, for instance, robs both boys and girls of MEI and both children will tend to be less mature, less resilient, and less adaptable.

Part of the immaturity and sense of entitlement (affluenza) of our millennials comes directly from unbalanced ratios of FEI and MEI in American child-development. A male business executive at a gender training at Cisco Systems—a man in his sixties who wished to remain nameless—put the idea this way, with a warning attached. "To me, when young people in our workplace, especially the young women, say they don't want to feel 'discomfort' I just see a 'me generation' orientation, like 'Stop! That hurts me!' I mean, sure, if there's real pain or overt hostility, then that's a good response, but most of the time this twenty-something isn't really hurt at all. The kid just wants everything to be cushy. But 'cushy' 'easy' and 'feeling good' isn't what life and hard work are about.

Everyone in a workplace this stressful needs to be able to handle tough times without blaming other people or taking things personally."

Robert Cole, CPA, the Controller of a major media group in the Midwest and Northwest, corroborated this observation. "Young people in general seem to be coming into the workplace less mature than they did a generation ago. It is becoming a significant issue in our industry."

Kathryn Kerns, a professor of psychological sciences at The Ohio State University, has studied children and adults to discover the ways in which bi-strategic parenting is useful to children's resilience and success. She has noticed that MEI, sometimes called "paternal nurturance" or "the father factor," (which moms can sometimes practice, of course) helps build resilience in these ways.

* Teasing. By teasing children more than moms tend to do, fathers, boys, and men compel more resilience later in life as long as the teasing does not become abusive or repetitively bullying—because teasing, like talking about feelings, is a bonding activity that compels pathways in the brain to develop between emotion and thinking centers. A lot of the neural pathways people have tended to believe can only be developed when children "talk about feelings" actually can develop through teasing behavior, and some of them can develop more quickly and permanently through this more "coercive" form of nurturance.
* Revving kids up. By throwing children up and down, startling them, for instance, and petrifying their moms, Dad is actually stimulating a wider range of emotions in the child's maturation than just sitting still would stimulate. The revving up and the physical fear factor is crucial for resilience-building in attention, focus, and emotion centers in the brain.
* Ending eye contact sooner but meanwhile scanning the environment. Moms not only tend to keep eye contact longer with children than fathers do but fathers tend to look out into the world more, compelling children to also look out into the world to measure themselves. Resilience-building needs both kinds of eye-contact—gaze into an intimate other's eyes, and gaze into the larger world in which the child will be tested.
* Exploration and building. Paternal nurturance tends to do more bonding through tasks, activities, building things,

experimenting on things, and exploring. Dr. Kerns has noticed that this gets nuanced between moms and dads even down to the way moms are more likely to teach a child a skill by helping him follow the established or written rules while dads are more likely to "throw the kid out there" to see how he problem-solves himself. Both ways are powerful resilience-builders.

* Compelling the rules of independence. Active fathers tend to challenge their children to take on big tasks, including hard ones, whereas moms tend to praise children more quickly for doing the minutiae of each task during each step in its process. Dr. Kern also noticed that dads will, more often than moms, pretend not to know how to build a toy either in full or at a crucial stage of the process so that the child is compelled to complete the building process himself. Not only does this build independence in the child, it also compels the child to realize one of the rules of resilience: while we parents might do a lot for you when you're young, in real life you have to be independent and strong to succeed.

Fathering, mothering, and bi-strategic parenting are as much spiritual as physical. MEI teaches:

> humility…
> "You're so wrong, you're inflating yourself, come on, grow up, be a man!"
> …loss…
> "I have failed, other men have failed, this is the way life is, get used to it"
> …grief…
> "My sorrows are so immeasurable sometimes I just don't know what to do, but I persevere"
> …pain…
> "Life is basically very painful so protect yourself and protect the people you love"
> …joy…
> "It's okay to feel happy sometimes, that's why you have a family"
> …and the male part of the meaning of life…

"Life is an adventure, a quest, and most of the time you just don't know what it all means but you keep pressing at it because there is something wonderful going on and you need to be a part of it."

Can moms teach all these things too? Of course! But, generally, Mom does this teaching in a more maternal and less coercive way. Moms who have become citizen scientists about their sons often tell me they notice a direct link between lack of child-resilience and a passive, inactive, absent or non-existent father or male mentor. The most frequent comment in our Gurian Institute surveys on this topic, "Children need their fathers," is supported by both scientific research and real life.

Question: Do female and male emotional intelligence approach bullying differently?

Answer: Yes, they often tend to, and it can be a healthy difference.

In *Blue Bloods*, the CBS cop drama set in NYC, Danny, a detective played by Donnie Wahlberg, is father to two adolescent sons. One of them, an eighth grader, comes home with a black eye. Danny learns why: the boy got called a nerd by a bully who had been cheating off the boy's tests. Sick of it, the boy decided to purposely get a test question wrong. As a result, the bully also got the question wrong and did badly on the test. In response, the bully hit Danny's son in front of a crowd of peers. The son felt embarrassed, ashamed, and just generally terrible—and he had a black eye.

Dad learns all this from his son and asks, "Okay, so, what did your mom say to do?"

"She said tell the principal, get the other parents involved, and go to peer-to-peer mediation. But there's no way I can snitch." This boy knows: things will get worse for him if he betrays the group that way. His father knows it too.

So, Dad takes a different tack. "When I was a kid like you I got in fights," he says, "and I lost my share. Here's what we did." He offers a secret weapon to his son as long as the boy promises not to tell mom.

The next day the boy comes home glowing—he has gone from depressed to very happy. His self-confidence has clearly returned, and Dad can see that.

"What happened?" Dad asks. "Did he make it to the bathroom?"

His son laughs. "No way!" and "It was great!"

The trick—the secret—was to sneak some ipecac syrup into the bully's lunch.

"He puked right in front of everyone!" the boy says, laughing.

Father and son share this triumph together. Mom, not privy to exactly what the coercive and somewhat brutal solution was, tells her husband in a later scene that she's glad everything got worked out. She can see that her son's self-confidence and resilience have taken a step forward. For the sake of the father-son bond, she wisely allows the secret between father and son to remain sacred, without prying, and clearly respects male emotional intelligence.

While this "solution" to bullying is fictionalized, it is also an example of how differently MEI and FEI often see bullying. For me as a boy and for my father as a man, when I was bullied, the solutions were "mom" solutions—try to talk it out—but then also moved, if necessary, toward "dad" options: "If you have to fight back, punch him back; that's the only way he'll stop bullying you."

Both Mom and Dad were right in various cases— sometimes, talking to the bully could help, sometimes, talking to other parents and teachers and principals helped. Other times, however, a more physical-kinesthetic approach was needed. Like Donnie Wahlberg's character in *Blue Bloods*, I got in a few fights as a boy. I lost some and won some. In more than one case, there was no other way for me to stop a bully than to fight back.

While I don't suggest that any school institute a policy in which fighting on school property is condoned, I do believe we've moved so far away from male emotional intelligence that we are pretending the American bullying problem, which is acute in many schools and neighborhoods, can be solely solved with words spoken to the bully, the witness, the victim, the adult, or the schoolchildren.

Sometimes healthy coercion is needed more than words—an aggressive, kinesthetic/physical action that will confront and thus nurture resilience in the victim and also, most likely, alter the bully's trajectory of domination and violence.

Trait 4: Male Emotional Intelligence seeks out weakness in order to compel healthy adaptation.

A deep asset of female emotional intelligence is that it is more protective than MEI is of feelings. Women who wish others would not put down boys for having feelings or for crying, like Jane Fonda did at the women's conference, are protective. As we've said, that protectiveness—that pro-social strategy—is good and crucial to human development. Put-downs and other dominance strategies can indeed hurt kids and certainly they can feel painful in the moment. And while some women, like my mother, are often coercive, MEI and FEI do tend to trend along gender lines so that, in most cases and situations, the tendency in nurturance toward an overriding focus on individual feelings trends more female than male.

As our society has developed the Dominant Gender Paradigm over the last fifty years, FEI protectiveness has risen in application throughout our social systems. In the United States especially, as the DGP has helped us uplift women's empowerment, the Big Three have moved toward a female emotional intelligence model in which "I am feeling hurt" is considered a paramount and essential statement of health. The assumption in this trend is that males' and females' self-esteem is significantly damaged by put-downs. Because women's mirror-neurons activate and remain active for many hours or for days when they see their son or daughter experience emotional pain from verbal attacks, they work very hard to try to "heal" the child's pain immediately with verbal responses of sympathy.

Despite this trend and despite the importance of this immediate expression of pro-sociality in children's lives, boys and men, for the most part, see things a bit differently. While we know it is true that put-downs can be damaging, we also tend to sense that emotional intelligence development *needs* put-downs, criticism, and coercion to *discover weaknesses* and build strengths in others and ourselves. Put-downs, to us, are a form of love. We males know from very early in life that most boys and girls don't suffer long-lasting or overwhelming damage from being made fun of, challenged, called names, even treated harshly at times by siblings or peers. Abuse/bullying is the exception to this, as is constant criticism of a sensitive child.

Boys seek out weakness in others and then attack it mercilessly to help one another grow up. This trait of MEI creates a conundrum for social systems that have decided to think uni-strategically toward only pro-social and against coercive strategies. For most males, the "fear of feeling vulnerable" that many people today say males shouldn't have is, in fact, a healthy trait of MEI; it is natural to male life. But for people who only want feeling-conversation and who only want the end of put-downs, males will seem defective. And while coercive put-downs can lead to dangerous repression of feelings—thus all of us must remain vigilant to make sure males can access feelings—most of the time this fourth trait is not dangerous. It's part of the male journey.

One reason lies in biochemistry. Because of higher amounts of testosterone, even the shyest boy whose mom says, "He's not aggressive at all," will likely become aggressive in some areas, for instance, while playing video games. He'll try to prove himself through and with aggression, and he will specifically target any area in the game or game theory where he's weak. This need for strength, status, and worthiness mitigates vulnerability, in general. One can't be highly aggressive and highly sensitive at the same time if one is to succeed at the aggressive act of proving oneself worthy in the world.

Expanding This Conversation in Your Community

Given how frightening this trait of MEI can feel to a protective parent, it can be difficult to engage this conversation in our communities, especially because bullying is constantly discussed and with good reason. Federal studies, available through the FBI, have discovered that about 13 percent of American children are severely bullied, and that is no small number. Trait 4 can become bullying and, even when it is a form of nurturance, it can be confused with bullying.

Our children are innocent and vulnerable, we know. To us parents they are perfect the way they are; they need constant comfort, not coercion. The world is hard enough on adults, we will say in our PTA meetings: why make it hard on kids? A parent myself, I completely understand this love of the innocent child. However, if we are to stave off the phenomenon of adult males remaining immature for decades and adult females taking things much too personally in workplaces and in communities, we'll need to expand our community conversations about what really needs to be done, including taking our present views away from extremes ("Hazing is great, there's no bullying in it, it's all good" or "If you feel even the least bit uncomfortable you should be able to litigate"). Both are crushing our children's ability to mature in healthy ways.

One way to expand conversation is to point out that most of the punishable offenses in hazing, teasing, one-upping, and aggression nurturance are male offenses. Our fear of male emotional intelligence forces us to neglect its virtues and benefits or systematically try to erase it from social life. In pretending "male nature" doesn't or shouldn't exist we're taking a culturally illiterate view of human development. Better would be to take the revolutionary view of pointing out in your meetings, your blogs, your posts, and your school and community conversations how essential MEI is.

The people who can support you in doing this are, often, your boys and the men you know. You can ask men to tell their stories of their own boyhood. They will not only have stories remembering when they felt hurt feelings and were told to suppress those feelings, but also stories of times when one-upping, proving themselves, and adaptation from weakness to strength built greater resilience, strength, and maturity in them. Let their stories help you make the case that nuance and thoroughness of study is needed as we discuss aggressive and coercive nurturing in school policies, in homes, in neighborhoods, and in all social institutions.

As you tell their stories, bring research to bear from this book, as well. In the Notes and Resources at the end, I've provided a notation of a fascinating new study out of Sweden that you can use. It tracked one million boys and men and showed that a lack of toughness-training during male adolescence predicted premature death of men later, at a rate of 30 percent higher suicide and disease rates in adulthood! This is the kind of science-based study you can post on your Facebook page to show that male "toughness," while potentially harmful, is also life-saving.

A mom wrote me an email about how she moved the conversation forward in her community.

I was at a PTA meeting and we had an expert speaker who kept talking about how much we should focus on teaching boys not to make fun of each other. I kept wanting more depth from the speaker because I have raised my son to feel his feelings, every mom I know has done that, but I stood up and said, 'Look, we have to get beyond that theme if we are going to really help our boys. I mean, I see boys having feelings all around me, like my sons can talk a blue streak about what they feel, so please speak to us about the deeper stuff going on inside boys, like, how they seem to resent how much I press at them about those very feelings! I used to think that meant they would grow up to be immature men but now I wonder if they are trying to tell me that I'm hovering so much to protect their feelings that they can't mature in other ways.'

The speaker wasn't too open to what I said so I have started writing blogs about my life as a mom of sons. It is a very freeing experience—I love it—and it helps me join this boys' movement I want to see everywhere now.

If you do not already do so, consider writing blogs about your life as a parent of sons. At your dinner tables, in your PTA and PTO groups, in your classrooms; while sitting and watching your kids play soccer or do their karate; in your Bible study groups or academic lectures open to the public, *talk and write about your sons.* As a citizen scientist, you can become a powerful voice for the new *complex systems approach*—the ethological and ecological approach—to male biology and male culture.

Trait 5: Male emotional intelligence does not focus on words-for-feelings (verbal emotional expression) as much as female emotional intelligence does, and that is okay.

We have hinted at some of the science that explains this trait already—now let's explore it more directly.

At Ohio State University in Columbus, Dr. Brad Bushman, a professor of communications and psychology, has been studying the various ways that we "vent and express our feelings" when we feel discomfort or pain. Coming as we all have in our academic training over the last five decades from the baseline idea that verbally expressing our feelings is the healthiest course, he decided to test the idea. To do so he created a series of studies and controls among various age groups to see if thinking about feelings (rumination) and using words for feelings (verbal expression) will lower our stress levels, assist us in our relationships, and help us act more successfully in groups at work and in our families. Measuring stress responses in both one-on-one/ group conversations and social media/email verbal expression, he got fascinating results.

The theory was borne out, to some extent, by Dr. Bushman's experiments, published in *Personality and Social Psychology*. But in a majority of cases, Dr. Bushman found, "the students in the rumination group were angrier and most aggressive while those in the control group, who did nothing to vent their feelings, were the least angry or aggressive." This result turned the debate about the sanctity of verbal expression of feelings on its heels. While it's certainly a good thing to "use your words," talking about feelings is not the panacea for human development some people have posited it to be.

Dr. Bushman's studies have been replicated by neuro-psychiatrist Daniel Amen who tracks rumination and feeling-expression in brain scans. Dr. Amen told me: "The more rumination about feelings in the brain we experience, the more risk of ANTs (Anxious Negative Thoughts), which just continue the stress cycle of more emotional distress and more likelihood of anxiety and depression. Girls and women have up to four times more activity in the rumination part of the brain—the cingulate gyrus—so there is a lot of gender involved in all of this. Without realizing it, women tend to value, sometimes too much, the constant processing and expressing of feelings."

The studies of Bushman and Amen teach us yet another piece of the puzzle. The male way of specifically *not* taking as much time as many females to think about their feelings or put feelings into words (their tendency toward emotional suppression) is just as functional as the FEI tendency to do the opposite. In other words, too much of one approach is not functional. Just like punching someone in the face is generally non-adaptive, too much "I feel uncomfortable, I feel sad, I feel scared," doesn't work either.

Question: You seem to be saying that emotional suppression is a good thing. Are you? Do you really want to say that?

Answer: While it can be harmful, at the same time, emotional suppression is also very helpful in ensuring success.

In a recent poll of managers and line workers in corporations the question was asked, "Who would you rather work for, a woman or a man?" The majority of women and men responded: "a man." In follow-up interviews, the question "Why?" received myriad answers, nearly all of which could be summed up in these two comments:

*   "Men are more direct, less behind-the-smile manipulative in how they lead."
*   "Women bosses create more drama between people because they focus so much more on talking out the emotional process."

I've recreated this poll in my training for women and men at corporations such as Frito-Lay/Pepsico, NASA, Cisco Systems, and the U.S. Department of the Treasury. I've asked the same question and the responses have been similar. When I further ask women, "What is one advantage you can think of when you think about the male brain,?" many responses come, but one that consistently brings smiles: "Men don't ruminate or express as much as women do; they just don't share as much in the workplace and, actually, that can be a good thing."

There is a deep sense of wonder in corporate audiences as I put brain scans up on the screen that light up with various colors. If you go onto YouTube and type in my name or names such as Ruben Gur (at the University of Pennsylvania) you'll see brain scans that show the differences between male and female emotive processing. Looking at those scans you might think, "Hmmm, it seems like males think it's okay not to feel something as much as females feel it." That is indeed a part of

MEI, as is the idea: "For males, it's very often also okay not to feel it in *a lot of words*." In fact, for males, it's actually very functional to suppress emotions and emotional expression, if that suppression is *best for the group*.

Let's look at both sides of this one coin together by admitting that the downside of this interior logic can show up in some males just "going it alone" when it comes to feelings. Protective of others and frustrating to some spouses and friends, these males find internal ways of processing feelings that never come to the light. They leave their children and spouses out of their emotional world by attaching very few words to feelings. In their lonely bedrooms or long walks or long drives to a seeming nowhere, these males feel and think, process and grow, yet without audience, without a friend, without a lover to help them. They're roamers and nomads through emotion, alone. That can be very hard on some marriages and relationships.

At the same time, that's not all of what's going on with males in their tendency to use fewer words for their feelings. The musician Russ Deniston illustrated another side of Trait 5 in an article he wrote in recollection of his emotional experiences in 1974 when the Supertramp album, *Crime of the Century*, came out. He recalls a difficult freshman year in high school in which he listened in the privacy of his bedroom to "School," the album's sad lament about educational conformity.

"I wouldn't understand what conformity meant for years to come, or that going through the public school system was designed to produce a certain kind of end-product. But I did know enough to identify with the feelings of fear, confusion, competition, and all the rest." He wrote further that this song and these memories helped him to become a musician not because he expressed them to others but because they so imprinted on his lonely experience of listening to the music without others. About the song "Hide in Your Shell," he recalls his feelings.

"The song's lyrics 'But what you see is just illusion,' 'You're surrounded by confusion,' and 'To feel that you are alone' described my interior condition, one of wondering what life was all about, because I wasn't figuring it out very well and I'd taken to hiding the real me, just like in the song." At 19, a young searcher for a self, his emotional core, his soul, opened wider than before. At a Supertramp concert he felt a great deal of intense emotion as he saw the screen picture for the lead song, "Crime of the Century."

"The outline of a prison cell window and fingers grasping the bars was the perfect picture for this album, the representation of our condition, our humanity hemmed inside of ourselves."

Deniston recalled feeling more feelings in that moment than he could describe in words to anyone around him, and words were not needed for those feelings until decades later when he wrote the very short article of words about the experience. My male friends, who speak aloud similar suppressions or delays of feelings, and men I see in therapy who often tell me how many feelings they had as boys that were never shared with mother or partner or spouse will often say two things at once to me about this:

* "I wish I had said more to other people."
* "What's wrong with just feeling these things myself—why do I have to share everything?"

Adolescent boys may have an especially hard time with this. Sharing feelings with others often feels to them like it lacks integrity. As much as it feels right and good to share feelings with the people who beg a boy to talk about his feelings (that person is often his mom) he may also sense that he's betraying something in himself by carrying on such an inner struggle to let his mom coerce spoken feelings out of him. Mothers, wives and partners in therapy often tell me how much this very same male non-sharing hurts them—that their adolescent son or spouse seems to be finished processing his feelings before he talks with her. It appears that he "just doesn't have any feelings to share," or "refuses to tell me what he's feeling." In this way, women often feel that the male is withholding his heart and soul from the people he loves.

Differences between the female and male brain can feel like a cruel joke on parents, children, and on lovers, especially the fact that females produce and connect words to feelings on both sides of their brain in far more brain centers for verbal processing than males have, and males only do it in the left hemisphere, mainly in the front left, with fewer verbal centers and less neural pathway connectivity between emotion centers and word centers.

While it is crucial that we continue as a modern culture to help men speak aloud their feelings, especially with those they love, we can't have a social revolution on behalf of our sons if we don't confront the tacit lack of integrity in the idea that gender equality in love cannot occur until males share all or even most of their feelings in words. This will never happen! To believe it is the gold standard of love will continue our social trend of calling males perennially defective for being who they are.

Trait 6: The male approach to friendship and love is often different from the female—males often emphasize challenge and the pursuit of valor together, and this kind of bonding is crucial to human survival and thriving.

I brought up male/female differences to a good friend, Gene, 65, at lunch a few years ago. He and I had been friends for 27 years. We sat on this afternoon across from one another at our favorite Thai restaurant in downtown Spokane and we caught each other up on our lives. Talking about himself he said, "You know, in some ways, I've never been happier. My life is just what it is, problems and all. I know who I am and I'm finally at peace as a man."

"Wow, Gene," I congratulated. "How great!" In his eyes I saw that he had arrived at the place William Wordsworth called, "the calm existence that is mine when I am worthy of myself." Ten years younger, I didn't quite feel yet what he felt.

"Yes," he smiled, "it is great."

Food came—Garlic Shrimp and Cashew Chicken. We dug in and he asked, "And what about you, Mike? How are *you* doing?"

"Fine, fine," I said, then we talked more and finally I sighed, "I envy you your peace, Gene. In some ways, I'm still a wounded boy trying to heal himself, that boy whose parents fight all the time, the boy in a battle with political forces, with male versus female forces, with subtleties unexpressed. I'm still trying to explain something, figure out something. *You*, though: you seem complete to me. For the last few months it has really seemed like you are not anxious anymore."

"Thank you," he said, accepting the compliment, "but you aren't doing so bad yourself, you know."

"Thanks, Gene," I said. "I know. You're right." And that was the end of this particular conversation.

In that friendship on that day—as in most of my interactions and friendships with men—a lot of depth of love and truth transpires but with little spoken about the deep subjects we are actually talking about. In fact, during our whole interaction of deep love and bonding that day, Gene and I talked mainly about whether the Seattle Seahawks would make it to the Super Bowl, a subject we still pondered the next time we saw one another, about a month later. Entering the restaurant, we gave each other our customary quick hug and high five, sat down to order food, and focused mainly on the Seahawks again, who had indeed, by then (January 2014), made it through the playoffs and into the Super Bowl.

When we got around to "deep things," we spoke briefly, and enjoyed our silences. Coincidentally, I had just read a passage in the Pulitzer Prize-winning novel *The Goldfinch* in which Donna Tartt has her young male narrator reflect on his friendship with an older mentor named Hobie. The male narrator writes: "Though our talk was casual and sporadic there was never anything simple about it. Even a light 'how are you' was a nuanced question, without it seeming to be; and my invariable answer ('Fine') he could read easily enough without my having to spell anything out."

I loved this passage because even a very verbal male like me—a writer who writes many words per day—can sense this male nuance. Gene and I talked about our own pursuit of worthiness, valor, success (the battle played out by the Seattle Seahawks) and attached it to a sense of peace without verbally connecting all the dots. Donna Tartt's characters sustain one another to survive and thrive even when they say very little about anything except to bond and be present to one another. This deeply resonates for males even though most of us can barely enunciate its depth in our maleness and MEI. I remember my best friend during late adolescence, a boy named Mike Garvey ("The Two Mikes" his mother called us). We often just sat silently on the beach or in his basement listening to records such as Supertramp's or watching television. When we talked about ourselves, it was usually while playing pinball, chess, or after swimming, or as part of the flow of life in which we tried to be strong and smart and, in our own ways, morally right. We talked a lot—both of us were high school debaters and could talk. But we talked about our task or game or our budding bravado, and not much about one another's feelings.

Yet we knew those lives well. We understood each other's souls. Years later I would read the American poet C.K. Williams, who wrote of men, "For our more abiding, ancient terrors we each have to find our own valor." The two Mikes' valor, our courage, came in large part from the depth of silent presence we experienced together.

This is an amazing part of MEI stimulated, biologists believe, by differing ways the chemical vasopressin joins testosterone in working through the male brain. By thriving in the silences, the unsaid, the oblique—and by bonding through tasks of valor as much as or more than words—boys and men find and feel a great deal of heart and soul—emotion and feeling. Mike and I understood this as Gene and I understand it. Connected to this trait—this emphasis in male friendship on the often unexpressed but shared feeling of *valor*—is the methodology for creating courage together and in one another.

Understanding this in our social systems will become revolutionary as we decide to value it as much as FEI. Not only Mike's and my silences, but also our banter and dissing of one another, was our male emotionally intelligent way of talking about building valor in one another without talking about it per se. Instead of giving one another an instruction manual on how to be courageous within and without, we coerced one another to learn courage. While we certainly gained—as Gene and I have—from watching how girls and women build friendships, we also, instinctively, tried to protect our own way of building friendship—male bonding.

This point affects all systems that give care to human beings. The health care system is one example. As everyone knows, boys and men occasionally need to get medical help, but many do not get into therapy or even go to the doctor. We've called this a defect in males yet we've missed something about Trait 6 in some of their reluctance. We've missed the sturdiness and functionality of male stoicism and we've missed the need of males to bond with the practitioner in a male-friendly way in order for the male to surrender his highest intentions for others as he receives care.

This is the hidden internal measurement of bonding-success in males: pair-bonding or group-bonding to sustain interpersonal valor of self-sacrifice. Males know they are somewhat disposable and will generally try to make sure everyone else is cared for first. When they do act to surrender the will to sacrifice the body/self, they will generally surrender that will in a pair-bond or group-bond (often among other males) that convinces them it is okay to make that surrender. If a male doesn't form a male-friendly bond with the doctor, nurse, or therapist in the context of not just talking about how he feels but 1) doing things to still care for others, and 2) doing things via MEI trait models, and 3) doing something he is convinced is important (and doing it together) he'll likely continue to avoid the therapy or doctor's office.

Internally, even if he's ill, he will continue to pursue valor, assume responsibility, "go internal," and continue his disposability and self-sacrifice, all of which will, practically speaking, mean facilitating a life for others, especially women and children in which they get needs met even if the man does not. In other words, absent male-friendly bonds and MEI environments in physical and mental health care facilities, men will continue to do what they do best: sacrifice their own health and well-being so as not to be a burden on others.

Many people, especially in the context of androphobic DGP ideas of intrinsically flawed "masculinity," will accuse this man of being inferior or defective, "He's too macho to tell us how he feels, he's too macho to get help," but this misses the fact that this man is taking care of us, intimately and lovingly, though he may not be able to express that to us, or the caregivers, in words.

We'll actually get more males into better health care when we realize, "One of the reasons guys don't go talk to a doctor or therapist is that the whole modality does not fit with many of their brains or their ways of bonding and getting help." Indeed, I believe the health gap—and especially the therapy/mental health gap—males experience is more likely to decrease, and more males are likely to seek help when personnel and systems are set up to include the specific ways male bonding works.

In your own citizen science, I hope you will study male bonding and male sacrifice for valor. I hope you will protect male kinship bonding. Our society's future depends on male bonding as much as female, but male bonding is, at times, more deeply nuanced into the healthy life of boys than we might be able to measure or track. We don't have quality or quantity of words available to us, quite often, by which to determine if it's working or not. Meanwhile, without our protecting healthy male bonding as a crucial human development modality, boys and men (and girls and women who interact successfully with MEI) will be less healthy and will receive less "worthiness" building—less character and emotional development—because there are some ways in which a boy cannot become a worthy and healthy man, a nurturer of children and spouse, a provider and protector, a whole person unless he is challenged to be whole through the love of other males.

Trait 7: Male emotional intelligence helps others "get to the gold"—the legacy.

The final trait of MEI involves the redirection, in the male brain, of feeling and emotion toward specific personal and group tasking around positive legacy. These motivational feelings are stimulated in the limbic area of the brain then parsed toward gray matter areas of the upper brain attached to goal setting and, in larger systems, a personal, familial, or communal purpose. A recent article about the Seattle Seahawks' final road game of the 2015–2016 season gives us an example.

Reporters asked quarterback Russell Wilson about returning to the Glendale, Arizona, stadium where, the year before, the Seahawks lost the Super Bowl on an intercepted pass in the final minute of the game. For the Seahawks and all their fans (myself included) this late fourth-quarter play created waves and waves of terrible feelings of anger and frustration. For weeks afterward it was discussed as many people experienced, expressed, and expelled feelings of anguish at the Super Bowl loss.

All the while Coach Pete Carroll, Russell Wilson, and many other team members were being interviewed about "the play," the loss, and their feelings. And nearly every time the matter came up for discussion, these team leaders referred to it as "something to build on...the right play with the wrong outcome...just another piece of the puzzle of winning next time."

While fans processed lots of feelings, the "gold" was not, for Carroll or Wilson, in processing the anguish verbally among the press, the fans, or even the teammates. Rather, the "gold" would come, these wise men knew, in using the anguish to win the next game and build the greater legacy.

Wilson put this powerfully on January 1, 2016, as he talked with Associated Press reporter Tim Booth. "Wilson again brought up the challenge of getting past a difficult moment in his career," Booth reported. "Wilson said, 'I think it builds you up. I think it helps you understand that the ball doesn't always bounce your way. But when it doesn't work out, how can you use that? How can you continue to build and evolve and progress? It's been a constant progression, this journey.'"

While "getting to the gold" can get taken to the point where traumatic feelings are never expressed in healthy ways, it's also true that many individuals misinterpreted the Seahawks' strategy as "unfeeling" or "not sharing the feelings themselves." The opposite is true. Wilson is feeling a great deal and sharing a great deal of feeling through the new and sacred *task*—the next game, the next goal. And he is sacrificing those feelings, too, for the sake of the legacy of the whole group, including all his fans.

This kind of love is active, what Harvard Psychologist William Pollock calls "action love." In this kind of love feelings are often *servants* of a goal, methodology, team, or legacy that will lead to caring for, nurturing, and protecting the future "gold" for the larger group, team, and society. The millions of fans of the Seahawks and of the NFL are the larger system that a particular individual (Wilson or Carroll) is serving—the gold is not just an individual treasure but a widening circle of success for everyone in the "group." Thus, for this team and men in general, their worth, their gold, often comes in their attachment to and transformation of their pain into a motivational and often shared passion for the task that the feelings are meant to serve.

This seventh trait is one of the reasons every scientific study of any credibility shows the need for male role models to help young males. An older male models goal-setting, legacy-building, and sacrifice of self for the group to younger males. Without that healthy modeling, males can become selfish, myopic, egoistic, and more dangerous. If they are well fathered in the trait and the others, however, they grow to become men of self-sacrifice. They commit to helping build safe worlds for others, in their families, homes, workplaces, communities, and beyond. They combine their energies with other males in goal-focused teams. They work harder, feel stronger, listen better, speak more clearly, and are more completely pro-social.

A New Path for Healthy Boys: Valuing and Employing MEI

In speaking with a group of therapists and mental health professionals recently, I explored these seven traits in the seminar format, then some of us talked together afterward. This exploration was important for us because we were all mental health professionals who work in a therapy profession most males find anathema, especially because it is a sit-still-in-a-chair-and-talk-to-me-for-fifty-minutes modality (not physical), thus a profession better suited for the female brain than the male.

A female therapist, Mary Engle, put her experience with the male therapy-avoidance phenomenon this way: "I've noticed that even the way males and females experience being victims is different so I need a different frame for a lot of my males. Sure, like my females, the males are victims, but most of them are not victims of their own dangerous or defective masculinity. If I lead with that approach to males, they'll flee. They know from deep within themselves that they 'do' emotions differently than I do and they need me to show them I know it, too. I can't pretend males and females are the same and then still expect males to stick with me."

Another therapist, Sammy Ortiz, agreed. "The challenge for us in the health professions, especially in mental health, is to bring more of the male emotional intelligence thinking in, which I think we can do by bringing in more sports psychology. I came to therapy via sports and athletics. In my practice, bonding with male clients is a big deal. I even teach the clients and couples different kinds of male brain psychology, like the PET scans. I really think if we don't pivot the mental health field towards more integration of *male* psychology, we will lose millions of males. But it's hard, you know," he lamented. "You bring up 'male psychology' and you get some backlash, unless you tow a party line on masculine gender roles and male emotional suppression as the main issues."

This led us to ask how it was that the Dominant Gender Paradigm became the dominant academic and psychological theory regarding emotionality and gender. Freud, Jung, Adler and most of the other original psychiatric theorists were male, so how did our profession become so female-centric, "un-male," and attached, when gender came up, to the idea that "males struggle because of masculine roles"? None of us in that room—a brain trust of multiple Ph.D.s, M.D.s, etc.—knew of an actual clinical study involving hard science (biology, neuro-science, genetics) that could prove that the increase in mental disorders, school failure, lack of motivation, and marital troubles in and around us were mainly caused by male emotional suppression or that they would be cured by "decreasing masculine stereotypes and norms." There were lots of "studies" giving opinions about this, but neuro-science and biological sciences did not prove it.

A psychiatrist, Patty Weist, said, "I think the problem is that we try to curtail or end most of the ways males approach feeling and emotion as if each one is defective but we're seeing the opposite result of what our forefathers in psychiatry wanted—they wanted *more* healing and help to *all* people. But today we're seeing more healing and help to *females* and less to males. This lack of gender diversity in our profession ends up putting us all in more danger because these guys don't get help."

This whole afternoon of discussion, interaction, and analysis affected us deeply. A therapist said toward the end of the day, "Okay, if not masculinity and masculine norms, which are easy for our profession to see and talk about, what should we protect our boys from?"

Many answers emerged and many of them were summed up in the word "immaturity." Asked a final question about this by the host, I answered honestly, "The thing that will break a civilization apart is not a stereotype or norm of males—it is a generation of males who do not mature into loving, wise, and successful men."

I believe this deeply. Maturation is the prime directive of childhood—it is the goal of boyhood. Ideologies are important. Protecting both females and males from male excess is important. Meanwhile, equally as important and, now, in the new millennium, even more universally important in the U.S. is male maturation.

Helping our sons to grow up well and on time will save our sons.

Chapter 6

The Science of Maturity: Ending the Male Motivation and Maturity Gap

> "A nation or civilization that continues to produce soft-minded men purchases its own spiritual death on the installment plan."
>
> –Dr. Martin Luther King, Jr.

AN EMAIL FROM A TEACHER AND MOTHER, Crystal, came to me from outside Atlanta, Georgia.

I'm a mom of three sons, 15, 13, and 10. I also teach middle school. I read your book, The Wonder of Boys, *when my kids were young and I saw you speak last year. I'm a strong black woman who raised my boys on my own for about four years. Now Dad is back in the picture but for a while, it was touch and go with all that very loud boy energy in my house.*

What I want to know from you now is what you think about how unmotivated and immature our boys are these days. I see it in my school. Too many boys are just floundering, not growing up, sitting around, getting bad grades, not caring much about it. They don't seem to feel responsible for much. They're not really pursuing any goals. It's a weird phenomenon. It's like these boys just don't have a reason, somehow, to grow up, or don't know how to do so.

The worst thing is, I also see the immaturity at home. One of my boys is king of the heap, he's the leader at school and God bless him. But my other two are floundering and it scares me. I've got six classroom periods a day of boys and girls in our school and I see maybe one girl in each period who is unmotivated and a mess, really sad, but the thing is, I see four or five boys every period getting Ds and Fs and just not doing a thing.

Reading your latest book, How Do I Help Him? *I am now thinking I have seen things all my life through the lens of what you call the 'Dominant Gender Paradigm'. I've bought into the idea that boys are unmotivated and immature as a result of masculine privilege and masculine norms, but that theory seems false to me in my own home. In my home I've raised all my sons to be responsible, to be mature, to be motivated, but, well, I'm worried.*

I want you to tell me the science of all of this because I see it in all kinds of boys—my own black sons but Latino boys, white boys, Asian boys. We're a pretty heterogeneous district in Atlanta, we've got all kinds of kids here. I used to think what you call 'the boy problem' was a black boy problem. I used to say, 'It's a leftover from racism,'' but the truth is, this is not a problem just for black boys or one group of boys. This maturity problem, this motivation problem, it is now a <u>boy</u> problem, and it scares me to death.

In the last ten years, I've received thousands of emails and comments like this via social media, online, and in-person in cities and counties across America. Parents, teachers, and professionals see deep issues in maturation and motivation of males today. While girls suffer many issues, this maturation and motivation issue is much more of a boy problem in America than a girl problem. Similarly, other industrialized countries have noticed it. China, Japan, Singapore, Britain, Germany, Italy, Oman, Australia—all over the world, people are starting to feel afraid of what is happening to their boys' motivation and maturation.

An American mom of East Indian descent sent me a number of emails about her 18-year-old son which I've compressed into this summary:

We got him through school, good enough so he could go to college but the basic immaturity I wrote about kept showing up. He surrounded himself with friends who were always in party mode and played video games instead of going to class. I think he just wanted to keep himself entertained to avoid loneliness and to show off as a grown up. Very soon, you can imagine, he got himself into academic probation and finally he had to drop out of college.

He's in the basement of our house now and we have become like some kind of very bad joke, the kid in the basement sitting at his computer doing God knows what and not doing anything else. We can see that his health is not good, he stays up all night playing video games and his father is sure he is using too much porn. It looks to us like he has completely lost motivation to try anything. He won't grow up.

We confront him but he avoids communicating with us. He is ashamed, but he is also unwilling to take guidance. He's an adult by age so we can't force him into counseling. To us, it is like he has a disease, like cancer, but there is no way to diagnose it in our house. My grown son is not a man, sir, I can tell you: his father agrees with me that this is a very tall boy.

Parents know: all races of boys are in distress. We don't just have an "unmotivated impoverished boy" problem or an "unmotivated boy of color" problem. We have a boy problem that afflicts even the most successful Caucasian and Asian-American boys—even the boys we have decided, culturally, are doing just fine.

The Male Maturity and Motivation Gap

Males mature later than females—physically, hormonally, emotionally, socially, and in nearly every other area of development. But the natural maturity gap has widened in the last fifty years to dangerous proportions. In 2005, I wrote an article about this for the *Washington Post* and received thousands of emails from parents and professionals who told stories like Crystal's from Atlanta. My colleague, physician and neurologist Leonard Sax, had the same experience in 2008 when he appeared on the NPR program, *Fresh Air*, to discuss this male maturity gap and received thousands of emails right afterward. All of us in this field are becoming increasingly worried. The millennial and Gen X/Y males are not growing into adults the way their predecessors did. They are living in parents' basements well into their late twenties, dropping out of college, holding a job for a while but then losing it, and, once bonded to a mate and children, leaving those bonds within a few years or being kicked out by more mature wives.

Gary Plep, who has been a therapist for both the U.S. military and in Silicon Valley for forty years, has led men's groups for the last thirty years. Over this span of three decades he has seen the situation worsening. Here is an excerpt of a recent email about examples of the phenomenon.

In my Wednesday men's group, one of the men (a 50+ mechanical engineer) shared that a friend and colleague was interested in hiring him to replace some of the young engineers he had in his company. The owner of the engineering business had to lay off 30 of these young guys over the last couple years not because they weren't smart but because they lacked maturity to do the job.

Another instance: in my Monday men's group the men are in their 50s except for one 25-year-old who I took in after his father died. He is addicted to video games. We have confronted him several times on his need to "show up," be on time, keep his agreements regarding his participation in group.

We challenge him to grow up or not be here. This is like pulling teeth. This young guy can see that he is immature and so are his friends and he wants to change but he just keeps giving in and being the little boy who, at best, can't quite even succeed at pale efforts to mature.

As I have talked extensively with Gary we agreed: the numbers of these young males are in the millions and they, in his words, "drive people crazy." He's right. We're all frustrated with them—women increasingly so. These boys and young men themselves feel ashamed and sense that they are a forgotten generation but can't muster the wherewithal to grow up. Technically, they are adults so their parents can't force medical or other solutions on them, but they are also psychological boys whose sense of failure compounds their own, their parents' and their society's anger and anguish. Yet we all know, at a deep level of instinct and experience, that a civilization is carried forward on the shoulders of mature men. Our new path in raising the next generation of these men involves confronting the present path of neglect of male maturation we are involved in now as a civilization.

The Four Rules of Healthy Male Maturation

In this chapter I will ask you to take a sixth step in our social revolution by giving you empowering science as well as insight and practical strategies you can use to help your son or any boy who is under-motivated and not maturing well. The life and legacy of this sixth step involves four rules for male maturation that I hope you will use to rescue the natural boy. In prescribing each of these "rules," I will deal with male maturation, but nothing in this chapter will be bad for girls and everything will be good for any child's journey to adulthood.

Rule 1: Male immaturity and lack of motivation are linked with ten areas of male development not just one—but one of them (often hidden from us) involves genetic neurotoxins that directly impact, to the negative, male motivation and maturity in our Industrial and Post-Industrial society.

In my own experience with boys, and corroborated and expanded in my meta-analysis of scholarly and field research in male development, I have identified ten factors that suppress American male maturation. I have already analyzed some in depth in other books and earlier in this book, but I will cover more of them now. As I do so, please see resources within this chapter and in the Notes and Resources section at the end of the book.

As you read these factors please do citizen science by taking a moment to put a check mark by any of these points that you feel instinctively may apply to your son or to a boy in your care. After you've gone through the list instinctively with check marks, we'll go into more depth on the factors.

1. *Neurotoxins* are negatively affecting male gene expression, including suppressing testosterone levels, increasing depression and anhedonia, and thus, decreasing self-motivation. The effect of these neurotoxins can be exacerbated by mental illness.

2. *Significant trauma,* including physical and sexual abuse or prolonged bullying, can raise male cortisol levels too high for too long, affecting brain development for maturation and motivation; this, too, can collaborate in a particular boy with gene expression of mental illness.

3. *The loss and devaluing of the "three family system" (nuclear, extended, communal) and of fathers and male role models specifically is* crippling our sons' development. This is especially detrimental during male adolescence when these attachment figures and identity/role models are primarily responsible for male maturation and motivation.

4. *American families, including social institutions, in general do far too much for boys and expect too little of them.* This social trend provides boys with a growth span of passive rather than active reward-gathering that limits male maturation in the male brain.

5. *Parents, teachers, and others intervene in normal male behavior patterns too much* for males to emote completely, learn impulse-control fully, motivate themselves intrinsically, and mature into men by the normal age of adulthood.

6. Many boys are *overstimulated by too many activities* for their own natural brain and genetic template—these boys often need us to help them cut back on multi-tasking so the boy can mature through specific activities and passions that match his natural talents most closely.

7. Many boys raised in poverty are *under-stimulated by opportunities and resources* (their bodies and minds are undernourished) while other boys who are raised with means and resources are undernourished in *purpose-driven activity, including healthy rites of passage.* In both the paucity of resources and under-focus on purpose-driven life, gray matter development in the brain is impeded.

8. *Our boys spend too much brain-time with technology (screen time) and too little brain-time in nature.* Hyper-use of screens and under-use of the natural world can diminish the full development of the neural centers for self-motivation and maturation in the brain.

9. Our boys as a demographic group *do not go to work, whether inside the home (chores) or outside the home early enough* to help them mature on time. In previous generations, males matured by entering natural work-related rewards systems that motivated them to succeed, thrive, and empathize with others in adolescence. Not now.

10. *Educational and faith community systems are becoming less and less boy friendly, bleeding boys out of them.* These systems have, in the past, mentored boys to maturity, self-motivation, character-development, and self-regulation but now, boys leave them (stop attending church or synagogue) at or near puberty, and thus lose a maturing force in their lives.

Did you put check marks beside any of these numbers? Our boys are very natural creatures—each of these elements affects their developing brain biology and so, anything we can do to address any or all of these will be helpful to their maturation and motivation.

The Science of Male Immaturity

One of the most hidden and destructive stressors on maturity and motivation of our natural boys is the mass of neurotoxins they absorb through food, drink, and other environmental sources—aluminum, artificial sweeteners, sugars and flours that may harm them, junk food, pesticides and other pollutants. If you checked this number 1, you have checked an issue that I believe is perhaps one of the least known yet most destructive to males—and to society as a whole. If you didn't check number 1, please don't skip over this section. Your son may be affected by number 1 but you can't see the root of this issue yet.

Until the Industrial Revolution, our sons ate and drank foods and beverages that were natural to their environment—what was grown around them. Their food fit, for the most part, their gene expression because its genetic makeup and the boy's genetic makeup were both natural. While a particular boy could be allergic to a particular food or drink, a boy's life overall was a nature, nurture, culture collaboration.

Since the Industrial Revolution, and especially in the last fifty years, our children are ingesting artificial chemicals unnatural to their genetic template. These are synthetic toxins that can disrupt male gene expression and brain development. These synthetics can come in a food or drink, lead in paint or pipes (as the beleaguered city of Flint, Michigan has discovered), inhaled air polluted by chemicals, or chemicals in plastics, fertilizer and cologne. Each or all of them can traumatize genetic templates for motivation-pathway development and maturation-activity in the mid and upper brain.

Because the same neurotoxins can harm girls, Gail and I were vigilant about the relationship between neurotoxins and obesity, female depression, and other issues for our daughters. However, we weren't too worried about motivation and maturation because females have more neural fail-safes for maturation and self-motivation than males. In other words, our girls' brains naturally develop these pathways earlier and more completely than boys—especially because of the white matter emphasis in the female brain and female neuro-chemistry. When it comes to maturation/motivation, the male brain is, on average, more fragile. This science has come to us over the last twenty years from studies in many of the seventy-two industrialized countries.

In this way, not only male and female brain-difference research, but also the research on neuro-toxins crosses cultures. In one set of studies reported in *Scientific American,* scientists analyzed 150 billion bits of genomic data from human tissues and cells from brain, heart, bone and blood in multiple countries.

"Myriad control switches help to arbitrate how genes get expressed in different cells and tissues," Dina Fine Maron, who reported the research, wrote in 2015, "and those switches are often triggered by maternal diet, toxic exposures, and many other environmental factors. To begin to understand what drives these complex epigenetic effects, scientists... located the switches by analyzing specific chemical modifications on the

DNA and the proteins that it wraps around. Then researchers took data comparing individuals who have specific biological traits with those who do not to see which traits are associated with which switches."

Maturity requires the switching on or off of certain proteins in certain cells and tissues. Unfortunately, if your son eats or imbibes neurotoxins found in plastics, fertilizer, foods and beverages—often called "industrial toxins"—the switches needed for full maturation of cells and brain tissue may either not turn on or may get turned off.

A new meta-study published in *The Lancet Neurology* revealed that a primary reason for brain disorders connected to immature male brain development are, indeed, these "under-regulated industrial chemicals and pesticides, in addition to exposure to heavy metals" which directly invade gene expression and have become a "major factor in the dramatic rise of neurodevelopmental disorders in children."

Dr. Philippe Grandjean is the co-author of both the *Lancet* study and *Only One Chance: How Environmental Pollution Impairs Brain Development—and How to Protect the Brains of the Next Generation.* He told the *Huffington Post*, "The world is facing a 'silent pandemic' of 'chemical brain drain'. We have an ethical duty to protect the next generation, in particular, the next generation's brains."

Dr. Grandjean and study co-author Dr. Philip Landrigan note that since 2006, when they first published their results, things are getting even worse. The list of "confirmed developmental neurotoxins doubled in ten years. At the top of the list of culprits: pesticides." Pesticides, though helpful in keeping insects away from crops, are harmful to the brains of children—and they touch nearly everything our children eat and drink.

So does plastic, which includes the estrogen-mimicking and potentially dangerous chemicals *plychlorinate biphenyla* and *bisphenol A.* This estrogen-mirroring sits at the heart of the neuro-chemical maturation issue for our sons because it disrupts their endocrine systems. While the endocrine disruptors are good for making greater financial profit off cows and crops, producing more than natural estrogen (and other biochemical agents) that will fatten the cow and "fatten" the crop, unfortunately, the endocrine disruptors also keep many of our boys' neural switches off when they should be on and on when they should be off. For at least a decade we have known that these neurotoxins were affecting girls toward early puberty and greater obesity (invading girls' natural menses and endocrinology) but more recently scientists have come to realize their potential effects on American boys.

It's impossible to say that every single boy's gene expression will be negatively affected by these chemicals. However, millions of boys will be, and your son may be among them. The interaction of the chemicals in food or fertilizer with his human cells may harm him at a hormonal and, therefore, cellular level. As the endocrine disrupting hormones attach to specific receptors in his body, they initiate a complex chain of events that impede cellular development and function.

Think of each hormone inside each cell as an artist at work—a sculptor who chisels at a blob of rock to create a Rodin statue. Natural gene expression, excited and assisted in a natural environment, is that chiseling, that sculpting, that art. Endocrine disruptors interfere with the artistic process because the disrupter can erase a natural function in some moments and in others, alter an action of cells completely. As the disruptor attaches to its unique receptor, it launches a different set of events in body and brain than what was naturally intended for this boy. We don't end up with Rodin's *The Thinker*—we end up with a statue without arm, knee, feet, hands, eyes, or other essential parts of the body.

One of the ways male maturation and motivation diminishes in this sculpting process hides in the profound effects the disruptors have on male and female reproductive functioning. The disruptors may have lowered dad's sperm motility and already affected reproductive cells in mom's ovaries. Thus, the neurotoxins may alter the parents' DNA in both the sperm and the egg before a child is born. Many brain disorders such as autism, anorexia/bulimia, and ADD/ADHD are linked back to these neurotoxin/sperm and egg issues. Depression, too, can be linked to these issues. On the depression genetics, under-motivation can linger because under-motivation is a form of social-emotional withdrawal (anhedonia) that depresses social cohesion and hierarchical advancement. It is sometimes co-morbid with high irritability and violence, but not always. As two extremes of immaturity—lethargy on the one hand and violence on the other—these are often both linked to *depression* in males from DNA invasion by endocrine disruptors that lower male testosterone levels significantly via "estrogen mimicking." This cellular mimicking happens when in the parent or, now, in a son, the industrial toxins drive too much estrogen into cells which creates a disruption that over-produces estrogen cells and under-produces androgenic (testosterone) cells.

Hence, a "First Cause" of male depression, violence, and under-motivation emerges. While there can be other primary causes of the depression (and anhedonia), such as genetic predilection (for instance, two short alleles on the 5-HTT chromosome), trauma response (chronic bullying or abuse), and situational reaction to grief or fear (a family member or spouse dies and we become depressed), industrial toxins are a hidden link to depression in males of the last two generations via decreased testosterone levels caused, we believe, by estrogen mimicking.

We began to see this link about thirty years ago. One of the first studies to focus on the problem came from the New England Research Institute in which Dr. Thomas Travison and colleagues noted a 1 – 2 percent decrease in testosterone levels among men. "Male serum testosterone levels appear to vary by generation, even after age is taken into account," said Dr. Travison. "This suggests that some factor other than age may be contributing to the observed declines in testosterone over time."

From this starting point, he continued to conduct research on males and discovered that estrogen receptors and endocrine disruption in neurotoxins lowered baseline testosterone levels in some males. Over the decades, the 1 – 2 percent annual decrease in male serum testosterone level has grown, by 2016, to what physician and neurologist Leonard Sax has called "a dangerous decline." Sax has noted that male testosterone baseline levels are now 30 – 40 percent lower than an average male in the 1970s.

Researchers in the U.S., Denmark, and Finland confirm Dr. Sax's math. They recently published their findings in *Physiological Reviews*.

"We are at a tipping point," warned Dr. Niels E. Skakkebaek from the Department of Growth and Reproduction (EDMaRC) at Rigshospitalet and the University of Copenhagen. "There is no doubt that environmental factors are playing a role. Many of the male reproductive problems could be due to damage to the testes during embryonic development. While the reproductive problems could arise from genetic changes, recent evidence suggests that most often they are related to environmental exposures."

Recent studies published in the *Journal of Clinical Endocrinology and Metabolism* have corroborated Dr. Travison's, Sax's, and the EDMaRC findings. Dr. Shalender Bhasin of the Boston Medical Center revealed: "The data in this study are important because they provide independent support for the concerns raised earlier about the reproductive health of males....It would be unwise to dismiss these reports as mere statistical aberrations because of the potential threat these trends...pose to the survival of the human race and other living residents of our planet."

While our popular culture often condemns high testosterone as dysfunctional, calling it "testosterone poisoning" or "toxic masculinity," and while high testosterone has indeed been linked to high risk-taking that can end up dangerous for individuals or groups, we've missed the fact that chronically low testosterone is equally or more dangerous because it is directly linked to male depression, which is a direct cause of both male violence and male under-motivation and immaturity. With too little testosterone in our cells, male body, biochemical, and neural development is at risk.

If you didn't check the first of the ten factors, above, I hope you'll consider, if it's appropriate, checking it now. One reason you may not have checked it is the lack of academic, governmental, or media discussion of this aspect of male development. In my meta-study, I found more than 95 percent of related studies and media reporting on male under-motivation did not mention "low testosterone" or "neurotoxins." In fact, while I was writing this chapter and these very words, an article came out by a social scientist in *The New York Times* (April 4, 2016) who wrote without scientific proof that males are staying away from college and maturing later than young women (or not at all) because "masculine stereotypes" keep them attached to their "privilege as a dominant group" and all this forces them to "not be emotionally honest" which then causes all the other ills. In this article, none of the factors listed above are discussed, nor is there any significant science in the article.

Yet the science of endocrine disruptors and male maturation holds a key to what is really going on. Artificially low testosterone levels are harming sperm and egg, and killing our sons and daughters. Neurotoxins invade male development at unprecedented rates today, and we must work together to end this unnatural social trend.

How Do I Know If My Son Has Been Affected?

When I meet an older adolescent boy or adult male for counseling who presents with trouble becoming motivated, I suggest immediately that his parents get blood/spit tests that provide genetic and other nature-based information, including a check of his testosterone levels. I explain that an endocrinologist or other related professional can do these tests and will do so, most likely, a number of times in a multi-week period so that a baseline for testosterone can be established. If that baseline is determined as "low," one cause of his under-motivation may be clearly neurochemical. While the neurochemical stress already activated in parental sperm or egg can't be controlled now, his parents can control the food he is eating, the drinks he imbibes, the plastics he drinks from, and other non-organic agents in his environment.

One way to know if any of this might affect your son is to check the three primary markers for male health—physical health, cognitive health, and social-emotional development. If your son is having trouble in any of these three areas, you may have very good reason to protect his growing body and brain by getting him off of plastics and thus saving him from the "estrogens" and BPA; giving him organic food, thus saving him from the fertilizer that carries the endocrine disruptors; taking soft drinks out of his diet thus saving him from the excess sugar, sweeteners, and endocrine disruptors in the chemicals in pop; and teaching him "neurotoxin literacy" so that he can become a citizen scientist on his own behalf throughout the rest of his life.

Rule 2: Boys mature their social-emotional brain pathways and centers as much from non-intervention by adults as intervention; if we want them to grow up well, we must intervene much less in their normal behavior than we currently do.

I received this email after speaking at a conference of Montessori teachers and parents in New Jersey. The organizer's friend and colleague sent her this email in the late evening after our conference, and I am grateful that she forwarded it to me.

Today at 5 p.m. we had Aiden's birthday party at Space Odyssey. The kids got to bounce, jump, and run around. Then it was time for pizza. The kids ate in the party room. Some kids eat faster than others. While we were waiting for all the kids to finish eating, a few boys found an empty space in the middle of the room and began wrestling around. Before we knew it ten or so boys joined in. Rose and I started to talk about Michael Gurian and what we heard from him about maturity, intervention, and aggression nurturance in the conference this morning. Christine (Zachary and Kyle's Mom) excitedly joined in on the conversation since she has read two of his books.

The horseplay began to get a little rougher. Tanay dragged Khalid across the floor by his arm. Rose and I wanted to step in but we instead collaboratively decided to observe and see what happens. At this point other parents got interested and joined in on our observation process. I looked across the room and Susan and Fahima were on the other side watching intently, pointing and discussing but never intervening. The boys themselves were hugging, wrestling, rolling, dragging, and kicking. I was getting nervous but the boys' faces were all smiling. Their eyes were on each other totally engaged, totally connected. No one was malicious. At this point even the party attendant had joined us in our fascination.

Then it was time for cake. The kids gathered around the table. No one was hurt; everyone was happy. None of the girls had joined in on the horseplay by the way, but most of the boys had. The kids sang happy birthday, first in English, then Spanish, Filipino, Chinese, Hebrew. The attendant was shocked and amazed and wanted to know what school we were from. Everyone had cake and said what a great party it was. We said goodbye and there were lots of hugs. It was great.

Thank you for the conference. We are all discussing, debating, wondering, calculating and thinking about Michael Gurian's words. I hope we can continue to unravel the mystery of boys—well, a mystery to us women anyway!

Montessori classrooms are peace-oriented and very high on the verbal-literacy scale, training children to use words as much as possible and avoid shows of aggression. My daughters went to Montessori school through sixth grade and loved the method. Gail and I are big fans of Montessori, as well. But many Montessori teachers and administrators have shared with me that there is a flaw in the daily practice of Montessori Method as regards *boys:* the schools often loses more boys than girls. When parents pull their boys out, they're unsure of why, because the Montessori Method should be, in theory, great for boys—it's very hands-on, kinesthetic, and project-based. But some of the boys don't seem to be flourishing.

I have worked with Montessori schools throughout the country to understand not only the way boys learn and what they need cognitively, but also male maturation, including the assets of male emotional intelligence and male motivation in the male maturation process. One major area of discussion in this consulting is: "Why didn't the girls join into the rough play of the males at that restaurant in the email?"

While some girls enjoy aggression more than others do, and even more than a boy might, most girls will not use it as the first choice for play and bonding, but many boys will. Given that natural boy, the question of when to intervene in playtime becomes very important. When adults intervene to stop rough (scary) play they curtail male maturation and motivation-development but often don't realize they are doing so.

The Montessori parents at the restaurant made a choice to help their boys become motivated rather than end their self-motivation. In their citizen science at the conference, then at that restaurant, they saw no danger to any child or community in the boys' physical nurturance and maturation of one another, so they chose to let male emotional intelligence and maturation guide the moment. They made a counter-cultural choice that pays off for boys' health and growth—*non-intervention*. It is counter-cultural not just to Montessori schools but to contemporary America.

We adults today, especially haunted by DGP ideas of "toxic masculinity," contribute to lack of male maturity and male motivation by generally creating social systems in our homes and schools that don't nurture the nature of boys as well as they could. In these systems, there is constant intervention—constant interruption—of natural male maturation.

The Neural Pathways of Growing Up

Maturation is a brain development process that occurs as the brain experiences limbic system (midbrain) to frontal lobe connections and pathways (pathways to the cerebral cortex). As little children, we are impulsive, mainly activating out limbic system. To grow up, we must learn to make executive decisions, choices, regarding our impulses by activating our upper brain. To continue our maturing, we develop the limbic-to-pre-frontal cortex pathways and better activate upper brain functioning through diverse "stressful" *every day experiences*. We will know we are mature when we have developed significant executive decision-making capability—making tough choices to direct impulses and impulsiveness. To gain that maturity we must experience millions of social-emotional stimuli that have a beginning, middle, and end all their own, most of them uninterrupted by adults.

Unfortunately, many of the popular culture child-raising decisions we've made as adults in the last fifty years have created less mature children, especially less mature, less motivated boys because those decisions have involved hyper-structuring our children's everyday lives. As we hyper-control and hyper-organize boys' interactions, including their playtime activities and their scuffles, they don't naturally grow neural pathways to full maturity because they don't engage in the full-length intimate experiences needed every day to mature those pathways.

In other words, even though our intentions are good, we "de-mature" our sons rather than fully maturing them.

Helicopter parenting is perhaps the most famous example of this neural problem. By our intervening in the child's every moment of existence, brain development is impeded because the helicopter parent does the brain development for the boy. The boy's brain is relegated to an unnatural and very passive existence because the parent thinks he has to be protected from harm. By doing that for their son on a consistent, even obsessive basis, the boy doesn't have to learn to take care of himself independently, grow courage or valor, or develop complex emotive problem-solving skills. In other words, he doesn't have to mature social-emotionally or even, with completeness, cognitively.

Zero tolerance policies in schools are the essence of helicopter parenting. Thinking that we, as adults, are the only or the most important maturation agents in children's lives, we assert ourselves into their existential development at every turn and in nearly every moment.

The author Meghan Cox Gurdon captures this beautifully in her article, "When Children Truly Ranged Free."

"American childhood today is a much more supervised and curtailed time of life than it was even a generation ago. Walking to school has become a rarity where once it was common; organized play dates have largely replaced spontaneous gatherings; and woe betide the child who bites a sandwich into the shape of a weapon or points a banana at a schoolmate: He may face suspension for an act of such proto-violence."

Like Crystal and the Montessori parents, she has seen first-hand how "de-maturing" constant intervention can be.

While some insertion of parents, teachers, and other adults into child maturation is, of course, essential, especially when a child is in danger (I will fully explore other strategically important developmental interventions in Chapter 7), much of what we do is detrimental, especially to the brains of males because males do not have the same maturation fail-safes the female brain has.

Neuroscience researcher Yuko Munakata of the University of Colorado recently presented findings at the Integrative Science Symposium in the Netherlands that explain some of this brain science. Using behavioral and neural data, she and her team studied thousands of children and adolescents to examine "how the increasingly structured activities and social lives of children may affect the development of executive control."

She found that "children who spent more time participating in unstructured activities scored higher on a verbal fluency task that measures executive functioning than those who spent more time on structured, externally directed activities." As she expanded her research she found that positive and strategic interventions can improve frontal lobe pathway development in children and, thus, executive decision-making, but, simultaneously, too much intervention and structure can harm that same brain development.

This research challenges us to rethink the social trend toward stopping rough play to *talk about what happened.* We have thought for many decades that if we invaded our sons' development to talk with them more, we would increase their verbal functioning. But Dr. Munakata's findings show us that while, yes, talking to boys is wonderful and useful, brain development is also very subtle—letting the child continue his play, learning, and growth experiences without intervention or verbalization will also help the boy develop verbal fluency and executive self-regulation (maturity) experientially.

Why?

Because stopping his existential experience to talk about it ends the holistic and multi-sensorial challenge activity in its tracks. On the other hand, leaving it unstructured and uninterrupted—active all the way through the whole life of the experience—allows the brain to grow even more verbal executive pathways. The message here is that "action" is often a better method for the brain's effort to mine the whole multi-sensorial, non-verbal, and verbal experience of the moment for its neural "gold" than stopping to talk. Obviously, like so much of the new brain-science research featured in this book, the science asks us to encourage our boys' health and development at deep non-mainstream levels of lived human experience.

In your own citizen science, take some time to list ways in which your son's life is constantly beleaguered by intervention. As you do this, think back to when your mom or dad used to just send you out onto the street or into a muddy field to "go play." Because of this freedom of play and unstructured time, you had to generate your own game, find your own game-mates, create and build your own "container" and space for the game, discover objects you needed for the game, some of which you ended up having to build with the help of your friends, and talk through, both in your heads and with playmates, the game itself, physical objects, and existential conditions.

This methodology stimulated lots of neural pathway development because back in that day, we couldn't remain passive if we wanted to play, grow, learn, compete, and prove ourselves. We had to move from brain-maturation moment to brain-maturation moment as we threw ourselves bravely into the daily mystery of our unstructured and relatively unsupervised play.

This methodology is something to ponder and emulate but it doesn't mean I am saying, "Never intervene in boys' play." Of course, if children are in danger, intervention must happen immediately. And in many cases, structured activity and learning is quite beneficial. But a new baseline for intervention in play and growth time will need to develop in America over the next decades if we are to save our sons. My rules of thumb are:

1. Unless there is real danger, consider rethinking the existential mystery of male play and growth by increasing non-intervention.
2. When you do intervene, use zero tolerance policies very minimally and maximally use "the three times rule."

If you see a boy in a group do something you don't like (but is not imminently dangerous), let it happen once to see what the other kids do. Generally, the boy himself or the other kids will force change in the behavior immediately or over time.

However, if the negative behavior doesn't change, watch it happen again and, this time, give a warning that doesn't stop the activities. In other words, yell out or give a warning but don't intervene.

If the behavior happens again after this warning, pull the boy out of the container for a verbal interaction (correct the behavior) then, after he has cooled off, send him back in. Even in this "third time" don't stop the game or interaction for the group, only the misbehaving boy.

After the third time, if the boy continues the bad behavior, more grave consequences (including not playing this game or time out for the boy) may be very appropriate.

At a school-parent evening recently I was discussing this and a parent said, "I think we intervene so quickly with boys because we use girls' behavior as the gold standard."

I think she's right. As research has shown, boys are five times more likely to be suspended or expelled from pre-school than girls quite often because *they are not acting like girls.* Untrained in male brain growth, male maturation, and male motivation-reward biology, preschool and K – 12 teachers and parents stop male growth from occurring in the very environment that parents believe is a safe container for that growth.

Conducting Your Own Study

Here is an experiment I have seen used in more than 200 communities. I hope you will consider using it to conduct your own anecdotal study.

Set up or find a place where young children will gather—a classroom, playground, or large group party at your home. Allow the play and learning to transpire for a long enough period of time that you notice conflicts arise. As the conflicts gain momentum prepare yourself to do all of these things at different times:

1. Intervene three times. Say "Stop that, don't do that, that's bad behavior."
2. Not intervene three times (unless the kids are in danger), just watch the whole process transpire.
3. Nurture with direct empathy using words three times during intervention or later.
4. Nurture with aggression and challenge three times –e.g., direct the boys to punch a punching bag, take a run, slam their left fist into their right palm to release tension—if words arise in the boy, they arise, but if not, you let the action speak alone.

As you conduct this experiment over a series of weeks, you should notice some very interesting findings. One thing you might corroborate through this experiment is "locus of control." When you do intervene, notice that the child's focus moves from the child to you. As this happens, notice how the boy will, quite often, stop his maturation process to watch you puzzle out what has happened. He may lower his head, fidget, wait to see what you do or say, then mirror it as best he can. Because of your intervention, his brain, his psyche, and even his body will basically stop.

While using good words that teach him how to apologize, for instance, we the adults who intervene go through a number of emotions—especially if the child is our own offspring—that the child will now need to help the adult with. The child may build a minute amount of empathy this way, but most of what the child will do is stop his own growth until the adult feels better, feels reassured, and finally moves away again to let the child play, learn, and grow in his more active and complex way in the game of other kids.

But if at other times you let him skin his knee and even cry in pain, the community of *other children* will come around in diverse ways to help him, and it will not be his job to help the other kids regain equilibrium and go through their own emotions. Our fallen child will be able to go through all his own complex array of emotions and neural pathway development. In fact, he will be *forced to do so* because he is not being rescued by an adult so he has no alternative—he must grow pathways in his own brain.

Think about our earlier scenario in which one empathy nurturer might ask, "Are you okay?" while an aggression nurturer yells, "Get up, we need you!"

While crying for a little while then getting back up again and playing the game, the child doesn't need to go to the periphery of his own growth experience to reassure the adult. He cries then he gets up. His brain feels a lot, and it decides positive next steps. If a parent or other adult rushes in out of sympathy for the boy, grabs the boy, lifts him up, hugs him, suggests he sit on the sidelines for a moment to recover, the boy is no longer an actor in his own neural drama. The locus of control of his life is back on the parent. The boy has to stop growing in order to do this thing the parent wants him to do despite the fact that the boy would rather cry then get back into the game.

Question: Does most book banning fit this category of "over-intervention?"

Answer: Yes. We must stop banning books boys will read.

Book banning is, generally, an example of too much parental intervention in male development because emotional intelligence, motivation, and maturity can develop through reading but we are intervening in that maturation by banning books the boy will likely read.

Ten years ago, in *What Stories Does My Son Need?*, young adult author Terry Trueman and the Gurian Institute team suggested 100 books and movies to build character in boys. Since then many of those titles have come up for censorship proceedings. *Harry Potter* has perhaps constituted the most notorious case of censorship, but there are many others.

The very books that boys might like to read often get banned, which decreases the development of verbal pathway development in the male brain. The boy goes online, into more passive environments that mature him less well. Sometimes twisted political correctness forces the ban, like banning *Huckleberry Finn* for using the word "nigger." But more often a book is banned because of some kind of prudishness or ideological moralizing among a few parents in a school system, so a tiny minority ends up harming the vast majority of children.

Rebecca Skloot, author of *The Immortal Life of Henrietta Lacks,* for example, saw her critically acclaimed and bestselling 2010 novel attacked because one parent in Knoxville requested that Knoxville high schools ban the book. The Christian parent was upset about a scene depicting a woman's discovery of her own cervical cancer. Her self-exam of her own vagina, the parent thought, was pornographic, and she wanted to protect her high school son and other students from reading it.

"The parent confused gynecology with pornography," Skloot pointed out, and she was right.

Meanwhile, Skloot's book was a book a boy might read, both for curiosity and scientific content. The scene in question is, in my opinion, generally appropriate for any child of any age who has the ability and maturity to read the book.

In New Zealand recently a young-adult novel by Ted Dawe called *Into the River* was placed on an interim ban because, Dawe reports, "a Christian group objected to sexually explicit content, drug use, and use of a slang term for female genitalia." Dawe, who is himself a school teacher, expressed dismay about the ban not only because of its unfairness to the book itself, but also because he knows, he wrote in the newspaper, *The*

Guardian, "the challenges teachers face trying to find books that will interest boys."

I implore legislatures to pass laws to support school systems by tempering parental overprotectiveness. A revolutionary law would be one that compels parents to provide "actual proof of harm" for the book they wish to have banned. Given that actual proof of harm will rarely be possible to show, schools may generally go forward, in the wake of this law, to provide authority and topics of interest to children. While this effort will help our daughters, too, it will especially help our sons, since boys already, on average, don't read as much or as variously as girls do.

Rule 3: To mature, boys need a three-family-system that includes bi-strategic attachment (both maternal and paternal nurturance) and also expands beyond them into multiple other adults who create and maintain a "safe emotional container" for the boy.

Human maturation and the development of healthy independence is a natural form of gene expression as our chromosomes carry markers for growth throughout the lifespan. This genetic template will grow and evolve somewhat no matter its nurturing environment because of the strength of gene expression itself, but in order to *fully mature* the child into healthy adulthood, this gene expression needs the help of diverse maturation influences.

In the last fifty years we've tended to argue over whether a child can get enough nurturing through two parents (a traditional or alternative "nuclear" family unit) or even one, a single parent. Scientific research, much of which is cited in this book, argues that two parents, or bi-strategic parenting, are better than one, though one parent can do heroic things to raise children.

Meanwhile, neuroscience also shows us the wisdom of our third rule of male maturity: more than one or two parents are needed to raise mature and motivated boys into adulthood.

Frank Biro of Cincinnati's Children's Hospital Medical Center tells us why: "There is really no correlation between onset of puberty and one's social or emotional maturation." While parts of a boy's body and brain will mature on their own even if he lives in isolation, and while one or even two parents can do a great deal to link puberty with maturation, the child will still not fully mature without other healthy attachments and relationships that combine with parents to form his *safe container for social-emotional growth.*

To get a handle on what we mean by "safe container" and "other healthy attachments," think of the word "tribe" in English or, even more subtle, the word "pueblo" in Spanish. "Pueblo" has no real equivalent in English—it is both place and people together in a state of being rooted in allegiances and common values. The Mexican pueblo, for instance, is traditionally comprised of Mom, Dad, and many other people who mentor the child. This pueblo, in my best translation, is what I call The Three Family System.

1. *The First Family.* This is the nuclear unit: Mom and Dad, or two Moms/two Dads, or single parent, or other configuration of individuals who have the primary food, shelter, clothing, and attachment responsibility for the child, as well as protective responsibility against substantial childhood trauma, and challenging the child toward the developmental milestones of maturation and self-motivation.

2. *The Second Family.* This is the extended family and other closely attached individuals such as grandparents, aunts and uncles, nannies, other child care providers, coaches, mentors, and friends who supplement the work of the primary parents in protecting the child from trauma and challenge the child to mature. Just like the first family, it's best if the second family includes coercive and prosocial mentors, i.e. both empathy and aggression nurturers.

3. *The Third Family.* This family is made up of institutions, groups of people and individuals who wrap around and scaffold the first two families, including teachers, school principals, school counselors, therapists, social service providers, faith communities, governmental agencies, organizations like Boy Scouts and Girls Scouts—all of whom help ensure that the child is further protected and challenged to mature in autonomy, independence, purpose and success.

Most of our children had not one or two but three families in the past. Many boys don't have this now. Yet we can identify the male instinct to find a pueblo by studying gang affiliations or extreme and dangerous religious communities. Jihadi activity is, in some part, a result of males seeking intense allegiances and affiliations in tribal groups within which the males can be assured of becoming mature and thus motivated and valued adults.

While girls and women, too, need a pueblo, the male genetic template, especially its Y chromosome orientation toward testosterone's role in male brain development, requires multi-systems, diverse nurturing influence in safe containers. To study this, check out boys playing team sports in your parks or schools. Notice how the males quickly develop the allegiances that will create the safe container of this "pueblo." For many of these boys, the values and allegiances of this sports team will become crucial to their self-worth development. In this pueblo, competition is a sophisticated form of cooperation. The boys read one another's feelings and actions to anticipate what to do next so that the team environment provides what they need—a constant communal challenge to maturation, and a constant source of motivational inspiration.

Even boys playing interactive video games in your home can illustrate this urge in boys. Video game technology became team-interactive (a virtual pueblo) as soon as the Wii and Nintendo technology evolved enough to expand to include this component. Boys can sit alone in their own room while they interact with other boys around the world. They try to do this inner work in this "pueblo" with relatively little adult supervision in order to mature themselves. While team sports and other kinds of "Three Family Systems" are better for boys than video games, all male activity can point to their need for the diverse Three Family System to mature them.

Some of our innovations in the last fifty years have been very good for our children, but the breakdown of the Three Family System, and male isolation from all the important components of maturation, is not one of them. In the past, your ancestors were raised in a Three Family System with lots of female and male influence and diverse parenting and mentoring techniques and strategies. In our new millennium— especially in our vast American geography and American penchant for child loneliness—the Three Family System is in dangerous flux.

As a result, maturation of both girls and boys is paralyzed because our children's natural gene expression is under-nurtured. Among males, the loss of fathers and elder men (masculinity) is a vast danger to male maturation. The "safe emotional container" that males need to work out and experience their maturation is not masculine and male enough to be fully safe and maturing. As the DGP and Big Three have guided us to move away from masculinity as a protective and maturing human force, we have also inadvertently left our sons more greatly exposed to failure to mature and become independent.

Meanwhile, another significant maturation-stressor is the paucity of second family bonds available for many children. In many cases, appropriate second mothers and fathers now live too far away to help us raise our children and while non-blood kin can become second family, this can be hit-and-miss. What we used to call "the neighborhood" was a second family (pueblo-like), a maturing influence that could substitute for extended family members, but it has disappeared in many parts of our country.

Similarly, today, some first family members feel alienated from certain values of third family—our cultural institutions—so the first family becomes isolated from both of these potential second and third family institutions. For example, there is more disconnection of many families from not only schools and neighborhoods but also faith communities today than there was fifty years ago. These faith communities used to provide safe containers by acting as both second and third family maturation influences. Many of these institutions do not feel to parents and children like they are part of the boy's Three Family System anymore.

One Piece of the Puzzle at a Time

At a recent K–12 school visit a group of parents and teachers talked together after the training. A middle school teacher, Sue Dalke, said, "Seventh-grade girls are like high school students in a lot of ways but seventh-grade boys are more like kids." A high school principal, Anne Wainmeyer echoed this observation. "Yes, I guess my ninth-grade boys are going to, one day, stitch their brains together into something mature but right now, they are light years behind the girls."

These educators noticed gender-brain maturation differences then they talked about the male maturation needs of boys that our social revolution must build into our national consciousness. Anne said, "It seems like boys' maturation is just more fragile than girls'. This isn't to say that our girls don't have significant difficulties—they do. But girls just reach out to form relationships better than a lot of the boys, so if the boy doesn't have a couple really good relationships at home or at school with at least one or two teachers, he can drift away pretty quickly."

Sue nodded agreement and said, "Especially, by the time they hit our ages—middle and high school—the boys seem very fragile without good relationships with men. I work in an inner city school where most of the boys have little or no contact with dads and male role models. A few years ago I worked at an elementary school. I remember when I would bring a male teacher or coach into my building or classroom to do a certain lesson some of the boys would literally cling to him."

It can feel overwhelming to us as parents, educators and citizens to try to fix everything all at once. The three-family-system is in flux and we can't change that right away. We have to look at one piece of the puzzle at a time. One piece of the puzzle we can all bring into our citizen science right away is the link between male maturation and male and masculine influence. If you can look at bringing just one more healthy adult male into a fun and complex bond with your son right now, you will be doing something structural to affect the safe container for maturation, the bi-strategic need of boys to have multiple influences, and the fragility of that male brain in its maturation process.

The idea of the fragility of male brain maturation in comparison to female has evolutionary roots: nature had to ensure that females matured more quickly than males in order to be neurally prepared to have children in early puberty. But our societies always met the evolutionary and natural male maturation disadvantage by giving them multiple female and male influences then, at puberty, giving them even more male influences. These male influences in first, second, and third family nurtured and even coerced maturation of young males.

In our day, consciously planning out this piece of the male puzzle—making family decisions about how to give boys of ten and older specific male mentoring—is even more important perhaps than in some past times because males in the past met their male mentors organically. The males among our ancestors were trained in hands-on, one-on-one work by men and teams of men. They engaged in masculine mentoring through groups engaged in challenging activities. They spent a lot of time in bi-strategic systems in which elder men were available and committed to the task of maturing young males.

The DGP and the Big Three, in struggling to assert women's rights, correctly noted that many of the masculine frameworks in our human past could be taken to extremes by some people but incorrectly asserted that masculinization is not needed as a bi-strategic component of maturation. Multi-family masculine and male influence is utterly needed. Here's an illustration of how paternal nurturance—not just from Dad but from many other males—helps boys build more neural pathways for maturation and motivation.

Columbia University researchers Noam Zerubavel, Kevin Ochsner, and their colleagues used brain scans to discover what happens in the male brain when males study others higher up than them in hierarchies (e.g. fathers, elders). Reporting in *Proceedings of the National Academy of Sciences* in 2015, the researchers explained that even just studying the face of a person more accomplished than us triggers activation of both the primary and secondary circuits in the frontal cortex (the evaluation and analysis circuits). As a boy studies, imitates, or even resists higher-up male role models, the male builds important mid to upper brain pathways via deployment of all seven traits of male emotional intelligence. If there isn't a male present, this inner work can't happen.

If there is, however, even in the silent presence of male role model—even who rarely or ever says a word—the boy's evaluation centers motivate him to try to increase his own status in the male's presence. The frontal cortex gets involved in directing his actions via activation of the *ventral striatum* (connected to reward-anticipation) and the *amygdala* (connected to the activation of emotions) in the limbic system. Then the secondary circuits in the frontal cortex (the *precuneus and temporoparietal junction*) activate as the boy sees and understands what the male role model or mentor has done to create status, success, self-motivation, and maturation. Then all of this is further activated as the boy goes out into the world and tries to imitate the maturation that he modeled off the father, grandfather, uncle, coach, older brother, friend, employer, teacher or other male.

As parental authority has shifted away from parent-authoritative families to child-centered families, we've lost one of the best ways to raise mature men: give them strong male authority in the first, second, and third families especially by the time they are ten years old (early puberty).

"But moms can teach all this," I've heard people say, or, "Moms can raise sons alone and they turn out great."

Single moms can raise very mature sons, but if you study those who do, you'll most often notice that these moms smartly found *male mentors for their adolescent boys.* You'll also notice that if they don't do this, their sons are missing a huge piece of the puzzle of manhood, and their sons are more likely as adults to be under-motivated, less likely to bond with spouse and offspring, and more likely to go to prison or suffer early death.

Question: Is it good or bad to tell boys, "Be a man!"

Answer: It is generally good to do so because it motivates and matures a boy.

In most cases when people (both women and men) tell boys to be a man, they mean:

* Grow up, stop acting like a kid.
* Stop thinking the world will tailor itself to little old you.
* Be strong, others need you, go help them—it's your duty.
* When you fall, get back up—you're a model for others.
* Don't whine—act with honor and integrity.
* Don't expect the world to give you anything—*earn* your success.
* Take care of the people who depend on you.
* Be responsible and compassionate.
* Be protective and caring, not cruel and heartless.
* Cry when you have to, laugh a lot, especially at yourself, and forgive others their faults.

"Be a man!" motivates and matures boys because in most cases the comment is warranted: the male is acting in an immature way and needs to be reminded and motivated to grow up to healthy manhood.

Certainly, "Be a man!" can be misused. Some people who want boys to show no feelings at all will say it. This part of "Be a man!" has come under attack by DGP adherents who have, unfortunately, expanded their attack to include all uses of the phrase. Videos and lectures have come out recently in which people say things like, "'Be a man' is the worst thing you can tell a boy." Or: "These are some of the worst words in the English language." To these people, as Garrison Keillor captured in a recent comment, "Manhood, which was once an opportunity for achievement, is now seen as a problem to be overcome."

The people who attack "Be a man" have no natural science research behind their position. Rather, they are so entrenched in ideology they can't see that their androphobia negatively affects boys' maturation and motivation—the very things none of us want to curtail. No one, even the most strident misandrist, wants the dangerous result of fomenting a culture of immature, undefined, and lost males.

When you hear "Be a man" attacked in the media or see it portrayed as a "cause" of violence or male immaturity, I hope you'll remind the speaker or writer that actual science shows the opposite. The more messaging to become a man a boy gets, the *less likely the boy is to remain dangerously impulsive.* Remind whoever attacks the "Be a man" piece of the puzzle that while it is useful to discuss "masculine stereotypes" with very macho males in order to try to help them become more empathic, most boys are not this macho type today. Just the opposite: Millions of American boys today have too little maturation challenge in their lives and actually do need "Be a man" to help them become loving, wise, and successful men.

Rule 4: Multi-Strategic maturation of boys is not just good for boys and girls but also helps parents let go of their guilt for being imperfect and immature parents—certain "failures" as a parent or a child are not the worst thing in the world!

The guilt of the imperfect parent is paralyzing our efforts to mature and motivate our sons. In a sense, we as parents remain immature as parents, without self-confidence or a sense of adequacy, and pass this lack to our children. This is a hidden stressor on all of us that grows, in some part, from the parenting trends in the Big Three that run counter to the actual Three Family Systems we need. Our social trends push us to see uniformity of parenting style as the best bet—which forces every parent to worry that she or he is not doing enough. Gail and I struggled with this while we parented our daughters.

Worrying about our parenting ability, we sought magazine articles, studies, and curricula that taught "the best way" to parent or teach, the "three best tips for how to raise a boy (or girl)," the top four teaching techniques that will create successful learners. We parents are conditioned to find a single-theory or "simple way" to ensure our child's mental and physical health when, in reality, children need us to confidently provide our best assets as parents while trusting others in our Three Family System to provide their equally important best assets to the maturation of the child.

Here's an example of the conundrum in a recent media report. A *Wall Street Journal* article by Nina Sovich called "The Hardest Game for Parents" (12/17/15) portrayed different approaches to parenting: Mom and Dad play Monopoly with their seven-year-old son. When the boy is about to lose, Dad teaches him a last-ditch strategy for winning—letting him beat Dad. Later Dad says to Mom, "It's okay. He saw me lose. We all lose."

Mom likes her way better. She didn't give the boy any help, letting him cry tears as he lost the game. As he cried, she reports to the reporter, she verbally supported the boy's expression of the grief of losing.

In revealing these different approaches to the incident, Ms. Sovich tells us that she was inspired to seek out experts to help her understand what is best for children. As she revealed the results of her search, she summed up the professional research this way: "Psychologists seem to agree that flat out throwing a game to a child over the age of four is a bad idea."

These parents practiced bi-strategic parenting, which is the best kind for our children, and they could differ on a given day in a given circumstance. They might help a child "win" in a game or in later life. They might build his resilience to lose and then keep playing again in their own unique ways.

Yet the will to find a single technique won out. Statements like, "Psychologists seem to agree that flat out throwing a game to a child over the age of four is a bad idea" is not necessarily wrong in some cases but it is the wrong tack—it drives us to try for *perfect parenting as individual parents* and neglect the pueblo reality of child development. Nature doesn't know or even like single absolute theories. Nature abhors uniformity and wants diversity. There is no single best way to handle the incident during Monopoly. The brains of our children need and want diverse natural influences so that gene expression, personality, and core-self can mature.

Imperfection, then, is perfection. For us as parents, unless a child is in actual danger from a particular person or situation, our children are best served by our enjoyment of—even insistence on—no single "tip" or "best practice" for parenting or controlling the behavior of our son or daughter. As we call on academics, government, and the media to revolutionize the lives of American boys, we will need to show them that the three-family container is much more important for a child's brain development than a singular technique. Indeed, in all areas of maturation, presence and authority are equally or more important than one specific tip.

One way to argue this is to point out the role of grandparents. Is there any expert in child development who would tell a grandparent that throwing a game to a seven-year-old is bad for the child? I'm guessing not. Rather, most of us in the field would agree that the child's *bond* with the grandparent is paramount; as the grandparent "spoils" the child through a particular bonding activity like throwing the game, the grandparent builds even more social-emotional safety for the child's growth. When the child needs even more maturation help from the grandparent in ever more complex areas of life later on, the grandparent is there, waiting at the intimate perimeter of multi-generational relationship to help the young adult move through the new challenge or vulnerability he faces in the long journey to maturity.

My daughter, Davita, 23, works at a climbing gym. She's talked with me frequently about how many young boys come into the gym unable to self-motivate or self-create the passion and direction to "climb a line," which is how the sport describes climbing up a wall. "It's like this boy expects the gym, or his friends or his parents or someone else, like me, to tailor everything to him. He doesn't just go figure it out!"

This is, to Davita, the "sense of entitlement" that has been often discussed in our culture. She's also described parents of these boys sitting on benches watching this happen, looking stricken as their son under-performs. Inspired by her insights, I came down to the climbing gym to observe. The deep parental fear of failure was palpable in some of the parents' faces—they seemed to feel that if the world is not tailored to the child, the child will fail at the tasks of the world. Behind sad eyes they were trying to figure out how to tailor the world to the child. Here was their son awkwardly climbing or misbehaving immaturely as he tried to push through his own anxiety or frustration and his parents sat in embarrassment at their own failure—and his.

Yet to be a parent is to always court failure—and persevere. Sometimes we are too harsh or too permissive, but if we keep our bond with the child strong and bi-strategic through attachment, presence, teaching, and modeling, we are the "perfect imperfect" parents who can most directly help children mature. Ultimately, that is our reason for parenting our kids: so they can become mature adults who survive and thrive on their own for the sake of the next generation of offspring they will produce and need to coerce and cajole into maturation.

So the fourth rule of male maturation and self-motivation gives, I hope, relief to us parents. Three Family Systems can take the single theory/perfect parenting burden off the single or nuclear parents by providing other personnel with different approaches—Davita, for instance, who lets the boy fail and thus invites him to succeed by figuring out the solution—and by appreciating the importance of failure in the developmental process.

The New Path

Even failure—both in child and parent—can teach children ways they must adapt in order to gain the confidence and motivation to climb the line and fit into a world that is, like a mountain or a high wall, always larger than themselves. In this vein I hope you will help all adults mature beyond single tips and techniques. We will all feel more liberated and more true to human nature when we do this and our boys will gain new paths to maturation that fit their lives in the new millennium.

In *The Whole Person in a Broken World*, psychologist Paul Tournier writes, "The efforts (the modern world) makes to heal itself may also bring it to ruin." Our efforts over the last decades to heal our society of its past defects have brought us to where we are now. Some of the efforts have led to good—our children are in some ways better off than a hundred years ago—but in some ways, our males are courting their own, and our, desperation. Until we revise our culture's understanding of male maturation, we'll keep trying to solve our problems without all our "pueblo" and natural assets available to us. We will continue to seek uniform single-theory ideas that are politically correct (and well argued in the Big Three) but just don't work once fully applied in a real family, real school, real home. We'll miss the diverse and complex biological systems our boys actually live in and neglect the clues hidden all around us in human nature and male genetics. Meanwhile, we will continue to see our boys withdrawing; we will continue to watch our boys get lost in environments that don't fully mature them.

One of those environments has become a de facto substitute for a number of fragile and somewhat lost natural systems—the electronics and technology movement that has entranced our sons, and all of us.

This system is both enhancing our son's lives and also crippling the development of their brains.

Chapter 7

The Digital Boy: Ensuring Seven Milestones of Male Development in the Digital Age

> "One time, discovering that his relief rider had been killed, Billy Cody completed a distance of 322 miles over rough, dangerous terrain in less than twenty-two hours, changing horses twenty-one times—a record in Pony Express history. (Previously), "at the age of 8 the boy could already operate an ox-wagon singlehandedly; at 9, he earned a man's wage as a cattle herder. His family needed the money."
>
> —Andrea Warren, author of
> *The Boy Who Became Buffalo Bill*

ANDREW IS 20. His mother, Sharon, an attorney, and his former middle school principal, Camille, a friend of Sharon's, asked to see me about Andrew who was having difficulty in college in another state. The "two mothers," one the biological and one a strong second mother, told me they knew of my expertise with young males. They knew I couldn't meet Andrew except via Skype, but wanted to get my advice because nothing seemed to help him. Sharon had tears in her eyes as we sat together in my office and the story of this boy's life unfolded.

"First of all, he's a great guy, really. He's gentle, he rarely loses his temper, he wants to succeed. He's stuck, yes, but for instance, he'll talk with me about anything I ask him. Don't you think, Camille?"

"He's very verbal, very open," Camille agrees. "A great kid."

"But he's got so many issues," Sharon said, opening Andrew's thick medical and psychological manila folder on her lap. "He's been seeing a psychiatrist on and off for seven years, since middle school. He's on Vyvanse for ADD/ADHD, and Wellbutrin and Zoloft for depression/anxiety—"

"How long has he been on each of those?" I interrupted to ask.

She consulted the file "He started on Ritalin seven years ago but then Dr. Lindowsky switched him to Vyvanse a year ago."

"And the others?"

"Wellbutrin for three years and Zoloft for four years."

"Okay," I nodded. "And do you think he's been depressed or anxious all those years?"

Sharon nodded. Camille added, "He's been depressed on and off, he gets anxious, he was bullied back in middle school for being 'different.'" She made quote marks in the air. "Meanwhile he's great with building things on his own, you know, like he built his own computer when he was 11, almost from scratch."

"He did," Sharon leaned in with a burst of joy in her wet eyes. "You should have seen it! His father and I were amazed. But he flunked out of math classes, I mean, it's strange to us that he's so smart but tests in math so badly."

"No matter what I or the teachers did," Camilla agreed, "we couldn't get him to do his math homework or much other homework, nor could Sharon or Andrew's father."

Sharon filled in more details. "We've been divorced five years now and Carl is pretty much out of the picture. He has a bunch of dreams he's pursuing, but I'm the breadwinner and Carl isn't too active in any kind of fathering sense with Andrew. I'm the one Andrew talks with about sex, guy stuff, at least most of it, which is another reason we need your opinion. Andrew is addicted to video games and he's addicted to porn."

"In what way?" I asked.

"In every way."

"Okay, for instance: how many hours a day is he playing video games or generally using his smartphone, tablet, or computer?"

Because many of our young males who play video games, bond with others online, and use internet porn are not so "fixated" that the technology use tragically disrupts the boy's physical, cognitive, and social development (addiction) I wanted to make sure we all meant the same thing by that word.

"His whole life is online," she responded immediately. "His psychiatrist lives far away from him now, so she can only prescribe his meds, but she says he is addicted, and the thing that really worries me is that he told me a few weeks ago he can't get an erection anymore without using porn. That's bad, right?"

"Yes generally, but are you sure he's being really accurate with you about his situation?"

Camille defended Sharon. "She's not making that up. Andrew and Sharon, especially because Carl is so distant, have an amazing relationship. They talk about everything. If Andrew told her that, it's true."

"It's true," Sharon said. "He told me it's been happening for about six months now. He's great at computers, you know, since he was a boy—maybe 9 or 10—and every year he just gets better at everything, like coding, programming, but he's just getting sucked deeper and deeper into that computer, those games, and that porn. It's like it happened fast, even though it took a few years."

Tears dropped down Sharon's cheeks and Camille reached to hold her hand. We talked more that day and then I Skyped with Andrew the next week.

I spent the next two months helping Andrew and his family through the various aspects of what seemed to be happening within him. As we talked, I also referred him to a neuro-psychiatrist for genetic testing and brain scans. Fortunately, because Andrew was a "science geek" (his words) he welcomed the testing and scans. His mother, too, had the financial resources to pursue them. But I continued to worry about Andrew. Even when he start seeing the neuro-psychiatrist, his mother, who still lived near me, came in to see me for continued emotional support three more times.

"I know Andrew's got problems," she said. "So if you could just give me the 'pros' and 'cons' of his situation. What is the best way to help him in the future with electronics? What did I do wrong before? I need takeaways from you—I need to know what the boundaries of helping him can be for me as a mom of a kid who everyone else treats as an adult but I know he's still a boy."

"First," I reassured her, "I know you worked with the information you had. You didn't know how video games and porn can affect males because the science on these things is only just now beginning to clarify itself. Ten, twenty years ago, none of us knew what we know now.

"Second, you are a good mom and you had good instincts about Andrew—you raised a very nice guy. He talks to you even about his intimate life. This is a gift—it means he is not afraid to reveal himself and get help. Nothing I will say should make you feel that in some way I think you have not been a wonderful mom.

"Third, you're right about the porn. If an older man can't get an erection without visual porn there's often nothing at all abnormal about that, and he's generally not addicted to it. But if a boy or young man at the peak of his testosterone functioning can't get an erection without visual porn there's generally an addiction or other problem.

"Fourth, there are actually some 'pros' to build on from Andrew's penchant for video games, technology, and his interest in building his own computer. That skill and life passion is way ahead of many other under-motivated young men. So, if he agrees to it, you might consider offering to pay for a vocational school that would focus him on building the visual-spatial skills in which he already shows promise and saving the money for college, where he's flunking."

This was a developmental idea that, at first, saddened Sharon who was a product of college, then law school. She believed deeply in college as the stepping stone to adulthood.

"Not every boy will flourish in college," I suggested, "especially a boy with the brain and genetic anomalies of your son. If you can place him in an experiential learning environment that builds mainly on his already established neural proclivities he may flourish in ways you can't imagine right now–and eventually get whatever college education he needs."

I put this in terms of Andrew's brain. "I think the reward centers in your son's brain don't connect very well to the same centers that yours do. Where you got a lot of reward in college from words he gets his dopamine rush from doing non-college related visual-spatial tasks more often than you do. While the video games and porn are addictive for him—and require treatment—they, along with the building of his own computer, show how brilliant his visual-spatial centers could make him one day."

This resonated for Sharon as she suddenly remembered something. "When he was 12, he absolutely loved working with his dad on some dream or other—something about a computer-generated invention I didn't really get, but the two of them worked on it in the basement all the time. Unfortunately all he got out of this were grandiose ideas about how life would turn out—that if you just dream, you'll have success. Andrew got that and it isn't working for him, but you're right, he also got those experimental parts of his brain that are probably really great."

"Yes," I encouraged. "He is a great combination of you both. He has your ability to talk about what he is feeling and he has this other spatial-mechanical proclivity. If you make a list of the times, jobs, and tasks that have stimulated Andrew's reward centers, I think you'll have a list in which a great number of incidents and tasks will involve his visual and spatial centers. This is a 'pro' and something to build on."

Andrew eventually did go to an in-patient rehab, and three years later Sharon told me that he had completed a two-year vocational school that specialized in computer coding. When he got out, Sharon told me he was still battling his addictions, though he was improving, she said. He would mature and succeed, she believed, "though most likely not until his thirties or later, I'm afraid," she said in a combination of sadness and hope that only a parent of a somewhat lost child has felt.

Andrew's case has in it many of the factors we will explore in this chapter. His brain functioning was re-wired from a developmental decade of video games, constant visual porn, and brain-changing medications; male educational trauma (the mismatch of his male brain with his classrooms); bullying at school during formative years; divorce trauma soon after that; and gradual decline of adequate paternal nurturance in his adolescent development.

In the wake of these factors, Andrew and his family were hungry for a developmental map for maturation that included a maturity map for electronics and technology use. Sharon and Andrew wished they'd had this map, they told me, much earlier in Andrew's life, so they could have followed it when this boy was born. They are a family that has inspired me to create and teach such a map. This chapter presents it for your use. It combines digital literacy with a foundational map for healthy male maturation.

American digital life can be a matter of life and death for our boys— the natural boy can be affronted by the digital boy, if we aren't careful. Technology can be a neurotoxin. If moderately used, our digital assets can be good assets—certainly video games are not evil. I play them and enjoy them. Nor is visual porn some kind of absolute evil. The point of this chapter will not be to take an extreme, unrealistic, or reactionary position on digital boyhood. The point is to save our sons from becoming Andrew—to start them out from the first stage of boyhood with lifestyles in which digital life does not *dominate* their maturation but is *integrated into* healthy male maturation.

Question: Can you give some general science-based advice about media and technology use with all children?

Answer: In general terms, here are a number of bottom lines to keep in mind for both boys and girls.

The American Association of Pediatrics is a good resource for understanding what is best for children *in general*. Because our children spend an average of seven hours a day on entertainment media like televisions, computers, tablets, and phones, first, second, and third family members should become citizen scientists regarding a child's media time. Remember that excessive screen time can turn into attention problems, cognitive and academic issues, problems with sleep and eating, as well as obesity and physiological health problems. Because most devices now allow access to the Internet, moral and character development of our children is at stake.

In general, we need to:

* Limit screen time (see the stages below).
* If we use screens, spend most of the screen time with educational media not entertainment.
* Focus childhood on non-electronic formats (books, comic books, graphic novels, nonfiction biographies and memoirs, newspapers, magazines, board games, chess, checkers, card games).
* When children (especially younger ones) watch media, we ought to deploy a family member (from any of the three families) to watch with the child as much as possible.
* Teach media literacy from the earliest ages so that children understand the connections between what they see and real life.
* Until the child is relatively mature, disallow screens in bedrooms (no televisions, computers, tablets or video games).
* If children use smartphones in bedrooms, they should be moved to the living room by one half to one hour before sleep time (depending on the age of the child/adolescent).

* No TVs on during dinner time and no cellphones either!
* No more than one or two hours per day for entertainment media (TV, video games, etc.) except, perhaps, on a weekend day.
* Never sacrifice one-on-one mentoring for screen time. For example, every adult in a child's life can potentially teach the child a hobby—this is preferable to screen time.
* Rarely sacrifice outside play time for media time. Outside play is more important.
* Rarely sacrifice reading time for media time. Reading is much more important for brain development than screen time, especially for the youngest brains.
* Rarely sacrifice imaginative free play with physical toys for media and screen time.
* Rarely sacrifice time in relational play and conversation with other human beings or care of animals (such as pets) for screen time.

The Stages of Male Maturation

The male brain matures in seven developmental stages. In these stages, individual gene expression occurs in diverse environments including technological. While characteristics in each of the stages might exist simultaneously, to some extent, each set of essential characteristics *peak* at different times in different boys, so they constitute a neuro-physiologically sequenced journey to mature adulthood. Because no two boys are exactly alike, this schedule of stages must be adjusted by you for best use.

The stages are:
Stage 1: Pre-birth to 2 years old.
Stage 2: 3 – 5.
Stage 3: 6 – 9.
Stage 4: 10 – 13.
Stage 5: 14 – 17.
Stage 6: 18 – 21.
Stage 7: 22 – 25 and beyond.

In previous books, *A Fine Young Man, The Good Son, Nurture the Nature* and *Raising Boys By Design,* you'll find developmental strategies for boys' and girls' social, emotional, cognitive, and character development in these stages. I won't repeat that work in this book. Over the last decade, however, new brain research has provided new knowledge and strategies for male maturation in the context of appropriate technology use during the seven stages.

As you read this chapter and absorb its Maturity Map I invite you to fulfill a seventh step in revolution—take control of and guide your son's use of screens and technology in seven stages so he can become a healthy man.

Stage 1: Pre-Birth to Two Years Old

Here are two key areas of male brain development to consider as you think about the use of technology in your bonding with your baby or toddler boy.

* Girls generally use complete sentences earlier than boys and tend to use more vocabulary words in speech than boys in Stage 1 and throughout life. This happens in part because of the verbal-emotive brain difference in gender we noted earlier: girls' brains are wired, in utero, to develop word centers, verbal facility, and emotive connections on both sides of the brain. From this XX driven brain formatting, girls become two years old with more access to neural pathways for word production, word use, and social-emotional word formation than, on average, boys do whose Y chromosome brain formatting lateralizes word production mainly to the front half of the left side of the male brain.

* Boys most often develop their gross motor skills earlier than girls, using more physical movement to communicate than girls might. The male cerebellum, the "doing" center of the brain, is genetically formatted by Y chromosome markers to be larger and more active in boys' brains than girls'. Furthermore, on the right side of the brain, boys develop significant spatial-mechanical and visual-graphic centers that girls often do not develop as completely there because they develop more word centers on that side.

Bottom line: Stage 1 girls tend to develop more use of words than boys and boys tend toward more emphasis on physical-kinesthetic movement and visual-spatial acuity. Knowing these basic maturation differences can help every home and preschool to protect boys. As we noted in the box above, time in front of screens for all children in Stage 1 should be kept to the bare minimum, but boys have a special vulnerability here because they're naturally more likely than females to attach their maturation to available visual stimuli and detach it from word production. This makes screen time a significant potential neurotoxin to them early in life.

It's essential that good visual habits are established for all children, both boys and girls, and especially for the boys who may later become like Andrew—hyper visually-spatially focused. While it's true that all brains are different and not all boys will become hyper-visual, it's also true that the child most likely to fit this negative possibility is a boy.

Therefore I advise the following guidelines.

Guideline 1: Be vigilant about passive visual stimuli and keep screen time to an absolute minimum.

Until Stage 2, avoid putting screens in front of boys. This means avoiding child-gaze on your smartphone (though we often think it isn't, a smartphone is a screen), and avoid letting your two-year-old play a game on your phone. Instead, interpret the environment around you with the boy verbally and help him to do so. At home or office, avoid putting boys in front of TV or laptop screens for entertainment and choose child care professionals who don't rely on screens to make the care-time easier for them.

Avoid the popular idea that if you start a boy using a screen device for his education early in life he will somehow gain an advantage later. There is no scientific proof for this, nor does it fit with findings in brain science. The brain at this stage of development doesn't need *any* screen to grow up capable of later cognitive tasks. Screens are therefore a privilege that can do damage. More than an hour every day in front of a screen for a Stage 1 boy will most likely do some damage to the naturally templated gene expression and development of his brain.

Why? Because our human brain development evolved for more than a million years of maturation in active nature, with all five senses activated in environmental contact. Screens are passive. Even if there's something active going on in them such as a visually acted story, they're less adequate for brain development than natural life.

Guideline 2: Read to boys and encourage boys to spend time in non-structured play.

Because many boys engage in more physical movement than girls, it's essential we don't see this maturation pattern in the negative. Instead, we can use it by continuing our reading (or other activity) and guiding the fidgeting boy to move around as he needs to during both his learning and play time.

Structure is important throughout a young boy's life, but wiggle room in structure is also important. Feeding him at the same time every day when he's two years old can be a very good structure. Playtime, however, needs very little structure at this age. The more he roams the better. You'll want to watch him like a hawk, of course, to keep him safe, especially if he is by nature a roamer or a runner, but meanwhile, much of what he needs now is the safe social-emotional container. He does not need helicopter style over-protection from us.

Put some music on and let him dance. Build a fence in the backyard and just let him toddle around, fall, cry, get comfort from you, get up and fall all over again. His brain learns naturally from these activities, as it does when seeing a cat and chasing it, laughing at the cackling of a squirrel, cuddling with Mom or Dad, getting thrown up in the air by Dad or Mom, being read to by Grandma or Grandpa and then rushing into the kitchen because the smell of cinnamon suddenly puts the brain into a joyful trance of sensorial excitement.

Guideline 3: Build purpose, mission, and independence into boys even at this age.

This first stage of life is one of utter dependence of child on adults and so we often miss the fact that we can and should teach independence. That independence can rarely be taught via screens. Here's an example: a two-year-old sitting in a high chair might throw his fork onto the floor. You might be tempted to bend down, pick up the fork, and save yourself the trouble of unhooking the high chair pad to help the boy down to the ground to do it himself.

In many cases, this easy fix will win the day. But in some cases at least, the boy would better mature in life if we don't do everything for him, and teach him instead to get out of his chair and pick up the fork himself. This gives the brain the lessons of maturation: independence, purpose, and self-motivation from very early in life.

Similarly, if you plunk him in front of a screen, he'll insist on repeating those habits in the next stages of growth. This more passive existence will be attractive to his visual brain, and so the boy is developing a relationship with passive media that duplicates passive forms of growth. By the time he is 20, he may be less independent, less healthy, less self-reliant, less self-motivated, and less mature.

Stage 2: Three to Five Years Old

Use of technology in the lives of American boys often increases exponentially as boys engage in the cultures of preschool and kindergarten. Even if the boy is usually at home, he may gravitate toward grabbing mom's phone. Mom and Dad, too, may put him in front of screens more now so that they can get things done. Be vigilant! Your son's maturation is at stake.

Guideline 4: Focus mainly on educational products.

What we've established in earlier chapters about the male brain affects this age brain, as do the gender differences you may have noticed in Stage 1. Just as in Stage 1, other ways of healthy growth are generally better for a child than screen time. For instance, it's more important than screen time to read to this boy, have him read to you once he's able; have him teach you about things he is learning; play board games with him; keep relating to him and verbalizing. Screen time should be strategically used for education—and still very little of it per day—and certainly not relied on as a major babysitter. If you find your son in a child care facility that puts kids in front of screens for many hours, I hope you will discuss the potential for screens to be neurotoxic babysitters with them.

Guideline 5: Do genetics tests if you are able in order to help you strategize screen time.

While strategic and low-amount screen time is generally best for this boy, it's often difficult for us as parents to pursue a single theory like "minimal screen time" if our son is using screens two or three hours a day at five years old but "seems to be doing fine."

"He's a great kid," parents of a five-year-old told me after a lecture. "We're not worried. We're in tech fields and we believe in what we create and what we do. We see no evidence that there's any harm to our son in screen time."

In that lecture I had mentioned the potential folly of huge tech organizations giving laptops or tablets to kindergartens and early elementary school children. Once they do, all or most learning moves to screens, for reasons of neural attraction and focus. When this happened, the child would be doing even less real world functioning. This is potentially dangerous, I had said.

But is it dangerous for every child? Every boy? Probably not, so how can a parent know for whom it could be dangerous? As with many potential neurotoxins, genetic testing might help resolve this question but it's not yet a simple thing to determine genetic testing for screen time danger. There is one way available to us, however: testing for obesity genes.

Obesity genes correlate directly with screen time issues in growing children. As we noted earlier, you can test for the three obesity genes: DRD2, an eating behavior gene, MC4R, an appetite gene, and FTO, a body fat gene. You can contact your physician or other professional to ask if they are able to order genetics test like those we've referred to in earlier chapters that will help you understand your son's genome.

If you discover that your son has the genetic template for higher body fat and weight gain, you can be especially vigilant about keeping him away from screen time. All science-based research is clear on the link between the sedentary time in front of screens and unhealthy weight gain, including the health problems as a result of that gain. This is a "back door" genetics test for unhealthy screen time with which you can prove that screen time will be potentially neuro-toxic for *your* child. Within the next decade, I hope, geneticists will be able to discover other "front door" genetics tests so that every family can determine the pluses and minuses of screen time for their individual child.

Stage 3: Six to Nine Years Old

There is a Waldorf school in Los Altos, California, in Silicon Valley's high tech country. This school uses no electronic technologies for learning. Pens, paper, knitting needles, animal parts, dirt, and other tools and elements of nature fill its classrooms—no screens. Parents of the kids in this school work at eBay, Google, Apple, Yahoo and Hewlett-Packard. In an article in The New York Times, Alan Eagle, 50, who works for Google, explained why he sends his children to this "no screen time" school.

"Technology," he says, "has its time and place. If I worked at Miramax and made good, artsy, rated R movies, I wouldn't want my kids to see them until they were 17. Remember: at Google and all these places, we make technology as brain-dead easy to use as possible. There's no reason why kids can't figure it out when they get older."

The two ideas here—that anything artificial can be both a boon and a toxin to the brain; and that the brain can learn any technology quite quickly later—are crucial to integrate into your male maturity guidelines. While you may not put your son in this particular school, the basic science behind the school is excellent, especially for many boys, who are 1) already brain-prone to overemphasize visual learning (screens), and 2) need lots of physical-kinesthetic time during the day to develop social-emotional skills and brain centers as well as cognitive fluency.

One of the teachers at the school, Cathy Waheed, a former computer engineer, teaches fractions "by having the children cut up food—apples, quesadillas, cake—into quarters, halves and sixteenths. 'For three weeks, we ate our way through fractions. When I made enough fractional pieces of cake to feed everyone, do you think I had their attention?'" She did.

In the third stage of its maturation, the male brain, like the female, develops pathways, tissues, and gray matter areas via sensorial contact—active hands-on touch, and proximal smell, taste, hearing, and sight. Interwoven through all this sensorial and kinesthetic stimulation is social-emotional interaction—verbal and nonverbal contact with peers and adults who teach and mentor. This combination of contact via senses and emotions stimulated by relationship helps develop the healthy brain. In the male brain, prolonged and hands-on contact can be even more essential for social-emotional development because male brains naturally develop fewer of these pathways without it.

If you think about ASD (autism spectrum disorder) you'll notice a reason why. Most ASD and children with ADD/ADHD and other brain-behavior disorders connected to attention, focus, organization, and social-emotional development are male because the Y chromosome and male brain put gender pressure on these areas of male life. That gender pressure exists in the reality we discussed earlier: the male brain does not have as many inborn fail-safes, such as a baseline of high activity in the cingulate cortex, for attention and social emotional development as the female. For the maturation/development reasons we noted in Chapter 6, males need urgent and extra attention to these social-emotional developmental experiences.

In this way, having boys spend many hours a day in elementary school (and then at home) in front of screens can be neurotoxic. While a boy who has one of the brain disorders can actually benefit from targeted screen time and specific electronic technologies, such as technologies that help him read social and facial cues, even for this boy, too many hours in front of screens will, in most cases, harm long-term development.

Guideline 6: As a citizen scientist and with professional aid, assess your son to determine whether a computerized school/life is good for him.

By 6 years old, it is crucial that you study the "nature" of your son; observe him, ask the three families to observe him; gather daily data over a period of one or more months; see what he needs. To begin your assessment, study these three markers of developmental health or difficulty.

* *Physical.* Is he developing physically in the normal range? Is he moving around in his home and other environments at least two hours a day? This standard is most easily attained if he is in a gender-friendly classroom where he can have recess and play sports. But the home, too, must be a center of physical movement. Study his daily life to see how much exercise he gets in the home. If you have any doubts at all about what would be a suitable amount of exercise for your son, ask your pediatrician for science-based standards that fit *him*.

* *Cognitive.* Is he developing his critical thinking skills and other cognitive abilities at the normal pace? Can he organize, think, feel, problem-solve, do a reasonable amount of homework, though he should have very little homework at this age. By 9 years old, you'll most likely be able to see some budding talents. He may be great at math or reading or both. Knowing his nature can help you decide healthy screen time limits for him and help him develop opportunity for maturation and mentoring in his strength area. If he needs extra help in a certain area, like math, a math program via the Internet might be helpful for him. You could focus some of his screen time on this kind of educational product but limit screen time for other entertainments.

* *Social-emotional.* Does he have a friend or two? Does he interact with parents and elders? Is he involved in interactive environments like Cub Scouts that help him grow social emotional pathways in the brain? On the other hand, perhaps he's not spending enough time with Mom, Dad, other "parents," other kids. If this is the case, he is likely spending too much time in front of screens. Study him for a few weeks and see where his screen time fits with his social-emotional development.

If your son is developing quite well in all three areas, you may have little to worry about in terms of his technology use. But if your son is having trouble in any of these areas, it's possible that curtailing his screen time and, simultaneously, increasing his physical, hands-on cognitive, and social interaction time may be a life saver for him—and for you.

For boys like this—and, indeed, for any child who shows a proclivity for logical thinking and competition—chess might be a good substitute for all or part of the screen time. Research in the neuroscience of chess has shown benefits in potential increase in IQ and math skills, attention span and memory, ability to concentrate, verbal skills development, strategic and critical thinking, development of patience, work ethic, and sportsmanship. Meanwhile, there is no neuroscience research to show that these benefits will come from spending excessive time in front of screens.

People often wonder how e-readers fit into a boy's developmental map.

"My son loves to read and likes the Kindle better than holding a book," a mom recently told me. "I want to promote his love of reading so I want to follow his preference, but is the e-reader considered 'screen time'? If so, is it dangerous?"

If a child is spending two hours with an e-reader and also four other hours in front of other screens, then the whole "screen time" as an aggregate must be dealt with; but outside of that kind of excessive screen use, the e-reader is the least dangerous screen-apparatus for the brain because it's merely a glass lens through which to see the original book. However, if the e-reader is used at bedtime, it can become detrimental.

Guideline 7: Beware of the effects of screens on sleep time.

The blue light in the e-reader, Tablet, or computer tricks the melatonin in a child's (and adult's) brain to think it's time to wake up. You want just the opposite near bedtime: you want the melatonin to put the boy to sleep because his maturation and health depend greatly on his getting the right amount of sleep. And sleep is crucial for mood control. Anxiety and stress can become a problem for school-age children. Among boys, this anxiety can get masked for a few years as the child seems happy enough—he's growing, he smiles, he is loved. We may not realize that screen time—perhaps in or near bedtime—is creating stress on his brain.

A licensed physical therapist, told me about "Headspace," an app that he uses with his two sons, 8 and 9. The app provides ten minutes of meditation and quiet every day via guided visualization, mindfulness guidance, inner focus, and guided breathing.

"Braden, 9, just goes right to sleep and seems to worry about nothing at all in life," the physician said. "I tried Headspace with him but right now he doesn't really need it. Jamie, 8, however, is my more anxious boy, and he loves it. He and I do it every night before bed for ten minutes. We turn the app on my phone and listen to the meditation and silence cues. We do this together for the ten minutes then I kiss him goodnight.

"Jamie used to have sleeping problems—he'd lay awake thinking about everything. Now he sleeps a lot better, falls asleep quicker. Life is just better for him. I highly recommend a parent does this app (or something similar) *with* the child—I think it helps that I or his mother do it with him. He's too young to really to do it himself, so doing it with him makes it happen, and it's also a great time for bonding. I feel like I'm modeling something good too—practicing what I preach—healthy mindfulness.

"Another thing we did was to cut out all electronics in the bedroom one hour before bed. The boys read or play with Legos or something else but no electronics. This has helped them both. The research on screen time and screen stimulation, as you know, is very clear. It can be dangerous to kids' brains.

"My wife and I had to be careful in this regard, though, because Braden tried to take his phone into his room by saying, 'But Dad, I'm just going to plug my phone in to recharge it, I won't use it.'

"We fell for this little fib at first but then we caught on. 'Plug it in in the kitchen,' we say, and that's that."

While keeping the screens away from a child's bedtime is good for all kids, for boys who are higher anxiety or higher strung and stressed out, it can be a life-saver.

Guideline 8: Study your son to decide when it is right to give him a cell phone.

Given the issues the male brain is naturally likely to have during its maturation, I wouldn't give anyone 9 years old or younger a cell phone and did not do so with my own kids. If you are thinking about giving your son a cell phone during Stage 3, I hope you'll study your son and his environments carefully. For all the reasons already noted, that male brain will, once it receives that phone, move a great deal of its learning and interaction into and through the phone.

This is potentially toxic for the boy.

I brought this up at a recent conference and some concerned parents came up to me afterwards. A dad said, "If we don't start our boys on these technologies, like the phones, early in life, they won't function well with technologies later—they'll be behind other kids."

A mom, who was an engineer, concurred: "The more time these guys get on devices the more 'natural' for them the devices become, which helps them to learn things like sequencing. The human brain is changing anyway, so what's the harm? I read an article in *The Wall Street Journal* about this, how coding can help with sequencing which can help brain development. What you said tonight about not giving them phones doesn't fit with the science."

This is a very reasonable set of assumptions, and sequencing is indeed an essential cognitive function that some boys need extra help with. But they can learn sequencing through hundreds of other cognitive tasks. They don't need a phone for it. So I put the weight of the argument back onto these parents.

"Study your sons carefully," I said, "and make your decision about giving them a cell phone based on seeing how they're maturing physically, cognitively, and emotionally. Ask yourselves 'Is learning sequencing skills with an electronic technology so important that I'd risk difficulties with my son's brain maturing in other areas of verbal skills and social-emotional development?'"

If you proceed from this parent-scientist perspective, you'll have powerful and accurate answers to your child's plea, "But Dad, Mom, I won't fit in, I won't belong, if I don't have a cell phone like my friends do!"

"Here are the reasons we're doing this," you can explain, and bring your son into a scientific discussion at this young age.

And the ultimate truth is: this boy and the other kids will get along just fine without cell phones.

Stage 4: Ten to Thirteen Years Old

A mom brought her 12-year-old son into my office. While describing the issues he was facing—not doing homework, less than adequate focus on schoolwork he wasn't interested in, getting lower grades than his intellect warranted—the boy pulled her cell phone out of her purse and began playing a game on it. From my angle I couldn't see the game but I could see his bent head and strained neck, his quick fingers, his intense focus, and his distraction from the adult conversation.

"Let's not play that now," I said. "We have a lot to talk about." The boy didn't notice me, or pretended not to.

His mom reached to take the phone away but the boy pulled the phone away from her, twisting his body to continue his play.

"Come on, sweetie," she said very nicely now. "Let me have the phone."

"Mom, leave me alone!" he hissed and continued to play the game.

This kind of interaction is common in today's families. Quite often a mom or dad of a 10-to-13-year-old boy comes into my office without the parental authority to alter a child's behavior pattern—and quite often the lack of parental authority connects to using technology. In this case, I intervened by telling the boy to give the phone back to his mother. The boy was a little bit shocked by my abrupt tone but his mother's hand was thrust out waiting and so the boy gave the phone back. While you might think this authoritative interchange from a near-stranger might harm rapport with the boy, it ended up building rapport. Though the boy initially sulked, he later bonded with me. This was a boy unconsciously needy of adult male authority. This boy's mother had lost some of her authority with the boy, especially because he had moved much of his brain development to screen time. A single mom, she hadn't realized that technology can undermine parental authority. Our family counseling focused, in part, on helping her get that authority back especially because of the stage of life he was entering.

The Stage 4 human brain is a masterpiece still in tatters, still un-sculpted. It's a period during which there's "a dramatic increase in connectivity among brain regions involved in judgment, getting along with others and long-range planning—abilities that profoundly influence the remainder of a person's life," according to Dr. Jay Giedd, Chair of the Department of Child and Adolescent Psychiatry at the University of California, San Diego.

Three very important things, beyond physical growth, are happening to the brains and biochemistry of these Stage 4 boys.

1. *Testosterone is flowing.* Puberty has begun in "pre-puberty" at nine or ten years old, then into puberty by about 12 or 13 for most boys. Some will hit puberty a bit later. Testosterone is an aggression and sex chemical. Teaching character to boys in Stage 4 is a primary function of all family and community systems because the male brain is awash with a chemical that will challenge the boundaries of character and morality. These boys need our strong and diverse authority.

2. Each brain is developing its own unique neural footprint for dopamine release. Dopamine, our brain's reward chemical, and the centers of the brain that handle it such as the *nucleus accumbens* and *caudate nucleus,* are now in a massive process of neural pathway development. This process needs our assistance in order to build neural pathways upward to the cerebral cortex in ways that will be most socially functional in the long-term. So this early adolescent needs the dopamine rush to happen from real life not mainly through screens because the screens don't fit as well with natural reward chemistry gene expression.

3. Stage 4 is a very active brain pruning time for adolescents. Pruning is the brain's way of getting rid of cells that are not being used to make room for the greater use of cells and brain activity that early adolescence anticipates and needs for maturation. So, for instance, if a boy is taking piano at 12 his brain will retain those cells. If he stops taking piano, his brain will get rid of a lot of the cells associated with practicing piano. Similarly, if he spends a lot of time in front of screens and curtails time in real-life situations, his brain will retain the "virtual activity" cells and lose the real life cells—to the potential detriment of his maturation.

In all these areas, gender in the brain is important because the male and female brain develop their hormonology, cellular activity, dopamine flow, and pruning tempo somewhat differently. A profound difference in all this is the quicker tempo of maturation for the female brain. The speedier maturation occurs in these areas:

1. Speedier myelination of cells that coat the brain, thus speedier development of more white matter activity in the female brain, making neural pathway development between the limbic emotional centers and frontal lobe thinking centers a speedier natural process in the brains of the natural girl than the natural boy.

2. More rapid and earlier pruning of unneeded and higher-risk brain cells and brain activity. The female brain starts its pruning back in Stage 3 and it peaks in Stage 4. The male brain may not begin its heavy pruning until Stage 4 and it may not peak until Stage 5.

3. Quicker development and completion of brain centers used for emotive processing, such as the *anterior cingulate cortex.* Complex social-emotional skills develop more quickly in the female brain than in the male and are naturally designed to do so, giving the male brain a disadvantage in social-emotional activities, especially when something like excessive technology invades brain development.

4. Quicker development by 2 to 4 years of connectivity between various limbic areas and the pre-frontal cortex. The natural boy and natural girl are not on the same page in maturation of executive decision-making. Male brains move slower to get some of their decision-making centers of the brain activated.

Guideline 9: A good standard of screen use should be character and moral development.
The typical American male today consumes 43 gigabytes of data per day which is an increase of 350 percent in the last three decades. Information is now mostly visual via television, YouTube, movies, games, and visual stimuli on websites. For adults, now, written words account for less than one-tenth of one percent of the total information we absorb in a day. For adolescents, the amount of word use is higher because of

schooling, but it is also diminishing every year, and is far lower than it was thirty years ago.

Our mission, then, is to flow with our times and its technologies while also staying focused on what the Stage 4 adolescent brain needs, which is age-appropriate cognitive, physical, and emotional development with an uptick of character and moral development. As the brain prunes, explodes dopamine centers, and builds pathways between emotional impulse and critical thinking centers, it needs guidance in how to become a mature adult—a person of character.

Study your son to see how much of his time is spent in character development. Connect the results of your study to technology and media in these two ways:

1. Direct as much of his time as you can towards websites, movies, and other visual stimuli that teach character—what a man is, how to become a good man, how to take on the responsibilities of adulthood and trust oneself to be confident throughout the process. Tell him, as I asked the mom in my office to do, that "if electronics invade character development (treating mom with disrespect) they become a privilege you lose."

2. If your son is getting too little character development in his real life, curtail his media use and get him into communities and programs that develop character. Explain to him the brain development process to justify this new direction in his life. While it may not be possible or prudent to take away his screen time to do this you'll most likely need to curtail it in order to connect him with more real people.

Fortunately, you can take control of all of this because every electronic product in the home is owned by *you*. Computers, cell phones, X box…all are *yours*. Even if your son paid for one of them with his own allowance money, you are still the parent. He doesn't have an inalienable right to digital privacy. If you have any concerns about his media use, you can go into his browser history. Of course, if you abuse this parental right, your son will sense you are over-using your power and he may lose respect for you. But if you practice your right to be his parent in kindness and moderation, you may save your son from becoming consumed in screens and video games that lead to his falling behind in character and emotional development.

Question: But isn't it sort of overkill? Aren't video games just games?

Answer: They are both games and potential maturation tools because they already deal with themes of character development and manhood.

Every video game—even ones that we might find despicable, like *Grand Theft Auto*—can become assets in a boy's moral development, especially if we discuss the games with the boys. Here's a quote from General George Patton that dads who play war games with sons can use to mentor their sons.

"Despite the impossibility of detecting the soul physically, its existence is proven by its tangible reflection in acts and thoughts. So with war, beyond its physical aspect of armed hosts there hovers an impalpable something which dominates the material. To understand this 'something' we should seek it in a manner analogous to our search for the soul."

"Your sons," I suggest to parents, "are not just playing a game—they're entering a world of soldiery in which, Patton says, they are searching for their souls. This fits the neuroscience." As males develop neural pathways between the limbic area and the temporal lobe, which is known as the spiritual part of the brain, the ineffable becomes meaningful to boys—it is a source of power, purpose, and independence. The boys can't generally talk about all this indescribable, transcendent feeling in depth yet, but it constitutes the manhood they search for in video games as these electric and electronic images are flung at the boy—images of soul, shadows of honor, ideas cast in light and darkness that motivate and grow a boy's soul.

If contextualized, they can help the journey. If played too much or never contextualized, they can create more neural distress, less light and more darkness in the male brain. And so, as with everything our son sees and feels, parents and the adult community have the power to direct a boy's maturation through his video games.

Here are some strategic ways you can do this.

* Ask your son to teach you the game he is playing;
* Ask him to interpret the game for you, not just for a minute or two, but in great depth; and
* Ask him, specifically, to interpret and integrate the games into the value systems you are teaching him in your family.

Video games are rife with doorways to these strategies because in many video games your son is already becoming a warrior who battles for good against evil.

Here's an example from *Halo*.

"We soldiers are simple things," the Colonel tells his troops. "We're taught honor: honor means sacrifice and sacrifice means death, our own or our enemy's. In some ways, beneath it all, that's what a soldier's really trained to do—to end God's work."

In this teaching, the video game is aiding temporal lobe connections by focus on God, the soul, manhood, and soldiering linked together in male maturation. Using this already extant linkage in the game or movie, we can help build the boy's mind as we talk with the boy about the video game. You can carry on this discussion with your son and add your own lessons in values, spirituality, suffering, death, life, and, ultimately, manhood. Especially if your son is playing an hour of video games every weekday and two or more hours every weekend, it's essential that you integrate video game play into this conscious character and manhood maturation.

A dad, who did two tours with the Marines in Iraq, accomplished this goal this way (I've summarized a number of our counseling sessions here).

"As you know, I came home messed up and you suggested I take the bull by the horns and talk to my 11-year-old son Cary about his video games. At first, I couldn't even play the games without getting flashbacks. But gradually, I could, and it was a way to bond with Cary. So I used Halo, like you suggested. It worked well because I could talk to Cary about my values.

"Like, there's a part where the Colonel tells Commander Locke what he believes: 'You give your life away so others will live in peace. These people who live on after what you did carry part of your deeds with them. In their final hours, they will have to answer the question you asked in yours: with your life, would you only create death or with your death would you create life? That is my question to you, Commander Locke: how will you die, and for what?'

"I asked Cary if he understood what this meant. He said, 'Yeah, Dad, it means you will sacrifice your life so other people can have their lives. It's like what you were doing in Iraq.' I cried right then, right in front of him, I cried and then he cried, too. We hugged each other. I was so proud of my boy."

As this father told me about this incident, tears came to his eyes and my own. What an amazing gift this father gave his son and that gift came through video games!

A dad or other mentor who has never been a soldier can do this with his son or mentee—indeed, I believe, he *must*. If an early adolescent boy is playing video games that can affect brain, heart, and soul without mentoring by fathers or father-figures, manhood will be defined for the boy without real men leading the self-definition. The boy may not mature into the fully loving, wise, and successful man we want him to be.

Guideline 10: Restrict the use of visual porn as needed.

Pornography is a natural attractant to most boys in this age group because most boys have begun to masturbate by thirteen, and male sexual function is directly linked, in the brain, to visual stimulation. Curiosity about erotica and porn is not generally dangerous to a boy. Every man you know most likely sought out some sort of porn when he was young and most of us turned out fine.

But life has changed from my boyhood, in which physical (and hard to get) magazines gave us our visual porn, to now, in which online life can addict boys to visual porn quickly and relatively easily. You may recall that Andrew could not get an erection without a visual porn stimulant. This exemplifies the dangers of online porn use. In the new millennium, many of our sons' brains are attaching sexual manhood development to visual porn stimulants. This can set them up to fail in later life in love, marriage, and even in healthy sexuality.

Porn, then, can be a neurotoxin even for boys who do not become sex addicts. So we must pay close enough attention to a boy's visual porn use. I hope you will pay attention by studying your son's porn use and, if needed, institute some of these strategies.

* Don't overreact to normal visual-sexual curiosity and normal masturbation. If you aren't sure what "normal" should be for your son, ask the men in your family, or ask a professional who knows your son. There is also a wonderful book on normal sexuality called *Slippery When Wet* by reproductive physiologist Dr. Joanna Ellington. Dr. Ellington has raised four boys and she has a powerful "mom-friendly" perspective—both as a scientist and a mother—on what is normal for adolescent boys.

* Keep strict tabs on the websites your son visits, both via his phone and his computer/tablet. If possible, keep parental controls on all visual devices (including television, Netflix, Hulu, etc.) but assume that your son may find a way around those, so keep checking everything to see where he went if you are at all worried about his visual porn use.

* If and when you discover that he visited a porn site, check the site out, talk with the men in your family, decide what should happen next. Should Dad or another man talk to your son about this, or, if you're a single mom without male assets right now, should you talk with him? As always, if you have any questions about what is normal for your son, talk with professionals, like school counselors, who know your son.

* When and if you approach your son about porn websites, avoid shaming him and if consequences are needed, give your son three chances. This will often be better than immediate anger or punitive consequences. Three chances to change his porn behavior helps him to self-regulate so he can develop his own mature response to the porn.

* If your son has been sexually abused, he may be even more attracted to porn than his friend or brother who hasn't been. If a boy seems inordinately attracted to porn, especially porn with a certain fetish or involving a certain population, you may not have known it, but he may have been sexually abused and the

porn use can be a gift to you—a clue to a greater conversation that needs to happen with this boy to discover and treat the source of his trauma. In these cases, get professional help immediately.

* Assume that no matter what you do to control porn in your home, he'll find some way, through friends or elsewhere to discover porn. And again, remember that some of this discovery is normal, so make sure to work together in your Three Family System to decide what is right for your son and his friends.

* Just as with video games, ask the trusted men in your family to look at the porn a boy discovers with the boy to teach lessons about objectification of women, healthy sexuality, and love and commitment.

You may have an 11, 12, or perhaps even 13-year-old who isn't seeking out or finding visual porn and your journey with porn may not begin with your boy until Stage 5. I hope you won't live in fear about porn, since most boys will never become porn or sex addicted, but I do hope, too, that you will be vigilant with this in Stage 4 or later, whenever the porn might become an issue.

Guideline 11: Be developmental rather than judgmental as your sons make mistakes—in their mistakes they are generally trying to create rites of passage into manhood.

Jim and Nicole, both in their late thirties, came to me about their 12-year-old son, Tyrell. They had intercepted messaging trails between him and a 17-year-old girl. In this relationship, he had pretended to be 18.

I dreamt 'bout u.
Cool. Like what?
'bout our first kiss, I can't wait.
Me too. I cant wait 2 be with u
Yeah. I really luv u.
U are sweet. I love u too.
Cool! (imogee)
Do u dream about me when you…you know?
Yeah. Is it weird?

No (imogee) it's so sweet.

Tyrell had not met this girl, Brie, who lived five states away, but it was clear that he was flirting sexually with her, trying out sexual language with her, and trying to help her through a tough time. His texts were at once flirtatious and empathic. She became the focus of risk-taking and rite-of-passage for him. The girl had no idea he wasn't 18 and she was ready to meet with him. In a text he sent just before his parents discovered this interaction, Tyrell promised to pay for Brie's airfare to come visit.

"Luckily, he has no money," Jim reported

His wife Nicole, on the other hand, was livid.

"How does my son decide to be this person? We raised him to be good, to be a good kid, and he's...he's masturbating, I mean, like this, it's like phone sex, and he's manipulating this girl, making false promises. Oh God, it's like he's sick, it's terrible."

Cases like this are becoming more common and they're very difficult to navigate because they exist in a new world, one in which the normal developmental imagination and experimentation of adolescence occurs on a potentially public canvas, and in virtual possibility. What was once only imaginable can now be real for our young boys and girls.

The male brain in particular is especially needy of both supervised and unsupervised rites-of-passage into adulthood. It rarely gets complex and supervised rites-of-passage today, and thus is even more prone to take large risks that mimic rites-of-passage.

Fifty years ago, a 12-year-old boy who fantasized a relationship with an older woman experienced the relationship only in his own imagination. He would picture that 17-year-old girl late at night in privacy as he masturbated. Then when he saw her at school or in the neighborhood, he felt embarrassment and appropriate anxiety about his immaturity and her out-of-reach status. Perhaps he planned out some kind of high-risk move to get closer to her but then, gradually, he let her go, maturing through some other imaginative story, this one non-sexual perhaps and involving his board games, his older brother's new car, or his own future as a sports hero.

In this way, his internal fantasies were developmentally appropriate as self-motivators to mature.

Now the digital boy can fulfill his normal internal life in ways that become dangerous to his own and others' normal development. Because of smartphones, Instagram, Pinterest, texting and sexting, cut and paste technology, anonymous servers, and all the other accoutrement of digital life, a 12-year-old can follow his natural maturation inclination into a rite-of-passage that has potential for actual harm. When his parents discover his activity, they feel naturally frightened and confused. Quite often, as in this case, they assume there's something wrong with him, become judgmental of their son and blame themselves for raising a boy of bad character.

Most often, though, the issue is not the boy, but the fact that we adults gave the boy the unfettered technology and access to virtual reality. In Tyrell's case, I worked with Jim and Nicole to discover if he had been sexually abused—which he had not—and we saw that there was nothing "wrong" with him. He was indeed a good kid developing normally at the higher end of the growth spectrum for twelve—tall and already starting to grow body hair—smart, adept technologically, and a boy with a good, empathic conscience.

When Jim and Nicole asked me what to do for their son I asked them to bring him back from the virtual world—take back the power and authority over his access to inappropriate porn sites by taking away his Internet access for a period of "grounding." This family chose not to give him Internet access for the foreseeable future but allow him to keep his smartphone. The parents also instituted a number of our earlier strategies for integrating screen time into character development.

Tyrell accepted the parents' judgments without much rebellion. He accepted the grounding from all electronics except smartphones for one month. He even accepted their shaming for his behavior. His parents were much harder on him emotionally than I would have been as a parent, but too soft (in my opinion) for refusing to take away his smartphone for at least another year.

But Nicole said, "I need him to have a cell phone so I can know where he is and I can always call him if I need to."

Jim said, "This is a moral issue. He needs to act in a trustworthy way. We're not going to make it easy on him by taking away all temptation. He needs to grow up."

Both parents operated out of deep love for this boy in different ways, but I left this case wishing I could have convinced them to be more developmentally appropriate, less judgmental of Tyrell, and more critical of the technology they trusted. The boy did not need a smartphone. Every 12-year-old boy survived quite well without one until a few years ago, and the smartphone would soon be used by Tyrell to circumvent the "grounding."

During a particular moving session, I remember helping Tyrell write a letter of apology to send to the girl. I sat with him as he wept gently in his chair. Caring for him there I remembered my own boyhood. I made many mistakes during my search for rites of passage into manhood, even though I had no access to this new world of potentially life-altering mistakes that has suddenly entered boys' and girls' lives.

Give Boys Non-Electronic Rites of Passage Along with or Instead of Technological Ones

As a Jew, the *bar mitzvah* was part of my upbringing, so I'm aware of the importance of rites of passage. Also, when I was 13, my father worked on the Southern Ute Reservation in Colorado, where I was introduced to Native American Vision Quest and the sweat lodge. Ever since these teen years, I've studied rites of passage. In *A Fine Young Man,* you'll find a number of rite-of-passage models you can use in your Three Family Systems. In *The Purpose of Boys,* you'll find a chapter on the HEROIC template for nature-based rite-of-passage development.

As you ponder taking greater control, if needed, of your son's use of technology, also consider giving him natural rites of passage.

If you're Christian, you might enjoy using a Christian rite of passage program I developed with Pastor Tim Wright, author of *Searching for Tom Sawyer.* Pastor Wright approached me ten years ago to help bring nature-based theory into Christian settings and he and I built a number of programs for Christian families and schools that you can review at www.timwrightministries.com. Two of these are the one-year rite-of-passage programs, *Following Jesus: A Heroic Quest for Boys* and *Following Jesus: A Wisdom Journey for Girls.*

To take technology away from boys without giving them sacred rites of passage through family, community, and faith systems is robbing Peter to pay Paul. As hormones flow, as pruning occurs, as white and gray matter activity increases and neural interconnections try to develop, the male brain is in dangerous flux. While this brain and soul need non-intervention from us to grow, they also need help directing development toward social-emotional and behavioral maturation.

Superheroes attract boys of this age in some part because they heal the chaos of adolescence by modeling rites of passage into manhood. Their stories direct the hormones and boy energy. The boy sees a piece of who he must become—a man of self-sacrifice. Superheroes are the pre-frontal cortex of the boy directing the rest of the chaotic brain to mastery and manhood.

When you look into the eyes of an 11-year-old boy, you can "see" the boy's ineffable yearning to fly to the stars and journey to the center of the earth, the need to hug someone one minute and yell at them the next, the shyness afflicted by the hormones of desire, an impulsive hunter preparing for cruelty. The male brain and body in Stage 4 of boyhood is a spectacular and magnificent mess of potential. It wants direction. Until about fifty years ago every human culture made two changes in the lives of males during Stage 4:

1. They began a concerted effort to seek out apprenticeships for young males in which the males would get rites of passage through crafting a life-work, even a self, in a mentor's workshop.
2. They instituted rites of passage by which the three families would test and measure the boy: give him direction on values and needed traits for maturity, compel him to grow in public settings, teach him how to treat females respectfully, and direct him toward a positive future.

You can do this today. Utilizing specific rites of passage tools can result in the rewarding process of seeing the light in a boy's eyes as maturation is almost literally "poured" into his soul by you and your community, and through his significant effort on the rafting trip, three-day hike, one week retreat with men, yearlong preparation for *bar mitzvah* or Confirmation, and other significant sacred challenge. As you commit to rites-of-passage for and with the boy, he'll begin to feel what it's like to start becoming one of those heroes himself—rather than just seeing them on screens—because he'll face the experiential maturation intrinsic to real-world rites-of-passage.

Stage 5: 14 – 17 Years old

Ahmad, 16, was a tall young man with a near-full black beard—strong looking but also bookish with his thick spectacles, and Muslim, which was frightening to some classmates, I learned quickly, and mysterious to others. He came into my office with his parents, all of Iranian descent.

His family members had brought him to me, they said, because they had read that I spent two years in Ankara, Turkey.

"We want an expert," they told me, "an expert in adolescent boys who would have at least a little bit of understanding of the kind of culture he has come from." Their son, they said, was failing to launch, and, especially, "addicted to technology." Ahmad himself admitted to the technological problem.

"It's the only thing that interests me," he confessed.

Getting this young man to open up took all the craft I possessed. Once he found out that I was Jewish, he became confused by his own feelings—suspicions deep in his cultural consciousness, tied to Iranian politics regarding Israel but, also, as he put his own stereotyping: "The Jews are smart like the Iranians."

Counseling went on in fits and starts over six months and I tried many things, including video games and movies, to help him. Asking him to teach me the games he liked, I also asked him to tell me what his favorite movies were. In learning their titles and working, through their lens, I sensed that Ahmad didn't know what a man could or should be— that he searched in the games and movies for his soul. But he wanted more than video games, movies, and digital life could give him.

One of Ahmad's favorite movies was the Tony Scott film, starring Denzel Washington, *Man on Fire*. I spent a lot of time discussing this movie with Ahmad.

Question: Can you please model exactly how we can use and exploit technological media to help an adolescent boy mature?

Answer: A direct way to do this is to use the movie, book, or other medium (e.g. YouTube video) to engage in conversation with the Stage 5 boy about the "manhood" in it.

In *Man on Fire*, Denzel Washington plays a retired counter-insurgency expert, Creasy. Haunted by his past, he comes to Mexico City to visit an old friend and soon takes a job as bodyguard for 10-year-old Pita (Dakota Fanning), who is then kidnapped and ransomed for 10 million dollars. The ransom deal goes horribly wrong. Creasy (who is shot and nearly killed during the kidnapping) and the authorities now believe Pita has been killed.

After Creasy recovers from his injuries, he vengefully and efficiently pursues everyone involved in the killing of the little girl, and he murders them. While finding all the bad guys, he discovers that Pita is still alive. In the end, he rescues her by making a deal with the lead kidnapper in which he promises to give up his life for Pita's. Among the most heart-wrenchingly beautiful scenes in the film is a final one in which Pita's mother clutches her little girl to her chest while Creasy dies in the kidnapper's car clutching a religious amulet, given to him earlier in the movie by Pita, hanging from his neck.

While Ahmad walked around the city with me or paced or sat in my counseling office, we discussed: Who is your little girl named Pita? What fragile person would you sacrifice your life for? Who have you felt this kind of empathy for, and when? We retraced times in his memory when he acted with empathic love for his sister, his parents, and his grandparents. Walking down this trail of memories helped this boy to think in mature terms. I didn't let him off the hook until he could give me good answers.

The movie helped us. In the middle portion of the film Creasy's best friend, a former soldier played by Christopher Walken, tells a federal policeman to let Creasy investigate Pita's abduction without interference. Walken calls Creasy an "artist" in his craft. In this film, the "art" is death but I asked Ahmad: "What is your art form?" Through it, we agreed, a man shows a lot of his love of others.

Ahmad first told me he wanted to get involved in video game software design as his career. We talked about that for a while but then I tried to move him into other issues of manhood as well. Not just work but relationships needed to become his art form as a man. We talked about how he could develop other parts of himself.

One afternoon we watched the final scene in which blood

drips from Creasy's gunshot wounds. Even dying, Creasy reassures Pita's mother, "You'll be okay."

Ahmad and I talked about how mature this show of strength was—it showed that Creasy could care for others to the very end. We talked about the difference between narcissism and heroism. Ahmad himself brought up his own issues with narcissism. He admired Creasy's utter lack of narcissism at his end.

We talked about something else: Walken's character says to the federal policeman that Creasy, who loathes himself for accidental killings of innocents in his earlier counter-insurgency career, follows this path of redemption now because "Pita gave him a reason to live again."

"What have been your acts against innocents?" I asked Ahmad. He told me about times he had acted like a bully to his sibling. He confessed regrets mainly about disappointing his parents and his culture.

Creasy redeems his past in his present, even unto death.

"How will you redeem yourself?" I asked Ahmad. "What good things should you do so you can replace memories of disappointing people with memories of helping them?"

We discussed self-forgiveness—what it is, how to build it into the mature self. We talked about how difficult life is and will be, how many mistakes an adult will make, how deep a man's grief and shame can go, but how deep redemption can go, too. I asked Ahmad to bring me quotes from the Qu'ran about all this, for ancient wisdom from his original culture that he could teach me. He came back the next week with a great deal of insight from the Qu'ran.

By now, we had spent five sessions using *Man on Fire* to help this young man open up his heart and soul. He now became focused on scenes in which Creasy trains little 10-year-old Pita to be a better swimmer.

"There's no such thing as tough," Creasy teaches her. "There's trained and untrained." Creasy makes her repeat this back to him as he pushes her very hard to be "trained" not "untrained." Ahmad noticed that she soaks in his tough love (aggression nurturance) and ends up winning a swimming contest.

Creasy's smile at her glory is priceless and in its glow I asked Ahmad: "Why does Creasy, who is clearly one of the toughest men you'll ever meet, slough off the 'tough' word and insist, instead, on 'trained'? In other words, why not say, 'Be tough!' How is 'trained not untrained' an even more subtle form of mentoring from this man?"

I asked this because I've found that every boy has his own answer to this and all of them are enlightening for each boy. Ahmad's answer involved talking about how much tougher on him his father was than his mother.

"I wish my mother was a little tougher on me," he said, with tears in his eyes.

In another scene early in the movie, where Creasy is bonding with Pita, she asks, "Does being black help you in this work (being a bodyguard)?"

He doesn't overreact to a white girl pointing out his race.

"We'll see," he says.

I asked Ahmad how this felt to him, especially as a Muslim.

"I used to get beaten up for being Muslim before I got bigger in fourth grade," he said. "But I never told my parents."

I asked him to do so. As we discussed this further, I asked him to consider how important religion and tradition, especially for a boy like him who was somewhat devout, can be in one's identity. I talked with him about the fact that adolescence was a time to explore every aspect of our identity, and to mine each part, in our own independent way, for its gold—our maturity.

Creasy cries in some very powerful scenes in the movie. His tears allowed Ahmad and me to talk about crying, tears, and all of the other forms of emotional expression available to him. Simultaneously, in another scene, when Pita complains about not wanting to practice piano, Creasy scolds tenderly: "Don't be a crybaby. You're tougher than that."

He then shows her an experiential way to avoid having

to play piano if she doesn't want to play it—an alternative to crying and whining—in which she burps in front of the piano teacher so that the artist's sensibility is offended. Thus, Pita succeeds in avoiding strict piano lessons and does so without tears—instead she acts, and thus solves her problem. Ahmad understood the worthiness of this kind of autonomy and creativity in problem-solving.

At the end of the movie, after Creasy has rescued Pita and now is dying, he gives Pita a final hug.

"Now, you go home," he tells her.

His last words to her are the command because he doesn't want her to linger near him since the bad men are just a few yards away, but she doesn't want to let go.

"Where are you going?" she asks him.

"I'm going home, too."

"You love me, don't you?" she says.

"Yes I do, with all my heart."

And then she runs to her mother's arms and he goes off to the car of the bad guys in which he will die.

Nearly every male, including Ahmad and me, becomes teary-eyed as he watches this. As the movie fades to credits we wonder together—man and boy, mentor and adolescent, counselor and client—what this love is that can be so strong that the toughest man in the world melts into the joy of dying.

Man on Fire is a leitmotif for a number of sessions of counseling with boys, weaving in and out of our other walking, pacing, and talking. Few conversations with adolescent boys go as well and go as deep as conversations that happen in a safe container connected to the media in which their unconscious minds are already invested.

Guideline 12: Focus family interactions on integrating the boy's media, when appropriate, into the search for a spiritual and non-narcissistic manhood.

To engage manhood training via technology and media, we will need to decide that there is no part of a son's culture that cannot help him mature; thus, we will have to avoid the idea that "it's just entertainment."

Yes, true, a lot of media is only entertainment, and yes, true, we can't keep up with everything an adolescent sees or does. But he is a boy of 14–17 so the most important internal question he is asking is: "What is a man?"

Understanding and exploiting the power of this question can take entertainment back into the realm of important stories for male maturation.

In Ahmad's case I also asked for heroes from his own Iranian culture. He mentioned that his father loved the 14th century Persian poet, Hafiz. I asked Ahmad if he had ever read this poet and he said he had. Because I couldn't read Hafiz in his original language, I bought a copy of the translation of Hafiz poems in English, *The Gift*, by Daniel Ladinsky. Over the course of the next few sessions, Ahmad and I used this book to ground our therapy. By the time we finished with Hafiz in our sessions, Ahmad understood much better the kind of hero—and male hero—he wanted to be.

Clients like Ahmad have taught me that no one need believe in God in the same way another person does but all boys can increase their maturation by investigating their own argument with God with and without technology. By arguing with the universe they stay humble, never believing they know the only truth.

Ahmad seemed to understand this as we ended our time studying *Man on Fire* and then Hafiz. "I see what you're doing, Mr. Gurian. You're trying to get me to be less narcissistic and humbler."

I agreed I was and Ahmad enjoyed "figuring out the gray-haired man."

Guideline 13: Teach Stage 5 boys the mindfulness they will need to thrive.

A future of mindful spiritual discipline—the ability to discover the quiet of soul and recharge the self there—is important to teach the brain in this developmental life-stage. These boys seek mindfulness already in their music, using those earphones and buds to stay "internal" for long periods of time. They go inward to find the songs of life around which to construct future success and love. They want to learn inward rhythms of meditative quiet. The brain wants these pathways to develop so maturity can take place. A boy who becomes mindful achieves a part of manhood—the setting of a spiritual, non-narcissistic path he can replicate, through meditation or prayer, throughout life.

This mindfulness is also very much about learning how to live in time rather than being constantly controlled by it. It is about discovering the expansiveness of space rather than being constantly battered about in the small space of home, street, and school. It is about building a mature relationship with the things and people of the world.

Rabbi Abraham Joshua Heschel, an author I use with Jewish adolescents, writes in *The Sabbath:* "Inner liberty depends upon being exempt from domination of things as well as from domination of people. There are many people who have acquired a high degree of political and social liberty, but only very few are not enslaved to things. This is our constant problem—how to live with people and remain free, how to live with things and remain independent."

For Stage 5 adolescent boys, "independence" and "freedom" are now possible, but so too is the sense that a man is always going to be enslaved by others, by responsibilities, by life. For this boy, it can feel like the only way to protect the budding self is to become narcissistic and self-absorbed. We want humility as well as strength in our Stage 5 boys, and so we teach mindfulness—the intimate connection to soul.

For Ahmad, Hafiz was the tool to help him develop mindfulness practice. I asked him to read a Hafiz poem once a day and then meditate and pray right afterwards. He didn't always stick to this regimen, but having the regimen, which was already a part of his five-times-a-day prayer cycle, echoed Islam for him. Whenever a Stage 5 boy has any kind of connection to religion, I try to use it to help him with mindfulness.

Fr. Bill Watson of the Sacred Story Institute, in collaboration with high school students, has done just that in developing a program, *True Heart*, to help build mindfulness in high school students. Even if you aren't Catholic you might still be fascinated by its regimen. In whatever way you decide to look at this Guideline 13, I hope you will—even if you are an atheist—study the scientific research available on mindfulness, and target your middle adolescent sons for education in that developmental milestone of maturity.

While your son may not need religion like Ahmad did to learn his lessons, your son will need some form of life that is like this religious kind of temporal lobe pathway development. If you don't help him find this mindfulness, he may well seek it in technology but technology cannot give it to him. Technology is an artificial and relatively frantic place of instant gratification and constant stimulation. He'll get enough of those later in life. He needs the practice of mindfulness now in order to sear it into his soul during adolescence, when his brain is perfectly tuned to habituate this practice, so that it will become a supportive and wise part of him as he faces life's inevitable ups and downs.

Guideline 14: Put these boys to work!

Every Stage 5 adolescent boy needs a path of self-discipline that earns him his independence and autonomy. He needs to build the sense that he is earning, not just being given, his life. Work outside the home has been and always should continue to be a primary testing place for financial independence, and the search for self. You can make this happen, even though it might take some time and effort.

With families and youth who become my clients, I sometimes tell my own story of working out of necessity because our family needed the money. First, I cleaned toilets in the Continental Trailways bus station in Durango, Colorado, where we lived during my father's time on the Southern Ute Reservation. Then I worked as a busboy in restaurants in Honolulu, Hawaii, where we moved for my last year of high school. I saved money, paid money to my parents to help with family expenses, and bought my own first car, a rusted old heap that became a talisman of independence. Today's smartphones, tablets, and computers were not available to me so I worked.

Many boys in Stage 5 need to work—and especially now, as a way of getting them away from technology overuse or addiction. A retired high school teacher, Jeanne Mark, 71, recently told me her sense of why this is true.

"For my forty years in schools I wished parents would see how different high school boys and girls are in the way they look at schooling. Some boys love high school but a lot of them hate how irrelevant the worksheets and sitting at lectures feel to them. I believe there should be some kind of diversion program starting at 16 for the boys who need it. Those boys—and I bet you there are millions of them—need more of the hands-on, one-on-one mentoring that young guys got back in my generation when they went to work at 15 or, by 17, ran off to the military. If we start the boys of the new generations working at that age, they will grow up, just like my brothers and I had to."

In her analysis, Jeanne is getting at something my own research confirms: millions of boys need to either be working at 16 or have a "work life" inculcated into their daily routine. This developmental advantage can be life-changing, not only because they'll spend less time in front of screens but also because working can provide "reward-system functionality" (dopamine release in the brain). Much of independence and autonomy building during adolescence is accomplished by the dual process in the brain of attaching limbic-to-frontal neural pathway development to the inspiration of dopamine release in the brain following activities, like work, that compel the pathway development. A boy works, gets praise (or critique and direction), improves, learns, grows, gets paid…all of this releases dopamine chemistry and builds neural pathways of maturation.

A program in Kansas City, Missouri Public Schools recognizes this process. The school district teamed with the Metropolitan Community College and the Kansas City Fire Department to offer training to high school students who want to explore becoming Emergency Medical Technicians or other related technicians. Interested students take the EMT class during their school year, then apprentice to the health departments at its completion. They spend some necessary time at computers learning basic health and doing simulations, but go into the real world to learn the rest of the craft.

This kind of program is especially important for the kinds of boys Jeanne mentioned—boys for whom high school and obsession with new technologies are not a fit with what their brains need for maturation. Programs like the EMT training can be especially important in many low-performing or low-achieving inner city schools in which the teachers and staff have never received training in how to educate boys. Personnel in fire departments, quite often, instinctively understand how to do that.

A further advantage to male maturation through work involves the narcissism we discussed previously. Many boys who are bored by school and waste many hours in front of screens build a grandiose sense of their own worth. Unfortunately, some of these boys need college and would flourish there but decide to avoid its rigors. If, however, they spend two years, from 16 to 18, working menial jobs (like cleaning toilets or bussing tables), their narcissism will be tempered and they may well realize the merits of college quite experientially.

Working at 16 is not for every boy, especially if the boy is clearly the best at a particular sport and needs many hours per day to train. But if we are to become revolutionaries on behalf of our sons, we must rethink Stage 5 to include the work option for millions of boys. Because of online schooling available to our children now, it is not difficult for a child to complete high school online while working 20 hours per week. He will get nearly all the screen time his brain needs via the online schooling and spend much of the rest of his day in responsible self-development and kinesthetic growth through work.

When I speak with audiences about this option, someone might raise the objection: "But where are the jobs for these kids? The workplace can't sustain this plan."

It's a logical objection. Each parent in the Three Family Systems will need to help a youth find a job or "create" a job somewhere within the community for the youth. This will be part of our social revolution, the creation of "new" jobs like hiring the youth to do filing, computing, clerking, delivery, maintenance, "assistant," "shadow," or just: "Okay, your job, son, will be whatever we need you to do." It will not be easy to find a job for each youth, but we must try.

And even if you don't decide to exercise this work option, I hope you will make sure your son's daily life (and, especially, technology use) is set up *as if he is working*, with many chores he must do, priorities on engaging school work and significant athletic life (for boys who are athletic) and significant relational time away from electronics, like spending time visiting elders in nursing homes and building relational skills experientially. Study your son's life. Ask yourself: if he were working, what would his day look like? Help him create a "work" day that fits.

Stage 6: 18 to 21

Immaturity for a boy in Stage 6 can feel like despair. He sees how vast the world really is, how deceptive its people can be, how confusing are its relationships, and feels insufficient as a young male because he also realizes that he lacks the inner resources for dealing with this complex life. If male anhedonia existed in this boy during earlier stages, it may become deeply entrenched now. If it did not exist previously, it may appear now. Technology and electronics can help "self-medicate" the boy's feelings of anxiety, fear, and lethargy, but they cannot fully give this sad, withdrawn or angry boy a defined and purposeful future.

Guideline 15: Make sure a Stage 6 male is learning or already knows how he is needed in his family, community, and the world.

Unless a Stage 6 male is physically or mentally disabled in some way that needs constant care, this early adult male brain needs to be working or studying with purpose in college or technical school. This is important in our present era when visual entertainment, screen time, and social media can stimulate Stage 6 males utterly and deceptively into releasing dopamine in the brain by convincing their brains that they're doing important things, like winning a game, even though they're not doing anything important in the real world.

Though we can't as parents control these males' use of media, we can at least help them structure lives that will bring them the right kinds of inner rewards—through college, vocational education, or work. If your son refuses to do anything "needed" in the world, you may need to marshal the forces of your Three Family System to re-orient him. One parent alone is generally not enough power or influence to change a Stage 6 boy's negative trajectory. A "parent team" of three or more people may be needed to lower the boom on this boy, and compel him toward a potent and honorable life.

Andrew, whom you met at the beginning of this chapter, was a lost Stage 6 male. For him and his parent team, vocational and technical school provided brain-friendly assets that fit this male's particular nature and self—he was able to come out of his video game addiction to discover how he was needed in the world after a long struggle in which not only he engaged himself, but his whole family team sacrificed a great deal of time, resources, and effort, as well.

Guideline 16: Where college is a negative place for young men, change college.

For many of our young men, college has become a place to avoid, either by not going, or once they go, by underperforming or dropping out. As Dr. Carrie Franklin pointed out in Chapter 4, college life has become, for many males in arts and sciences especially, a place of either attack or negligence. Even more subtle, college life today de-escalates male maturation by over emphasis on constant multi-tasking and de-emphasis on in-depth project-based learning. While many young people gain from doing and studying twenty things at once using words, many maturing brains (both male and female) also need emphasis on a few highly relevant tasks, some of which are not judged by essay tests and in-class verbal participation.

For males this can be especially true because the male brain generally matures certain gray matter areas and brain-myelination later than female brains do. Colleges so highly emphasize sitting in chairs and regurgitating words, with so little experiential learning, that other pathway development and basic brain growth for males is often curtailed. Instinctively, many males will gravitate away from this kind of environment, even though the college environment should help ensure that an adult will earn better wages and be better prepared for the workplace.

To help males in college we will need to revolutionize colleges in one or more of these ways.

We need to increase experiential and workplace-friendly learning. Those students who do well in the present highly verbal-emotive, regurgitative college frameworks can continue in that framework through classes that emphasize that approach. Meanwhile, more project-based learning, and learning connected to workplaces, must develop to help the other students flourish—and thus increase enrollments and graduation at college.

The hyper-reactivity to micro-aggressions and grotesque immaturity it inculcates in both young women and men will need to be curtailed. This can be done immediately as "real life" is returned to college. Perhaps most helpful in the area of sexual confusion and misconduct will be to focus on the clearest path to sexual assault prevention in every college—alcohol and drug use—rather than deceptive "rape culture" attacks on males that infantilize many females and also drive males away from college.

Every college that has a Women's Studies program (or set of classes) should have a Male Studies program. A diverse approach to "What is a man?" should be a major subject of college life, integrated into existing courses as women's studies and feminism have been. It can also be taught separately—as are women's studies in a separate department or sub-department. This innovation will not only help young males and females to better understand adult life but also help curtail the lopsided college conversations in many universities today in which only the Dominant Gender Paradigm of masculine defect is taught—sending young males away from college for sheer self-protection.

These programs might also bravely look at the boy crisis through the lens of our young people. My daughter, Gabrielle, then 26 and entering law school, responded to my discussion with her about the need for "Male Studies programs," by saying, "Dad, most of us know, white females are the new white males. It's the universities themselves that still live in the past. Of course we need this kind of program." In Chapter 1 we noticed that, in most ways, girls are doing better than boys in all demographics. Hopefully, bridges can get built between women's and male studies programs so our youth can look somewhat less ideologically than we have at what is really happening in the lives of males and females.

Teach young men a balanced used of technology and media—I call this "life/technology balance" as an echo of "work/life balance." A tech executive shared this story: "Millennials have grown up with Google and then in college they think Google is their best research source. Many times I've had young millennial software engineers ask me a question about how to do X after doing a Google search for X. The kid doesn't find his simple and immediate answer there because, frankly, there isn't one. The kid turns to me and asks me how to do X. I say, 'Listen, kid, you have to invest the time to read the specs of the systems involved and figure it out.' The kid frowns—it's too much effort for him. Even in college he was used to getting answers quickly from Google."

Online tools can be great for our college students. At the same time, college professors and staff are in a perfect position to mentor our youth in appropriate balance between technology and life. When in doubt, real life work and engagement should win the day. The maturation of our sons depends on it.

Guideline 17: Help each young man find peer and elder mentors, both male and female, and make sure each young man is also mentoring one or more younger children.

Technology when overused in the developmental years and continually overused in Stage 6 becomes a nearly sole source of "mentoring" but is an inadequate actual mentoring source. Young males need real mentors to fully mature their brains. Meanwhile, their brains also mature by teaching what they know to others, especially younger kids, so they can develop pathways for compassion, critical thinking, responsibility, and family-life skills.

One area of great distress for younger people today involves word-development in low income and impoverished environments. Low-income children come to schools with fewer words than their peers from more affluent homes and communities. One way each college can help meet all needs is to build volunteer or service programs into curricula and structure to help connect young people to these low-income children. Reading to and with these kids can change not only their lives but the lives of the college students who become the mentors of these young children. To fully satisfy the developmental needs of Stage 6 males, I hope all of us will lobby colleges and universities to include significant service activities like this one into college curricula.

Stage 7: 22 and beyond

By the time a boy is in his early twenties, you may have very little leverage anymore to help him with technology or maturation. Hopefully, your son is launched by now but if he is not, I hope you will get support from second and third family members, including mental health practitioners, to help you design and manage your son's still-open maturity map. When looking for a therapist to help you with a technology-obsessed young man, make sure—via Yelp, other websites, or personal conversation—that this professional knows how to treat *media or technology addiction/overuse.*

Guideline 18: Move academic training in graduate schools to a gender neuroscience base that utilizes innovative technologies.

Most graduate schools of education and psychology can get access to brain scans and other technologies but, generally, don't use them in classes that involve gender—education, psychology, psychiatry, and medicine. Academic politics and the DGP create obstacles and so the professors avoid the new sciences. The outcome of this avoidance is that most pediatricians, psychiatrists, psychologists, educators, and therapists won't have seen scans of male and female brains back in college or graduate/medical school; they won't have received training in boy or girl brain difference.

This paucity of appropriate technology-use means that people being trained to care for our boys often do not have full training in how boys or girls develop. You may go to a pediatrician who means well and is brilliant in many ways but will not know about the male brain *per se.* He or she may quickly prescribe a drug for ADD/ADHD in your son's case but spend little time ascertaining, via brain scans, which kind of ADD/ADHD your son has or, via genetics testing, what the right medication or supplemental treatment, if any, should be. She or he may not have any training in the connections between media use and the male brain and not be able to help you design a technology-use plan to help your son adjust away from chronic technology use and toward brain-strategic technology use.

To revolutionize child development to include the nature of gender, we will need to pressure every School of Education, School of

Psychology, and related medical or other graduate department to provide a one semester course—either in the university itself or for online and digital modalities—that teaches male/female brain/genetic development. Trained in gender neuroscience—using the technology, viewing the brain scans, realizing the effects of screens on brains, and learning the genetic side of gender—every teacher, mental-health worker, and medical professional would understand every child far better than they often do now. In this way, new technologies can become a positive part of our gender revolution.

Guideline 19: Train and find therapists and mentors who can help Stage 7 males to look into the abyss.

Young men in Stage 7 who are failing to launch carry within themselves an already deep abyss. It is the abyss we hinted at earlier, an abyss stimulating fear, anxiety, and shame at their own immaturity. These males need therapists especially to be trained in how to treat *males*. Male or female, this good mentor of this immature young man must know how to help the boy look into the abyss of past male trauma, male mental illness, male substance or technology addiction, lost love, or the anguish of male failure. In *How Do I Help Him?* I present dozens of strategies and techniques therapists can use to re-train themselves toward the male brain, and help boys and young men specifically to grow up. I've modeled a few of those for you already in this book.

As you get training to become a therapist, or as you, a parent, seek therapeutic help for your young man, I hope you will insist on non-shaming training programs that help everyone become more insightful about working with immature young men in general. We have created the phenomenon of the immature Stage 7 male; our boys did not do it, we did. As a citizen scientist, you can know the deep worth (or negligence) of the male-friendly program by studying the ability of the practitioner to discuss with the young man the deep truth of manhood: the abyss never leaves us, we are always staring into it, but that gaze will, ultimately, inspire rather than debilitate us if we can develop a calling and a mission.

This is what therapists and all mentors must help emerging males with in our digital world—getting beyond the confused boy, discovering the man who strives to shine beyond endless entertainments and distractions. Stage 7 males who drift, fail to launch, turn away from success, hide in basements with porn and video games yearn to apprentice their souls to a male-sensitive mentor. This lost young man longs to bind his heart to a gifted master and engage his mind in this safe relationship with such completeness that he can imprint his calling, find his mission, develop his unique and original art, and commit his nature to others with so much love, wisdom, and power that he will, when he is dying, be able to say, "I have lived."

The gift of the abyss is the inspiration it can provide if those who love the Stage 7 male know how to mentor him as a male—first a boy, then an adolescent boy, then a young man, then a man. To know how to do this, a mentor needs his or her own good instincts, and, in today's digital world, a good deal of training in the abyss and the inspiration that are natural and real for our new generations of young men.

Guideline 20: Use the Life-Review and Self-Made Maturity Map to help a young man to mature.

If your son is struggling to launch, finding the right therapist or mentor can be crucial; meanwhile, you can also help him to do both a *life-review* and *a map of manhood.* Both of these will deal with four areas of focus:

> Identity
> Autonomy
> Morality
> Intimacy.

This is what I call the "I AM I" model. You can find a very detailed application of it for the whole of male adolescence in *A Fine Young Man.* With any Stage 7 male, you can use the I AM I topic to challenge your son to talk into a video camera to help him map out his journey to manhood—past and present. Ask him to answer these kinds of questions:

Who am I? What are my strengths and weaknesses? Where do I fit on the gender spectrum? Am I a man yet?

Am I capable of being independent of my parents yet? If not, why not? What motivation am I lacking? What power do I still need to develop? What daily parts of my life keep me immature?

Do I know what a good man is? Am I a good man? When have I done wrong things? Why did I do those things? When have I done right things? How do I feel about those actions of empathy and service?

Do I know how to love? In what ways do I feel that I deserve to be loved, and in what ways do I feel that I don't deserve to be loved? Have I experienced significant past traumas that have derailed my ability to love and be loved? What are they? Do I need to get the help of a mentor so that I can feel, as I must have when I was born, that I do deserve to be loved?

Because your son will no doubt love his technologies, encouraging him to use those technologies to do his life-review and plot his future course will be a positive way of integrating electronics and technology into maturation. Ask him to blog (privately, if necessary) or create a Power Point file, a set of video clips, a video with music, such as we see at rites of passages, weddings, or funerals, that encapsulates his life as a male so far.

Help your son to understand what you yourself know: his manhood is not a discernible thing or ideology that one conversation or modality will capture. Manhood is an ontology, a way of being, discovered by each male in his lived-out life story. As you help boys find their own version of this ontology, recall your own past, your own youth, your own story. Tell it to your son in sacred times and places—on camping trips, retreats, long journeys, travels around the world or around the community.

As you talk with your son, you can also use the Manhood Quartet tool, which I've developed as an outgrowth of I AM I. You can discuss with your son that while no one can define for him what a "man" is (because "man" is a developmental end-goal, not a gender stereotype), still, there are some *natural standards* that have been in place for hundreds of thousands of years. He will know he is a man when he experiences this Quartet of male gene expression:

* He physically matures past puberty so that he can live independent of parents or the state unless he has a prevailing disability that requires lifelong parental or state care.
* He's capable of expressing love, compassion, and sense of service to family, mate, children, and society.
* He possesses adult critical thinking and emotional intelligence skills that will ensure he can develop an adult place in his world.
* He has developed his specific talents, skills, and purposeful work ethic to a level of growth that can lead to job success.

The quartet of manhood (independence, love, wisdom, and work-success) forms "maturity" and that is our end goal with our sons. We can measure our son's "manhood" by his success in that quartet, and so can our son measure himself.

If accomplishment of the quartet is well in your sights in your son's Stage 7 years, I hope you will celebrate and enjoy that. If your son has a deep (though still growing) sense of identity, autonomy, morality, and intimacy, I hope you will feel very proud. To the extent that any of this is still undeveloped, you and your son have a mission, still, to fulfill.

As you help your son measure his manhood carefully, through the technological assets he has—video, blogging, and online resources—you will be helping him make a pilgrimage through manhood that every young man, no matter where he fits in the development of his own ontology and being, yearns to make, both without and within, as he strives to become a loving, wise, and successful man.

The Strife of Accidental Manhood, and the Pilgrimage

Males have always waited in doorways between nature, nurture, and culture for mothers and fathers and everyone else to place in their hands the tools of manhood. Whatever personal and cultural needs the boys were given in the past, whatever gifts they received, they carried into a pilgrimage of adventures they yearned to live out for the sake of community and tribe, family and society. Boys make this quest of personal responsibility in order to build a self and then, in adulthood, give its strongest parts to those they love and those who are in need. In the video game that harkens back five centuries, Assassin's Creed, the "heroes" say, "We work in the dark to serve the light." Boys were willing to take on even this self-denying commitment.

In these journeys our ancestors' sons were strong and weak, courageous and kind, and, yes, sometimes villainous, dominating, and bullying. In doing their daily work of maturation these males asked for help to discover who they were because disasters and wars, treachery and fate, mistakes and immoralities often crippled them or killed them. Life is dangerous for males. Boys knew they must battle for their place in the world. In that battle they have hoped, ultimately, that the people who love them, especially those who benefit from their hard work, will reward them with respect.

But things have changed. Our present-day sons receive a lot of artificial "maturation"—artificial in pollutants that affect DNA; artificial in developmental structures that specifically define maleness as an affront to the good life; artificial in imagery and stimulation that reduces boys to visual consumers. Once our American young men were doers; now they watch. Once they learned through deep inquiry and rewarding action; now they literally "lose themselves" in artificial worlds. Social and daily life today can fracture their healthy gene expression, brain development, and socialization. They can grow into listless or seething adult males who sense that they are not men at all.

This strife of accidental manhood—the shame of not knowing if one is a mature male until one's midlife or even later—is a post-modern phenomenon. It did not exist in hunter-gatherer or agrarian times. It barely existed in industrial times, though it did emerge in certain pockets of society where families had gained wealth and immense entitlement. In these families, some self-entertaining immature boys could avoid manhood for long periods of time but, still, their accidental manhood was very much the exception.

Now, it is a norm in the United States where the rise of a relatively wealthy middle class—wealthy by world standards—allows for experiments in human development, including the end to patriarchal social roles, new industries, new ways of human pair-bonding and marriage, educational experiments, family life changes, and the attachment of human development to technologies.

From the viewpoint of systems biology, each of our modern experiments adds both a "positive effect" to millennial life (expanding ideas of what a male is and what the male gender roles can be) but also a cumulative "negative" effect (making maturation of our men not a directed pilgrimage of self, but often an unrealized or accidental stasis without foundation in the shared human reality of maleness).

Fortunately, as a nation, we can keep the good of the last fifty to a hundred years of social change but end the bad because our sin (accidental or negative manhood) is not one of commission but omission. We have "omitted" a lot of what the natural boy needs, but once we fully realize this and decide to act against this trend, we can actually utilize artificial resources like online, technological, and other electronics to help us ascertain what our children need to be whole.

As we integrate technology and nature-friendly developmental milestones into our discovery of boys' maturation, we can join together in three families to nurture boys through adolescence so that, by the time a boy leaves the seventh stage of maturation, he will be a good and whole man able to live in gender symbiosis with women and children.

This new gender symbiosis between males and females—a bridge between past, present, and future—is the subject of our final chapter.

Chapter 8

Saving Both Our Sons and Daughters: Toward a New Gender Equity Paradigm

> "We should offer ourselves to Fortune in order that, struggling with her, we may be hardened by her. Gradually she will make us a match for herself."
> —Seneca, *On Providence*

IN OCTOBER OF 2015 I was asked by the Men's Health Caucus to brief U.S. Congress members and staffers on the Boy Crisis. Previously, I had been involved in providing information to various White Houses, but never directly to Congress. Honored to be asked, I traveled to Washington, D.C. with excitement. On the plane I thought I could do something to help Congress awaken to the need for full gender equity. All the people in D.C. were kind and considerate—good people—but I came home a couple days later deeply saddened.

From the meetings with Congress members and staffers I saw no clear way much-needed political change regarding the Dominant Gender Paradigm could happen anytime soon in Washington. The Congress members and staffers were grossly under-educated and their system kept them that way: briefers, like me, were only allowed 15 minutes to make a case. Good people listened for a few minutes then moved to the next briefing or meeting. Meanwhile, many of the key people themselves were politicized between extreme Left and extreme Right. They could not see how to take on the gender minefield to fully support boys. I got onto an airplane with a heavy heart. The first line of this book came to me as we steadied in the air over Virginia: "In thirty years of advocating for children, I have never been more worried than I am right now about the state of boyhood in America."

In that sentence, the trip inspired me, too, with new mission. As I began writing notes for *Saving Our Sons,* I thought back two decades. In 1995, it was almost impossible to get *The Wonder of Boys* published. All the major publishers—twenty-five at that time—rejected my proposal by utilizing a GDP frame for gender equity. "Gender equity is about females, not males," an editor told my agent. Another: "Boys have privilege—they don't need a book to show off their dominance." Others: "Gender science is all gender stereotypes anyway." "People won't read about boys—we need books on girls." I was raising two daughters so I felt glad, of course, that so much attention was focused on girls, but I knew from my clinical practice that boys were struggling.

Now, flying toward home, I thought: "Even though many boys' books have come out in the last twenty years, still, 'gender equity'— the two words that control social change—have not yet become a revolution." As I wrote my notes in 2015 I realized: In some ways, the DGP is even stronger today than it was two decades ago—even more entrenched in the academic, governmental, and media worlds. It has had twenty more years to build momentum—some of that good for our children, some of it not.

A hundred years ago, journalist H.L. Mencken observed, "The aim of practical politics is to keep the populace alarmed (and hence clamorous to be led to safety) by an endless series of hobgoblins, most of them imaginary." We've looked already in this book at some of the hobgoblins about males thrown up in our culture in order to make sure males keep their place as the privileged sex and females as the only gender in need. In this chapter, I want to challenge and inspire you to take the fight for our children to another level. I will help you answer hobgoblin arguments tossed into our culture about "gender equity." This will constitute an eighth action-step in our social revolution.

Redefining Gender Equity

This chapter involves questions and answers that I hope will help you, as a citizen scientist and child advocate, to redefine gender equity. These are the kinds of questions I'm asked in meetings with leaders and teams that have power over the assets and forces of positive change in our culture. They're not easy questions or answers, but they do have information you can use to fight for the health of boys in America. The questions come from all sides; the answers are built on the foundation for healthy boyhood we've explored in this book.

Here is a summary of what we've looked at so far.

1. *Boys and men are mainly invisible to us even though we see them everywhere* because we see mainly the alpha males and the dangerous males. Our prevailing social criticism tosses all boys and men into the two camps, thus blinding us to the developmental needs of the 90 percent or more males who fit in neither category.

2. *Just as the patriarchal paradigm ruled our gender lives in the past with its insistence on old gender roles, a Dominant Gender Paradigm has ruled our last fifty years* of gender study in the Big Three—academics, government, and the media. This paradigm insists that the old gender roles and stereotypes are the most significant issues facing gender development today.

3. *While unequal gender roles and toxic gender stereotypes should remain an important concern in America they are no longer the primary causes* of male or female distress, such as violence against women and children. The primary causes of gender distress today are male epigenetics, neurotoxins, and mental illness; acute trauma experienced by males in broken or fatherless families and incomplete communities; and under-nurturance of boys that, attacking their nature in our social institutions, constitutes a climate of cruelty to male health.

4. *The natural sciences, including DNA research, neurobiology, and other "hard sciences" are a revolutionary way to study and fulfill actual gender needs in the new millennium.* Because of scientific transparency and access via online technologies, each of us can now work to become a citizen scientist who pursues positive approaches to child development, including protecting our boys and girls from under-diagnosis or misdiagnosis.

5. *Differences in male and female brains, biochemistry, developmental tempos, and emotional intelligence can now be taught to all parents, caregivers, and policy-makers who, as a result of training, can help toss out the notion that gender equity can't happen without "gender sameness."* While expanding male emotional and relational interactions to accommodate female brain standards for emotional communication is a positive communal step, we must be careful about devaluing male emotional intelligence.

6. *Lack of motivation and maturity among young American boys and men is an epidemic that affects all other national and human*

systems. As millions of young males don't receive developmental milestones and the attachments and challenges they need to grow up, their immaturity combines with anti-male economic factors to create a perfect storm of distress for our civilization, including increased mental illness for both genders.

7. *Electronic technologies can be both neurotoxic for our children and also crucial to a new path for young males.* We can and must establish developmental boundaries for technology use among our children while simultaneously using technologies in healthy ways to manage new gender equity movements that protect and nurture the natural boy and the natural girl.

8. *And finally (the topic of this chapter), we must transform our culture's language and resource allocation around gender equity to include boys and men.* Unhealthy males both directly harm and dangerously underserve females. We must bring gender equity and equal social attention to the needs of both genders into public discourse and policy-making.

Question: How do you answer androphobic and misandrist straw man arguments in personal conversations, community forums, and the Big Three?

Answer: By taking each one on directly, pointing out their flaws, then helping a group move toward new gender equity first, with awareness of our paralysis.

At a Helping Boys Thrive Summit® in a large American city, I sat during a break with a representative of the governor's office. To protect everyone involved, as I've done throughout this book, I'm not revealing the names and location, but the conversation could have happened anywhere. We had been discussing how we could bring a Helping Boys Thrive® Initiative into this state, and the need for it. This high-ranking official noted that he and his team had been disaggregating data in the state and found that while both females and males were suffering, all groups of males were doing worse than females—Black, Hispanic, Native, Asian, and White. The markers used were "physical, mental, and social health."

"We've been seeing this trend grow for some time," the executive said, "but we're paralyzed to do anything. People like you suggest a program or a gender initiative, but there are always people with power who get offended that we would even consider investing in this. They point to things like 'a cultural climate of male dominance' and 'a culture that favors males.' They say, 'Look around the room at this meeting—who's running things here, it's the men.' There are actually a lot of women in the room, too, of course, and lots of women in leadership positions, but there are lots of men, too. And our governor is male."

He paused as he recalled the scenes, a man in a suit and tie, a white professional with decades of political experience, who was also, I knew, the father of two sons and a daughter.

"It seems like this is a little bit personal for you," I said "—a sense of mission."

"Yes," he nodded. "It is personal. I want to know how to shepherd something like this through the political battlefield. We have to stop pretending we live in a culture that favors males and destroys females, but we can't..." he opened his arms out like two fans, "...we can't seem to get through the gender equity ideas that males have all the power so it's females we have to always focus on. In every meeting, a few big themes and equity questions come up and the conversation about social change is paralyzed. The result is the inability to go forward with funding or with programs that would help our young males."

"What themes?"

"Oh, like: 'But how can you say males are in trouble—women don't get equal pay for equal work, they make 77 cents for every dollar a man makes'; or 'There's no science to back up the fact that males and females are different, so what works for girls should work for boys,' or 'Talking about boys and men just ends up in masculine stereotypes and sets us all back a century'; or, 'Until we stop male violence against women in our rape culture, we won't have gender equity. How anti-woman can you be that you don't see that?'

"My colleagues and I don't have readily available answers to these charges and all their political momentum out there in the media and in our gender politics, so we can't make a good case for helping boys. People end up just saying, 'Our culture is male-dominated' and that's that."

He went silent again, looking past my head into the middle distance. His eyes had begun to shine slightly with wetness. For this high-powered man in high office, these moments in this little room were moments of deep memory and pain. He was confused by the paralysis, angry about the disconnection between DGP culture-conversation and the reality of boys' increasingly desperate lives. He had children, so there was nothing about boys or girls that didn't touch his soul.

This government official is not alone in wanting to find answers that will work in grassroot community efforts. Gene Dire, Associate Director of Catholic Charities in Spokane, told me something similar: "I'm at a not-for-profit that sees how boys and men are suffering, but doesn't have an action plan to show donors, funders, and foundation boards that we're on the side of gender equity. I need help getting past the naysayers, I need new language, and I need new tools because when I try to advocate for boys, the language trips us up. Someone always talks about 'male domination' and we don't have language and theory to counter that statement. The attack politics against helping males ends up winning out."

The system we've developed for tracking and discussing gender equity is flawed but well entrenched in the Big Three. It is difficult for politicians, judges, academics, government employees, legislators or others in institutions such as schools, academe, governmental agencies, and the media to battle the DGP. As "experts" repeat ideological headlines about male and female pay, rape culture, and others, they believe the ends justify the means in their pursuit of gender equity for women and girls. Having seen the damage this "gender war" has done—the criminalization and loss of males from so many of the systems that they desperately need for survival and thriving—my approach calls on you and others like you to pressure the Big Three with the science-based logic you've read in this book.

Question: Okay, yes, but since equity-competition between women and men for basic resources has helped empower women and girls, how do we not go backward?

Answer: We don't need to—women and men can continue to compete for jobs and equal pay, but women and children desperately need men to succeed equal to women, too.

Over the last three decades, thousands of moms have said, each in their own way, "Let's not throw the baby out with the bathwater. We need healthy, powerful, and successful men!" A physician and mother of two boys and one girl, Deb Gore, 51, expressed this powerfully in a recent conversation.

"Women are taking over the biological sciences, medicine, that whole part of the STEM world," she said, "with more women getting medical degrees than men now and more women going into medical research. But what's worrisome is that, while our hard work to bring more women into sciences worked, there's something we didn't foresee: we need the men!

"Here's what I mean. When women enter these sciences, they enter them gung ho, but once kids come, a lot of us (me included) want to work part-time. We want choices, freedom, opportunity to be with our kids—isn't this what feminism fought for, to give women choices and opportunities? It is. But we forgot that if we want that, we need lots of successful, mature, well-paid men to give us that choice. We must keep fighting for women's causes, and I will keep doing that, but gender equity cuts both ways, and for me, helping boys and men has also become a 'women's cause.' I would now call myself a 'choice' feminist rather than a 'power' feminist. Or maybe I'm just a 'common-sense feminist.' Whatever I am, I need men!"

Deb has enunciated beautifully the need for a balanced gender equity debate. As feminists and political leaders champion women's causes, they must see males as a part of that need. When they see the statistics in Chapter 1, and see how invisible the needs of boys are (despite some very visible and powerful men in leadership roles), everyone can do what Deb is doing: expand definitions of gender equity because her own need for healthy and successful boys and men is clear to her.

A Gender Diagnostic Tool

You can do your own citizen science in this regard. Bring at least five professionals from various academic and governmental fields into your discussion group, Facebook community, or list serve. Ask them to bring data from their organizations on what is going on with both boys and girls, and women and men in your community. Over a series of meetings, ask these friends and colleagues to develop a list of the major issues facing both genders locally.

Here is a list developed in one community.

Females:
>   Females are victims of domestic violence and rape
>   Fewer females in the engineering/high tech fields
>   Less pay than males
>   Less representation of females at the top of corporations
>   Fewer females in government
>   More anorexia/bulimia and overt depression
>   A lot of mental illness issues and substance abuse issues
>   Girl drama, bullying, cyberbullying
>   Lack of aggression and competition to take on alpha males
>   Four times more likely to attempt suicide than males
>   Lots of young women can't get jobs or can only get low paying "female" jobs

Males:
>   More males are victims and perpetrators of violence
>   More boys failing in preschool, K – 12, higher education, and beyond
>   More boys failing to launch, without purpose, without direction, immature
>   More unemployment among males
>   More homeless people are male
>   Less governmental funding for males
>   More males leaving churches and faith communities than females
>   More autism spectrum, conduct disorders, anti-social personality disorders, and higher numbers of nearly every other

brain disorder among males
More covert depression (usually disguised as substance abuse)
More males than females are brain injured
Much higher suicide success rate among males
More males die on the job.
More males unable to get VA help for adjustment problems
(some females are suffering certainly, but males have held
most of the wartime jobs with more brain injuries, concussive
disorders, and PTSD)
Males die younger overall—we keep females alive much better
than males
Ethnic group statistics show Native and boys of color are in
terrible shape, many black males in our community die by
25 years old and more females than males are thriving on our
Reservation
More emotional disturbance, learning disabilities, behavioral
disorders among males than females
More imprisoned males, more substance abuse and alcoholism

As you develop these lists, ask these questions:

Which of these lists hurts America—financially and in terms of
stability?
Which causes abject crisis in American life?
Which have we let get absolutely out of hand in its distress?

Hopefully we will respond, "They are both important lists. Boys
and girls suffer equally and need our help equally, though in somewhat
different ways. We can and must address both lists right away."

One mom used the gender diagnostic tool in her book group and wrote
me this email: "We looked objectively at these columns and were
shocked to realize that the male column actually scared us the most. We
are not gender warriors on either side of the aisle so we decided not to
go public with that conclusion because, the truth is, we should never say
that one person's suffering is worse than anyone else's, but as we looked
locally from an economic point of view, we could see that male crisis in
our state costs the most money and it was male distress that caused most
of the female distress."

Question: To advocate for boys as much as we do girls, we will need to change the general measurement for gender equity used in the Big Three—power—but since men at the top obviously have more power than women, how do we change the measurement standard?

Answer: Retain "power" and "money" as important standards of equity but now also assert *choice theory* (qualitative analysis) as an equal form of equity measurement in the gender debate.

The predominant measurement for gender equity has been "power." Both patriarchal/traditionalist gender theory ("strict gender roles are required for women and men to survive and thrive"), such as we still see in some parts of the Muslim world, and more recent feminist theory ("strict gender roles take power away from women so that women can't thrive") are both theories of power. The power in question is often measured by financial compensation and net personal worth. This measurement happens in a couple obvious ways. Males as a group make more money than females ("women in America make 77 cents for every dollar men make") and specific men—alpha males—have more money or higher paying CEO positions than specific women. The DGP approach to these realities is to argue that there is no need for revolutionary change on behalf of boys until all women have as much personal money as males, and as many females as males have alpha status.

Unspoken in this approach to gender differences are the kinds of realities Dr. Gore hinted at. Men on the average work more hours away from home than women, they tend to want to climb hierarchies toward higher pay more than women, on average (especially once women have children), and women will always want men, on the average, to do more of the dangerous jobs that will reward men financially but also kill men early. Individual men will, indeed, always earn more, on average, than individual women if aggregate male earning and aggregate female earning are kept separate in the gender debate. Gradually, individual women, especially those before and after their child-raising years, will continue to close the 77 cents on the dollar aggregate male/female wage earning gap, but the realities of human life and gender partnership will never allow the gap to fully close. For more analysis of this issue please see page 301.

So if our measurement of success for women is solely a standard of equal quantitative amount of personal status and money for every individual woman, we will continue to adhere to an ideological approach that paralyzes change. Men will continue to earn a greater amount of aggregate money in comparison to women because women themselves have asserted that millions of them do not want to see money individually—they want to see money *and* choice in partnership. We will continue to systemically neglect this women's reality—and continue to attack males as inherently dominant and unfair at their masculine core. In this mode, we will never be able to help the millions of boys and men who are struggling. In fact, we will consider ourselves righteous and protective of girls and women as we pursue this framework in our government meetings, academic studies, and popular press, neglectful of the fact that we have posited a gender war in which girls and women will always be one-down to men, and men will always be the oppressors.

This paralysis calls for social change in intellectual debate at all levels. In the Notes and Resources section of this chapter I have provided you even more detail from a number of social activists who provide even more language and data to support the following argument: the solution to this problem is to account "freedom to choose" (qualitative power) as equal to personal pay or hierarchical (quantitative) power. Once we add qualitative power to the social debate, we take a major step forward. This addition moves us beyond the 1960s gender equity paradigm of pure quantitative measurement toward choice theory. Most women today, while enjoying power and money, also equally want and value choice. Many, in fact, value it more than personal net money-earning and personal hierarchical power. This was confirmed by a comprehensive study based on Pew Research published in 2011 that found two-thirds of American women wanted to be able to choose to stay at home when they have children or work away from home part-time while one-third wanted to work full-time outside the home while raising their children.

The majority of American women, this study found, replicate Dr. Gore's standard of gender equity. They would rather not work 60 hours a week to earn six figures in their personal bank accounts; they would rather take the 77 cents on the dollar in the aggregate and partner with males for the rest of the 100 cents on the dollar, as long as 1) males share the extra financial assets (which most males do, all the way through and past retirement) and 2) women can work 25 or fewer hours away from home while spending the rest of their time with their children, family, and community. In this model, women value their ability to live and care for others at a deep, primal level that is not counted in DGP gender equity conversations about power and money.

Most males, I believe, understand this. We know that girls and women have as much or more power than we do in various ways and less in others, just like we have more quantitative power in some ways (more personal net financial earning, for instance) and less in others (less time spent alive, for instance, as well as less time spent with children, on average, than their mother has). We respect women's choice and women's power. Our moms were very powerful and guided our lives until independence. Now, for many or most of us, wives and partners run much of our lives. In college, in graduate school, in law school, in medical school, in the workplace, in the corporation, in the neighborhood, in the PTA, in the counseling office, in the hospital, even in the church or synagogue, we see that women have as much or more "power" than men do, each in their own way. So, to us, the pure insistence that quantitative power is more important than qualitative power, which is the ground of the DGP gender equity paradigm, is a kind of white lie, and we avoid too much affiliation with it.

Yet we love and support women and girls. As we observe so many of our daughters, wives, and mothers also avoiding the DGP now, we see that the DGP does not fit the grassroots of American life. American women, we also realize, are mainly seeing the world the same way men do in the new millennium (and vice versa), not calling themselves feminists anymore. But the quantitative personal power and personal net worth theory still controls social thought. Now all of us in the grassroots will need to rise up together, female and male, to assert our own vision and power in this debate until the Big Three fully and deeply adds our choice and qualitative theory to its various research and legislative platforms.

Question: Given the fact that it is usually boys and men who "misbehave," how do we answer critics who criminalize male behavior in order to protect girls and women?

Answer: If we can move these well-intentioned people toward a more scientific approach to human behavior, we can stop criminalizing and gender profiling natural male behavior and simultaneously, we can de-criminalize and mentor immature behaviors that have by now become criminalized.

In American towns, in corporations, and nearly everywhere we turn, dramas unfold between women and men that rise to alleged criminal assault. Most often, these actions are impulsive, immature, even aggressive but not dangerous impulses among males. Here is a real life scenario reported recently in the press.

A community leader, a woman, reported to her supervisor that another supervisor tried to kiss her at a party at which everyone had been drinking. Her supervisor asked her if she felt sexually harassed and invited her to file a sexual harassment complaint if she did. That filing was not only the procedure put in place in the company, but also, the supervisor advised, the law, since the U.S. Department of Health and Human Services Office of Women's Health's definition of sexual harassment or assault, includes "unwanted touching above or under clothes."

The woman contemplated filing a claim but then decided not to. Instead, she confronted the man the next day. Realizing she had no romantic interest in him, he apologized and explained, "I thought there was something there between us but I guess not," which was an accurate assessment and moved on.

From a nature-based, non-ideological and scientific standpoint, there was nothing violent or criminal in this interaction. To rise to violence or criminality, an action must 1) put another person in danger or 2) rob another person of property or rights. This unwanted act did neither. The woman and man were two human beings between whom one person misinterpreted sexual signals and flirtation. This happens a million times a day all over the world. Human interactions are awkward, not perfect. Impulses are acted on and the two actors generate responses.

Furthermore, the woman in this interchange was already empowered so she didn't need to put the man into the grievance system to gain personal power. The discomfort the interaction caused in the woman was handled maturely by her. She told the man she didn't like his attempt to kiss her and he acted maturely by apologizing and moving on. He, we can be sure, has experienced discomfort some other time from her or someone else; he would have then been challenged, as she had been by him this time, to act with mature response to that micro aggression. If he didn't, he would no doubt suffer the same micro aggression some other time and gradually, through these interactions, learn to mature. Similarly, this woman showed that she was grown up, a mature adult—and an empowered woman—by her response to the attempt at the kiss.

When I was asked for my opinion on this case, I applauded the woman and man for their maturity—hers in speaking her mind to the man, and he in apologizing and moving on. I agreed with both of them that the unwanted touch had been communicative of potential romantic relationship rather than an act of dominance. We agreed that it was good that no grievance had been filed. Over the course of the next month, however, word leaked out about this incident, and a great deal of trouble followed. "Gender profiling" occurred—while mainly the man was gender profiled as "dangerous," gender profiling affected the woman, as well, as "victim."

Various ideological constituencies in the community and beyond descended on the company, accused the woman of neither fighting hard enough for her rights nor confronting the "culture of male dominance" in the company adequately. Media got involved and the man was gradually put in the position of fighting charges of sexual harassment. The boss who didn't fire him ultimately had to resign, even though he had done the right thing—asked the woman to file a complaint. It was she who refused to do so, and for good reason—the man had done nothing that required criminalization. But the androphobic gender profiling won the day.

As the invectives flew, the "system" was accused of being "good old boy." Hundreds of thousands of dollars were spent on the legal disputes, and on the resulting dysfunction of the company over the next year. As all of these attacks ensued and the view of the DGP dominated the personal, social, and legal interactions, I hoped people in power would consider two dangerous ironies:

1. Women are *less* protected by this kind of gender profiling, both in its overreaction and its insistence on female fragility. Women would be better protected by developing resilience skills in which they confront unwanted but not dangerous behavior without institutional invasion. Men, too, need to develop this resilience. For actually dangerous behavior, of course, institutional intervention is absolutely necessary, but most unwanted behavior is not dangerous.

2. As males become criminalized for behavior that both women and men know to be natural and necessary to human success and survival, such as romantic flirting, both women and men will lose their ability to feel safe and comfortable with one another. Gender profiling lowers productivity in corporations and our culture continually loses assets and increases gender confusion and ennui.

The American criminalization of natural male behavior starts in preschool and extends into elementary school when normal male aggression (for example, physically bumping a friend into a locker) is seen as a gateway to violence instead of what it often is, a form of affection.

Similarly, when drugs are found in an adolescent's car, under the laws in most states today, all the kids in the car are convicted of a crime. In 90 percent of cases, these new criminals are males. Once these males go into the system they are traumatized by prison. With American recidivism rates at around 80 percent, once the criminalized male enters the system he will generally get very little treatment but a lot of new criminal skills and developmental affiliations. He will also now have a record and become nearly unemployable. This is a systematic attack on male maturation, beginning in the earliest years of life.

What we must do

We must make structural changes in all our systems—corporate, governmental, legal, and educational.

In corporate and governmental services, we can:
—Contract with consultants to diagnose gender relations in our company from a scientific rather than ideological lens.
—Adjust sexual harassment policies to de-emphasize punitive results of peer-peer interactions that do not endanger another person.
—Provide gender sensitivity training that is nature-based rather than solely or mainly androphobic.
—Provide discipline and growth on a case-by-case basis, empowering both women and men toward self-reliance and resilience rather than immediate supervisor intervention.
—Use a "three times" rule rather than immediate probation or suspension (or termination) for behavior that is diagnosed to be "normal-but-unwanted."

In courts and legislatures, we can:
—De-criminalize immature behavior that does not endanger another person—move it immediately to treatment interventions and generally order more treatment and less incarceration

—Contract with consultants to provide gender diagnostics that are science based and non-ideological regarding how each judge is treating male and female behavior.

—Provide gender sensitivity training to judges and legislators that is developmental and nature-based rather than solely or mainly androphobic.

—Provide encouragement for lawyers to develop maturity and resilience profiles for clients and judges and use these on a case-by-case basis when making sentencing and other decisions.

—Use a "three times" rule for non-felonies (or non-dangerous crimes) rather than immediate criminalization of behavior that is diagnosed to be "normal-but-unwanted."

—Pass new laws to protect natural human development and overturn old laws that criminalize normal male maturation behavior.

In our educational systems, beginning in preschool and advancing all the way through higher education, we can:

—Contract in house or with consultants to provide a cultural diagnostic that is science based and non-ideological regarding gender relations in the individual school building and its classrooms.

—Develop a new system for monitoring all discipline referrals for gender, following or during the diagnostic.

—Adjust intervention and punishment policies to de-emphasize punitive results of peer-peer interactions that don't endanger another person.

—Provide gender sensitivity training to staff that is developmental and nature-based rather than solely or primarily androphobic.

—Use a "three times" rule rather than immediate probation or suspension or expulsion for behavior that is diagnosed to be "normal-but-unwanted," like sculpting mud into a gun or pushing another child.

—Provide newsletters and other educational vehicles to parents that educate them on natural-science based developmental and intervention paradigms.

In our family systems, we must support all of these efforts by behaving in a manner consistent with ending our litigious approach to our children's social institutions. If families press charges or sue schools for normal distresses like pushing/shoving, "discomfort," or other non-violent offenses, we can't save our sons. Since, in most cases, the litigated events involve male behavior, we must see the invisible neglect and abandonment of male development inherent in this litigious overreach, and change the way we approach our legal and tort system accordingly. In this vein, I hope parents and teachers will work together to establish "unwanted touch" baseline standards in reflection of sibling contact standards. Our siblings use aggression nurturance with each other at home and we generally let them. What kids can do at home they can, within reason, do at school. Because many American children are bullied, our standards of behavior and procedures for child management must remain vigilant and, when necessary, punitive regarding that kind of dangerous harassment, but for the other majority of behaviors in school, sibling rivalry provides a good metaphor for "acceptable behavior."

Remember this: once kids are bonded at school they become like siblings in a Three Family System; so they have the potential to mature one another through their awkward, random, and even aggressive contact—as siblings do.

"Was the child in danger?"

That's the standard to employ at home and in school when punishing or criminalizing. If a child is not in danger, we can let as much touch as possible, within limits, occur at school just as we do at home. This doesn't mean allowing classrooms to be unruly, unsafe places. It means creating safe character-developing containers for children in families, classrooms, playgrounds, where children can teach one another how to love and be loved, get hurt and get back up; become strong and become tender, and discover who they really are, what their talents really are, who they can be in the future.

Over the last decade, this revolutionary new consciousness is growing in some schools and states. A number of those schools appear on www.gurianinstitute.com. As my team and I work with them—in Hillsboro County Schools, in Tampa, Florida, at the Army and Navy Academy in Carlsbad, California, at the McCallie School in Chattanooga, Tennessee, and in communities throughout the country—we see staff and parents transforming discipline systems from punishment to purpose development for both boys and girls.

Some changes are also beginning at state and federal levels regarding incarceration overloads, as well. In Utah in 2013 the legislature passed laws to:

* reduce drug penalties
* lower sentencing guidelines for nonviolent offenses
* scale back punishment for minor parole violations.

Data brought to the legislature showed $500 million in savings to state budgets via these new de-criminalization practices. Not surprisingly, more than 90 percent of the lives directly affected are males, with their families receiving indirect positive effects and, thus, female lives are more greatly empowered as well.

At the federal level, Sen. Charles Grassley (R., Iowa), Chair of the Senate Judiciary Committee, has been watching Utah and other states. He recently told the *Wall Street Journal* that he introduced the Sentencing Reform and Corrections Act of 2015 because Utah, Georgia, Texas and other states appear to be moving in a successful direction with these sorts of reforms—with reductions in recidivism as well as a lowered taxpayer burden to house prisoners.

The federal legislation allows for:

* cuts in mandatory sentences for drug violations
* increase in treatment options for prisons
* early release credit for participation in rehabilitation programs.

The federal bill has bi-partisan support.

So there is some awakening nationwide. You and I and everyone we know can now make reform revolutionary by pointing out to every stakeholder that each reform will positively affect the lives of girls and women by decriminalizing males and, even better, guiding males better than we are doing toward mature life.

Question: Are men naturally protective and caring of women, or is feminist theory correct that males have always been dominators of women?

Answer: Even in the context of bad behavior and dominance behavior among many males in the past (and some in the present), males are also inherently protective and caring of women and children, though they do it in ways we may not notice too well in our present gender paradigm.

The past has definitely been prologue. Warrior-based patriarchal cultures of the last 5,000 years inculcated a social system that denigrated women and rewarded alpha, especially warrior males. The alpha males in these systems also coached some beta and other males to model their de-valuing of women's roles and women, so that some beta males, especially those not married to strong females, further denigrated females. In the Victorian era and into the feminist 20th century, these alpha male practices became transparent and society moved through the feminist revolution. In human evolution, the feminist revolution has opened up huge gains for both females and males and so, in academe, the government, and media, it's become most sympathetic to say, "The past has been an institutional degradation of women by men so gender equity requires helping women not men." This, too, is prologue.

Revolutionary, now, in the new millennium, would be to accept the past while going deeper into the present. Even if you end up saying, "The patriarchy was a time when males dominated females, period," we must also notice: in the industrialized and post-industrial West, even with some alpha males behaving badly, (e.g. Ray Rice hitting his wife and dragging her unconscious body into an elevator) most males work in partnership with women.

Most males and male systems bend over backwards to give women what women need and want. Most men quickly relinquish social and personal power to women they care about, whether giving control of many domains to wives at home and in the community, giving power to and mentoring women in the workplace, or compelling a violent man to change his behavior. In fact, throughout our faith communities—which guide the lives of most Americans— we are seeing a systematic relinquishing of power by males to females. According to two decades of research on church attendance and leadership, meta-analyzed by Pastor Tim Wright and his staff, attendance and leadership in American churches is now majority female. Similarly, females now comprise the majority of law and medical school students— both areas were previously male centric professions.

As women ask for more power and nurturance, most males give it.

So I hope that, even if you see the past solely through the lens of feminist theory, you will become revolutionary in your vision of the present. If someone claims that an institutionalized patriarchal masculine social system in the U.S. denigrates females *now*, ask them for holistic, not ideological or anecdotal proof. Ask if they have studied millions of males and females rather than the small percentage of males who do bad or dominant things. Challenge them to tell you if they believe males are inherently protective and caring of women or inherently domineering of women. If they say the latter, you can then decide whether to believe any more of what they say.

This is a crucial point for redefining gender equity. The past approach to gender equity—the Dominant Gender Paradigm—is built on not only the need to redress past wrongs but in claiming that males are inherently domineering of women, which is far too simplistic a notion to stand up to hard science. To help your community go deeper, study your own life and the lives of those around you. With a large sample size, it will be difficult to find an institutionalized masculine system that purposefully denigrates or endangers women and children so that males can be the victors, succeed, and take the majority of human resources. Though certain alpha males still run certain systems and certain males tacitly or directly denigrate females, their actions don't rob all or most women of their power today. If they did, women would not be succeeding in the ways they are succeeding and males would not be falling behind today in the myriad ways, enunciated in Chapter 1, that they are failing to thrive.

Question: Until females occupy 50 percent of each job, especially all STEM fields and the top of hierarchies, can we really say that males need gender equity assistance?

Answer: Males and females will never occupy 50 percent of every job or level of hierarchy unless governments and laws compel quotas (which America will not allow), so to base social policy on that false goal is a straw man we must confront without harming females.

Billions of dollars, especially through the National Science Foundation, are spent to help girls and women penetrate STEM fields. My daughter, Davita, went to one of the MESA science classes during her K–12 schooling, a positive result of that girls-and-STEM spending. She enjoyed it and it helped her in her life work; there seems to be no scenario now culturally in which this kind of spending will end, nor should it.

However, the inequitable spending of taxpayer dollars almost solely on girls is becoming less necessary, as girls outpace boys in grades in many of our nation's math and science classes. Increasing the budget within educational systems for new ways of getting girls involved in leadership is also unnecessary. Girls are encouraged now to become leaders in all fields, from medicine to business, politics to law and every other field. This is wonderful and should and must continue, but, simultaneously, girls now dominate school leadership positions. There are more female merit scholars, club leaders, class presidents, school leaders. Rarely does a K-12 principal or college president ask, "Where have the girls gone? Why aren't they leading?" Just the opposite: "Where are the boy leaders?" is the normal question.

"But men get the best jobs, including the top leadership positions," someone will counter in a meeting or media interview. "Until we remove that gender bias, all gender equity focus needs to be on female development."

This perspective assumes that girls and women are, like minorities, already systemically behind boys and men and should therefore continue to be a protected class. Thus, our commissionable social resources—governmental, academic, and media—must go toward uplifting them rather than boys and men.

When I consult with governmental and non-profit leaders I challenge them to see beyond this thinking in two ways:

* As all new scientific data shows, the primary reason more males in America dominate the highest leadership positions is the fact that they have chosen that life-path. Fewer women want to climb hierarchies to occupy high positions of power that will take them away from their children. While some women, in climbing these hierarchies, have the resources to request that husbands stay at home raising the kids or that well-attached nannies and others help with child-raising, most do not. Hence, there is a gender gap in the highest hierarchical positions.

* For the most part, more males dominate spatial-mechanical work such as high paying mechanical engineering jobs, because they have chosen that life-path. While some women are brilliant in the spatial fields, there are distinct elements of the male and female brain and choice theory that attract more males than females to mechanical engineering. Even when young women are guided to these fields through helpful college and graduate school scholarships and mentoring, fewer women choose to stay in the highly isolative, non-relational, non-verbal science fields as compared to men.

Isaac Cohen, of *Forbes Magazine*, bucked the DGP in 2014 when he provided in-depth investigative reporting on both of these points.

"Non-physical (brain) or behavioral differences between the sexes have become the *mokita* of our era; they are the 'truth we all know but agree not to talk about.' Certain types of findings are routinely ignored, slighted, or repressed (in the media). Social science that points to discrimination against women is shouted from the rooftops, but research that casts doubt on such sources or identifies other causes is hastily shoved under the rug."

"Disparate preferences," preferences that follow innate personality types and gender differences, are what Cohen is talking about. A great example came to me from a grandmother who is also a nurse, Joanne Nestor, who talked with me about her visit, with husband Alan, a retired physician, to see their grandchildren, age 3 and 4.

"You could see the disparate preferences already—the spatial brains of these boys are already at work! 'Grandma, come play cars and trucks!' 'Grandma, look at me!' That little boy was climbing all over everything, up and down the high chair, the davenport, the stairs! The whole day was building, knocking things down, vrooming the cars and trucks around. I was both absolutely pleased and joyful by the end of the day, but also very exhausted!"

As we've shown earlier in this book, while there is certainly some gender bias in some fields somewhere, disparate preferences go back to chromosomal and in utero development of the male and female brain.

In 2013, Cohen discovered that even at universities that have committed massive resources to empowering women in certain STEM fields, women comprised the minority of enrollees in Harvard and MIT online courses, "including computer science (19%), circuits and electronics (9%), and elements of structures, a physics course with a side of linear programming (5%). Women who do take these courses get the same grades as men, and they actually have higher completion rates than their male counterparts. But on average, even in the privacy of their own homes and without the pressures and publicity of the classroom, they don't seem as eager to develop these skills."

New research shows us another brain-related reason for disparate preferences.

"Female professors reported that they enjoyed childcare much more than male professors," Cohen wrote. "The gender

gap in enjoyment of childrearing was not associated with
gender role attitudes or leave-taking. Rather, it seemed to
reflect genuine differences in how professionally committed
men and women felt about the day-to-day experience of taking
care of kids."

Most of the jobs in the fields that we call "spatial sciences,"
like those listed by Cohen at Harvard, are highly isolative and
require long hours away from children.

Women's preferences have an impact not just in certain
STEM jobs but on hierarchy climbing. At John Hopkins,
professors Camilla Benbow and David Lubinski confirmed
that gender differences in preference skew percentages of
males and females in hierarchy-climbing. Women tend to
be less acutely focused on climbing to the highest leadership
positions, even in areas where they are highly gifted. Benbow
and Lubinski followed thousands of gifted teen girls and boys
over a twenty-year period, well into their careers. Both the
boys and girls (then men and women) thought of themselves
as "successful in their chosen professions," liked their career,
including homemaker careers, enjoyed "continuing to develop
my intellectual interests," "continuing to develop my skills and
talents," "having leisure time to enjoy avocational interests," or
"having time to socialize," among others. But as the children
became adults, the males "placed greater importance than
women on 'being successful in my line of work,' 'inventing or
creating something that will have an impact,' and 'having lots
of money.'"

The women, however, tended to stress "having strong
friendships," "living close to parents and relatives," and "having
children."

"The sexes were similar in self-esteem and other self-
concept indicators. Most importantly, men and women, on
average, entered different fields and professions, and they
varied in how they chose to allocate their time."

Cohen also wrote: "Some people may find these results
discomfiting. Resistors are tempted to set up a straw man: 'Are
you saying you want women to be 1950s housewives again?'
But that's not what these data imply. It helps to remember,
as Steven Pinker has written, that 'equity feminism is a moral

doctrine about equal treatment that makes no commitments regarding open empirical issues in psychology or biology.' This sort of common sense feminism, which stresses equality of choice over equality of outcome, tends to get lost in the breast-beating over diversity."

If we are to help our boys and men, we must continue to support girls and women in becoming politicians and business leaders, but the expectation of 50/50 in engineering or CEO jobs is one that girls and women themselves, in their daily choices, caution us to avoid as the basis of social policy.

Interesting proof of disparate preference comes to us from Scandinavian countries such as Denmark and Sweden. In these, governments have developed quotas to ensure equal leadership positioning for women in high government positions. But their free market sector, which is more reflective of our American free market system, still shows only 10 percent females in the C suite of corporations.

Women have the freedom to say: "I don't want to kill my quality of life to climb to the top for those jobs."

A Gender Tool: Use "Centric" more than "Dominant"

A very practical way of instituting a new kind of gender equity language in your home, office and neighborhood is to substitute "centric" for "dominated" where appropriate. This can help your meetings and discussions retain the DGP where there is actual oppression of females, but also, meanwhile, move into new gender equity conversations.

In this new language, spatial sciences will be called "male centric" not male dominant.

Pre-K through sixth-grade educational environments will become "female-centric."

Football will always be male centric, as is much of the financial services industry, especially at the alpha levels.

Social services and human services are generally, today, female centric.

Let's keep "male dominance" as the correct term for countries under oppressive Sharia law, for instance, but let's curtail the use of "dominance" in America where male dominance is not the correct term. As each of us pressures media contacts, governmental personnel, and academic researchers to deepen gender language to be accurate to our present world, we will increase the chances of a new gender equity conversation

Developing Gender Symbiosis

I hope this book as a whole and the Q & A in this chapter provide you with ideas, strategies, and theory that will help you battle for your sons and the boys and men you love. I know, too, from fighting this battle for thirty years that we can fight this new battle simultaneous to our ongoing battle for girls. Gender is not a win/lose game. It is a natural asset in human development.

I also hope you will notice support for our social revolution growing around you. At first, your supporters may be invisible, but once you assert yourself and stick with your self-assertion to the end, support will emerge. That support may need you to take it to the next level—really build and fund it in your community, your mission, your world

I think support is growing because young women and men of these last two generations are relatively unimpressed by the "gender norms" that we, their parents and grandparents, battled in the 1960s, '70s, and beyond. These two generations of children—millennials and Gen X and Y—are plagued much more by psychological, physical, social health and justice issues borne of genetic difficulties, broken attachments, and limited resources than by "gender norms." While gender stereotypes exist and perhaps always will (boys and men shutting emotions in action movie plots, girls feeling pressure to look pretty, dress in pink and hate math), these optics and images don't compare in negative consequence to the loss of the father or the addicted mother or the increase in autism, joblessness, male suicide, and other mental health issues among boys and girls in our era.

Our young people want, I believe, *gender symbiosis*. I suggest this term in the context of systems biology. Symbiosis is the natural pattern of mutual dependency among organisms. It allows for the needs of both genders to be met so that the needs of the other gender can be met. Many of our young people want this redefined gender equity, because they feel they live in both a post-patriarchal and a post-feminist era.

When Theodore Roosevelt wrote, in 1919, that only men not women should work outside the home, and Betty Friedan, in *The Feminine Mystique,* captured the sorrow of that old patriarchal trap, Roosevelt was taking the light out of women's souls and Friedan promised to bring that light back. But since Friedan's wonderful book, the Dominant Gender Paradigm and its attacks on boys have emerged to control social dialogue about gender in a dangerous way. Our grown children see that. They are leaving college and entering workforces and marriage seeing a new reality: in their real world, light can no longer be returned to girls and women by removing it from boys and men.

Symbiosis, or *biological mutualism*, is a way of moving forward. While symbiosis can, at its extreme, denote a parasitic relationship— like a barber fish attaching to a shark to live off the detritus on the shark's skin—or hyper-dependency of an infant and mother, it most often connotes a close relationship between two interdependent people in which each person is dependent on the other for survival and thriving.

"Symbiosis" sounds a lot like marriage because—whatever your sexual orientation—it's a symbiotic relationship, a biological partnership of mutual dependency. Dependency is indeed a key word—men and women are dependent on one another! The idea that gender equity will not have been achieved until women are completely "gender independent from men" is false. We need one another in symbiotic ways. Where she has a weakness, he needs to be strong. Where he is weak, she can provide assets. We need this symbiosis now if we are to save both our daughters and our sons.

Until about fifty years ago, America's standard for marital and relational success was: will my child do better than I did? In our Gen X/Y/Z generations, many of our children are not doing better than we did, and we must change that by creating new and improved gender equity. While doing this we can still absolutely focus on "what is best for women and children." I know of no man who would argue against this focus.

Epilogue

IN 1914, FEMINIST ACTIVIST ELLA WHEELER WILCOX wrote, "To sin by silence when we should protest makes cowards (of us)."

In 2013, feminist activist Christina Hoff Sommers wrote, "The rise of women, however long overdue, does not require the fall of men."

In 2016, an anonymous feminist author wrote: "As a result of enculturated gynocentrism (hyper-protection of females) and misandry (hatred of males), if you take the side of men in an argument today, expect other men and women to instinctively, irrationally hate you for it."

They were all correct and each of these writers sought a way past the "certainties" of their days. They sought a way to be the servant of helpful ideology, but not its slave.

One of my own models in this work has been biologist and entomologist E.O. Wilson. From his research in Africa and back home in the hallways of Harvard's Museum of Comparative Zoology, he has been generating ideas about human nature for decades, including books like *Sociobiology* and theories such as "Consilience."

His latest book, *The Meaning of Human Existence*, published near his 85th birthday, continues his ethological exploration in a political-academic context.

"During the civil rights movement and rise of resentment against the Vietnam War," he recalls, "the country's intellectuals and its professors shifted far left. As part of this we adopted a belief that everything is due to culture and history, and nothing is due to the way the brain is wired."

He goes on to talk about bucking this trend by remaining adamant about the role of genetics. He became a man among a minority of academics who studied human nature itself, and received attacks as a racist, sexist, and old-fashioned thinker. He was, of course, none of these, but "if you could have a genetic basis for your behavior," he recalls, "then somebody could say there could be a genetic basis for differences from one race to the other, and that is what frightened the academics."

I first discovered his work in the 1980s as I was reading the ethologist Konrad Lorenz. Studying Lorenz, Wilson, and the work of neurobiologist Ruben Gur at the University of Pennsylvania, I began to posit my own theories of gender symbiosis. Meanwhile, as genetics research and other research in the neural sciences has evolved over the decades, some of the "politically correct" view Wilson lamented has receded in the sciences, but not in the field of gender.

In gender studies especially in the Big Three, to suggest that nature plays as large a part as culture in gender equity still results in being called sexist, old-fashioned, and patriarchal. Even knowing this, E.O. Wilson still argues for clarity. He writes wisely, "There's nothing more satisfying than that slaughter of an old theory, provided you can replace it."

We can now replace feminist theory just like feminist theory replaced patriarchal theory before it. Feminist theory, however, does not need slaughtering. Gender symbiosis, nature-based theory, and feminist theory can run parallel. Similarly, traditionalist theory still exists in some parts of American life, especially in some religious communities, running parallel to feminist theory. Now both theories must also accept new thinking based in the natural sciences or we will continue to create families that disintegrate before children are raised.

Our boys can help us become the revolutionaries they need us to be because, when this book ends, you can lift your eyes from its pages and find males around you. You can look at every boy and man you know; study his eyes and shoulders, hands and feet, clothes and masks, listen to his words and silences. Watch him, observe him, be silent with him, feel his energy, enjoy his grace, and when the time is right, talk with him about boyhood and manhood.

Ask him how he wants to measure himself, what legacy he hopes to leave, how he wants to love his family, partner, spouse, friends, children, and himself. Do this fearlessly with him, informing him of the lines you will not cross with him, but also letting him know that you trust him for the long haul. Let him know you understand: He loves home, but he's also an explorer on an infinite ocean, a seeker in lands of adversity and experimentation, a wanderer in the ancient wilderness of heroes and villains, a male who needs to nurture us in many settings, on many quests, with many people, among many sacrifices, in many games and challenges, and often without words to explain to us what we wish he would explain in words.

As you connect with this boy or man, I hope you'll see that he is involved in a journey that embodies the gravitas hidden inside all of us—the dark Unknown, the abyss, what theologian Barbara Brown Taylor argues beautifully, in *Learning to Walk in the Dark,* grounds all religion, all theology, every God, and every person's real life who says, "Don't turn away from the abyss—stare it down and you will prevail."

This is what boys and men want to do, and they want to be raised by us to do it for us, the people who love them. Boys who are loved well give love in ways no civilization can ever fully measure.

My own boyhood and manhood have been lived between worlds. I work almost completely with women, and my own family, Gail, Gabrielle, and Davita, are all female. But I also work with and advocate for boys and men in conferences, schools, prisons, my clinical practice, and in communities. I've learned the ways of both genders in both women's and men's worlds. But I'm a man, so I live in a life-long search for my own manhood.

As a boy, then man, I've looked into male eyes and understood that some boys are able to perceive, consciously, their angels and demons, warriors and friends, goddesses and gods, but not all do, and no man perceives everything he's facing as he faces it. From the first colorful toy he threw into the air to his first kiss, he makes a quest for truth within a plethora of disguised and, often, complex, self-deceiving experiences.

His manhood is, thus, not mainly a set of masculine norms but mainly a male container, a consilience that he makes into a safe and secure home for others as he battles his own abyss. It is not a thing but an amorphous bubble, like a field of light wrapped around a constantly changing body. This evolving nature of manhood gives men their purpose in the midst of a real life that seems to possess a bottomless passion for surprises and dangers.

As a writer, I try to verbalize what I learn about manhood more than most men and each time I use words I know I'm trying to speak for other males and females who can't. As I work to spread a mission of societal change and success for both boys and girls, I know: If I pretend that all of us are all just "people," my feet will be stuck in the quicksand of "nothing" and "anything," lost between poles of real being. At some point, each of us must step out of the muck of confusion to understand the differences between a "man" and a "woman." So despite the fact that "gender" will always evolve and grow, gender is also male and female.

To forget or neglect that is to create dangerous social systems— dangerous in the past for females and now becoming more dangerous for males. Gender is an experiment and an adventure and the end point of every adventure is the accumulation of a particular, functional, loving, and sacrificial self that attaches us to others. That self is not a thing to be defined generally as "just a person" or "masculine norms," but the immensity felt when a woman and man sit near a stream or ocean, play with dolls and trucks, make love, hold children in their arms, sign an important lease or contract: in these settings they realize manhood as a theme that has been pouring itself into their lives for decades.

Study this around you. Notice the complex love each man feels, not only for his loved ones but also his competitors. Help encourage manhood's part in gender symbiosis by honoring the deep ways that males discover both humility and self-confidence then sacrifice all their self-discovery for the sake of women and children without question, without whining, and unto death.

I love to watch football and I remember Peyton Manning's various and innovate and deceptive audibles-under-center that humbled defenses until a defensive line (for instance, the Seahawks in the Super Bowl, 2014) pierced through the armor of those audibles to defeat their foe. Manning, meanwhile, was already planning new ways to defeat defenses, and Manning did, in Super Bowl 50.

And while some football players ask God—in their prayerful, motivational circle—to help them vanquish their foe, if those men are steeped in manhood they won't believe that their God is the only right God and their competitor's God is wrong. That would be child's play—not a man's truth.

Manhood, these players know, is built by lovers, enemies, foes, sorrow-bringers, grief-wielders, dark forces, feminine graces, women's wisdom, children's needs, animal urges, hidden secrets, and most of all, the conjunction of male and female.

God doesn't choose sides between women and men, nor should culture.

One way is not better—both ways are necessary and beautiful.

One half of emotional intelligence is female, but the other half is male.

Many times in a male journey, a man will face down God—life, nature, being—with only a tiny sword in his hand. I can tell you from my own manhood, those are brilliant days—to be David against Goliath yet know that Goliath is not one's enemy but the source of one's strength, love, and wisdom—this touch of self to infinity is electric. As the poet Rilke put it, "This is how a man grows—by being defeated, decisively, by infinitely greater beings." It is this "defeat" during heroic meeting that boys seek in games and men seek in their risks and searches for the truth of love.

This is the primal "victory" of being a man—serving others relentlessly and willfully without ever fully winning or losing…but, in the service itself, finally becoming whole.

Acknowledgments

SAVING OUR SONS culminates three decades of research, practice, and advocacy in applied gender science. I stand on the shoulders of many others working in the field. You know who you are, too many to name, but each one of you played a huge part of my vision and theory. I am deeply grateful.

Each of us from our different angles—gender studies, women's studies, men's studies, male development research, pure neuroscience, gender neuroscience, epigenetics, psychiatry and psychology, as well as anthropology and social science—is able, now, to build bridges with one another. This devotion toward mutual dependency of disciplines will ultimately save our children.

My deep thanks also to my Gurian Institute co-authors and co-researchers: Kathy Stevens (of blessed memory), Katey McPherson, Dakota Hoyt, Patricia Henley, Adie Goldberg, Gregory Jantz, Ann McMurray, Tim Wright, Peggy Daniels, Stacie Behring, Arlette Ballew, Kelley King, Terry Trueman, Gary Plep, and Barbara Annis. You have strengthened my ability to think strategically and practically about the needs of boys and girls, and women and men, from the trenches and "on the ground." Your perspectives have been essential to our movement and our quest for a social revolution on behalf of boys.

To all the other people in the trenches who have aided us in the Gurian Institute's wisdom-of-practice research over the last twenty years, I wish to express my deep gratitude. We could not conduct our research without your help. Special thanks to Executive Director Katey McPherson for facilitating so much of this research on a daily and weekly basis.

Special thanks also to Troy Kemp and the team at the National Center for the Development of Boys, Paul Garro and the team at the Center for Excellence in Educating Boys and Girls at Central Catholic High School in San Antonio, Texas, Carla Sparks and the team in Hillsboro Schools in Tampa, Florida, and the Army and Navy High School team in Carlsbad, California.

Many thanks also to our coauthors and colleagues in faith communities including Pastor Tim Wright in Peoria, Arizona, Fr. William Watson at the Sacred Story Institute in Seattle, Washington, and Dr. Gregory Jantz in Edmonds, Washington. I am grateful for the grace with which they work with a mainly secular writer like myself. They remind me how important it is to avoid moving science and religion too far away from one another. The two disciplines are both, after all, the parents of our civilization.

To all the parents, teachers, citizens, leaders, and fans who have written letters (back when we did that!) and e-mails more recently, I express my humble gratitude. Among the many gifts your correspondence has offered me, one that influenced this book, is your ongoing challenge that I provide a resource for every possible reader that not only dives deep into what boys need to thrive but also takes on the acute challenges of advocating for boys in our present political climate. I hope this book fulfills some of that challenge.

My thanks also extend to colleagues in publishing, including my editors, Alan Rinzler, Dennis Held, Jon Gosch, and Russ Davis.

To my clients: thank you for allowing me to serve you. You have helped me become more effective with both women and men, and boys and girls.

To Gail and our daughters, Gabrielle and Davita, I extend the kind of gratitude that can barely be expressed in words. As women, you have insisted I work diligently for females and males, and, throughout this insistence, you have kept me focused on seeing diverse sides of various gender equations.

Everyone I have thanked here has taught me that there is a great deal at stake in our work now. The aggregate result we hope to achieve with the diverse people we serve is a whole culture's discovery of essential science-based and common sense strategies for every child. My thanks to all of you for helping me to do this for three decades—I couldn't do what I do without you.

Notes and Resources

Preface

This book integrates the following sources:
* Results from my meta-analysis of 1,924 studies on male development.
* Statistical benchmarks and analysis from think-tanks and governmental agencies such as the Department of Justice, the Pell Institute, the OECD, the WHO, and the United Nations. As one of the lead authors of the meta-study, *The Proposal to Create a White House Council on Boys and Men,* I have been honored to work with leading thinkers and researchers throughout the world who have gathered data under one roof.
* Action and wisdom-of-practice research from the Gurian Institute. We have trained more than 60,000 professionals and reached more than one million parents. In meetings with stakeholders in hundreds of communities, and in our data and analysis from social services and educational clients, we have thousands of responses to surveys and questionnaires, some of which appear in this book. These emails, correspondence, and research come from ordinary people like you who are battling for boys and girls around the world.
* Interviews and interactions with members of the legislative and executive branches, executives, government officials, and corporate leaders from Fortune 500 companies who are concerned about the holes in the new male workforce, and the male psyche.
* Case studies and clinical research from my own counseling clients, with details changed for confidentiality. My own clients, as well as clients of others in our Gurian Institute team, have been generous sources of information about the boy crisis and of possible solutions.

Chapter 1

With a few exceptions, I have taken the epigraph quotes from the remarkable anthology, *The Rag and Bone Shop of the Heart,* edited by Robert Bly, Michael Meade, and James Hillman, New York: Harper Perennial, 1993.

Gregg Zoroya, "The Tragic Tide of Suicide: 4 an Hour," *USA Today,* October 10, 2014.

Mark Emmons, "Williams' Death Opens Discussion on Often-Private Issue of Suicide," *McClatchy-Tribune,* August 14, 2014.

Betsy McKay, "Suicides Climb After Years of Declines," *The Wall Street Journal,* April 22, 2016.

The Proposal to Create a White House Commission on Boys and Men (updated, 2016). This meta-analysis provides data and analysis for five primary areas of male distress: Mental and Emotional Distress; Educational Failure; Physical Health Issues; Decline of Fathering; Significant Work Decline for males. These are presented in the statistics of this chapter. You can access our study at www.whitehouseboysmen.org and deploy it in your community.

Please note that this book was published just as the new Trump administration was taking over the White House. I hope my team and I will be able to work with the new administration and Congress to help both boys and girls. I hope, also, that you will lobby these new administrations and Committees to deal with male issues in depth.

See also Susan Chira, "Men Need Help," *The New York Times,* October 21, 2016. "More than a fifth of American men—about 20 million people—between 20 and 65 had no paid work last year. Seven million men between 25 and 55 are no longer even looking for work....There are 20 million men with felony records who are not in jail, with dim prospects of employment."

David Autor and Melanie Wasserman, *Wayward Sons: The Emerging Gender Gap in Labor Markets and Education,* for The Third Way Think Tank. See www.thirdway.org.

Along with these meta-analyses, you can type in my name on YouTube and there you will find a four-minute video called "The Boy Crisis" created by one of our Gurian Institute Certified Trainers, Craig Foster, for public showing.

See also Schott 50 State Report on Public Education and Black Males, Schott Foundation, http://black-boys-report.org/national-summary. "In the 2012-13 school year, graduation rates were 59% for black males, 65% for Latinos males, and 80% for white males."

I have also included blogs in the Appendix that you can pass out to friends, families, and other concerned professionals and citizens. Don't worry about copyright restrictions on this blog as I am waiving them for this piece as long as credit is given.

The work of the Pell Institute for the Study of Opportunity in Higher

Education has produced another important set of resources. At the Institute, Tom Mortenson's forty-year study of gender trends in America has led to a number of meta-studies you can peruse, including "The State of American Manhood," published in *Post Secondary Education*, March 2011. Mr. Mortenson works annually to update the statistics and has provided his 2015 update to me. I thank him for giving me permission to publish these findings.

Males, the Pell Institute has revealed, are doing badly in the aggregate, and also, in the aggregate, they are doing worse than females. This is true, as you've seen in the chapter, in all ethnic groups.

While the general trends in the Big Three—our academic institutions, government, and media—lean toward insisting that females are generally victims of masculinized social roles and male dominance, the truth is more nuanced: in some areas, they remain victims, but in the aggregate, females are now better off in America than males.

OECD – PISA data can be accessed via www.oecd.org/Pisa and by exploring the oecd.org site. Particularly instructive is to go back over the last few decades and watch the evolution of the loss of males over that time span.

The WHO study and Global Disease Reports are very instructive and can be accessed via various sites and links. One to start with: http://www.who.int/gho/publications/world_health_statistics/2015/en/.

Even among gifted students we see trends that should worry us. Professors Barbara Kerr and Karen Multon, from the Department of Psychology and Research in Education at the University of Kansas, pointed out two very important things in their 2015 study of gifted underachieving students. First: more gifted boys fail or fall behind in school than gifted girls; and second: the most gifted underachievers are white males. Gifted white boys presumably come to school with more demographic privilege than others, but they are the in the most distress among gifted students.

I see two things here: 1) it is not good for a society to have even its most gifted children (no matter their gender or race) failing in the environment we charge with shaping and educating them; and, 2) the boy problem my daughter Gabrielle and I were discussing—the disappearing American boy—is not just a one-race problem. It affects *all* boys, including all colors, and white males.

The aggregate conclusion from worldwide studies must be: *in most of the world, girls and women are doing better than boys and men in both physical and mental health indicators.* Even when statistics regarding female depression, eating disorders, and violence-against-females such as rape and genital mutilation are included, males are doing worse. Perhaps most surprising to people is the WHO study's wide reach: the health and wellness gender gap favoring females exists in *all 72 industrialized countries, including countries like China or Oman* that we have tended to believe are still patriarchal, and thus should be harder on females than males.

These statements may come as a shock to some people because the national headlines don't fit reality. In the last week this has been echoed in my email box as I have received emails from government officials and concerned parents in China, Singapore and Nigeria. These emails were preceded by emails and calls over the last two years from leaders and citizens of nearly every industrialized country. The latest came from Lagos, Nigeria where a parent wrote, "I have 4 boys—20, 17 ,16 and 15 and see the troubles they have in my country. I am passionate about this and would like to help boys thrive in Nigeria. This boy problem is not only an American problem; it is our problem, too, in Africa."

When you are talking with others at the water cooler or somewhere else in your community, you could remind them that, yes, women have significant areas of distress, but we must *see* boys, too. A stark example of our inability to see male pain showed up in the kidnapping of 300 schoolgirls in Burkino Faso in 2014. The kidnap of the girls was the headline. As a father of daughters (and as a human being touched by pain) I was glued to the screen, praying for these girls' safety. But at the same time, the headlines and the media reports did not feature the fact that simultaneous to the kidnapping of the girls was the *murder of 300 boys*. The girls were rescued, able to return to their lives and loves, while the boys were dead. The girls were visible; the boys were invisible.

So, too, with most headlines regarding gender pain. They take us where they take us and we must remain sympathetic to girls and women always, but we must also journey farther into reality. The WHO study asks us to do this as soon as possible: "*In most parts of the world, health outcomes among boys and men continue to be substantially worse than among girls and women. Yet this gender-based disparity in health has received little national, regional or global acknowledgement or attention from health policy-makers or health-care providers.*" The study concludes: "*Including both women and men in efforts to reduce gender inequalities in health as part of the post-2015 sustainable development agenda would improve everyone's health and well-being.*"

This is very logical. But the headlines we read and discuss at the water cooler are generally about female distress and male privilege. I hope you will use the information in this chapter to help people around you to see past the headlines. We truly can do this without robbing females of the real health they need.

As a father of daughters, I know we can't have a social revolution on behalf of our sons if we backlash against feminists or the purveyors of the typical headlines. These people are just as protective and caring of human beings as are people who advocate for boys. Our job is to provide facts and right wrongs without attacking the basic cause of women's equality. We can do this because, as MIT's, Pell Institute's, the Gurian Institute's, and all other studies of male development point out: there is no separation of women's well-being and men's well-being.

Claire Cain Miller, "A Disadvantaged Start in Life Harms Boys More Than Girls," *The New York Times*, October 22, 2016.

Neil Shah, "Unmarried….With Children," *The Wall Street Journal*, March 11, 2015.

Ryan D'Agostino, "The Drugging of the American Boy," *Esquire*, March, 2014.

Fortin, Nicole M., et al. "Leaving Boys Behind: Gender Disparities in High Academic Achievement, *Journal of Human Resources*, Vol. 50, Summer, 2015. "Using data from the 'Monitoring the Future' surveys, this paper shows that from the 1980s to the 2000s, the mode of girls' high school GPA distribution has shifted from "B" to "A," essentially "leaving boys behind" as the mode of boys' GPA distribution stayed at "B." In a reweighted Oaxaca-Blinder decomposition of achievement at each GPA level, we find that changes to gender differences in post-secondary expectations...occur as early as the eighth grade.

In her fascinating book, *Unbroken Brain,* Maia Szalavitz points out that it is mainly men and boys who go to prison for addiction. What I have called "gender profiling" allows for this practice, though much of the practice in the criminal justice system is unconscious, not malicious.

Kerr, B.A. and Multon, K.D. "The Development of Gender Identity, Gender Roles, and Gender Relations in Gifted Students," *Journal of Counseling and Development,* April 2015, Vol 3: 163-191.

National Science Foundation (2003). "Gender Differences in the careers of academic scientists and engineers." Retrieved from http://www.nsf.gov/statistics/nsf03322/pdf/nsf03322.pdf.

Melissa Healy, "U.S. Tops in Mass Shootings," *Los Angeles Times,* August 26, 2015.

Sarah Skidmore Sell, "Women Top CFO Pay Chart," *Associated Press,* December 19, 2015.

Denisa R. Superville, "Locked-Up Youths See Grim Prospects in Many States," *Education Week,* December 9, 2015.

Fareed Zakaria, "America's Self-Destructive Whites," *The Washington Post,* January 1, 2016.

An article by Heather MacDonald in *The Wall Street Journal* (February 12, 2016) displays one of the ways that "headlines" distort reality. In "The Myths of Black Lives Matter," the implication of the headline (no doubt created by Journal staff to incite readers) is that MacDonald does not think black lives matter. Her article clearly speaks to the needs of blacks and all groups. Within the article, too, are statistics of interest, that might get lost in all the extreme headlines on both sides of the Black Lives Matter debate. *The Washington Post*, she notes, has been collecting data on fatal police shootings because of "deficiencies in federal tallies."

She writes, "According to the *Post* database, in 2015 officers killed 662 whites and Hispanics and 258 blacks. (The overwhelming majority of all those police-shooting victims were attacking the officer, often with a gun). Using the 2014 homicide numbers as an approximation of 2015's, those 662 white and Hispanic victims of police shootings would make up 12% of all white and Hispanic homicide deaths. That is three times the proportion of black deaths that result from police shootings."

She compares this statistic with black-on-black homicide rates, which are 6,095 black homicide deaths. "Almost all of those black homicide victims had black killers."

The race issues here are much more nuanced than headlines allow. Black lives matter a great deal, but we have to be wary of casting white policeman into yet another masculine system that destroys vulnerable groups. And we have to be wary of missing the constantly high rates of white homicide and white male privation in our zeal to help other needy populations. The constant casting of males into villains and our blindness to what is going on with white males keeps the Dominant Gender Paradigm (subject of Chapter 2) going strong while millions of males and, thus, females, end up suffering.

See also Kathleen Parker, "The White Guys' White Knight," *The Washington Post,* December 23, 2015. Parker powerfully seconds the importance of seeing that the boy crisis affects all demographics, including white boys and men. She writes, "Based on my research and observations in writing, '*Save the Males,*' conservative white guys aren't so much trying to hold onto power and privilege as much as they're trying to find their footing in a culture they feel devalues and disrespects them. They're tired of hearing that they're the source of all problems. They're sick of being the single demographic about which one can say anything at all and suffer only the annoyance of deafening applause."

For more statistics and analysis on what is happening to American boys across the demographics please also see:

* Richard Whitmire's *Why Boys Fai.*
* Christina Hoff Sommers's *The War Against Boys.* (Also please see her short video clips, "The Factual Feminist," produced by the American Enterprise Institute, where she is a resident scholar)
* Warren Farrell's work, including *The Myth of Male Power* and his upcoming book, with John Gray, *The Boy Crisis*
* *Raising Cain* by Dan Kindlon and Michael Thompson (put into a powerful video for PBS of the same name)
* William Pollock's *Real Boys*
* *Boys Adrift* by Leonard Sax
* *Stiffed* by Susan Faludi
* *Manning Up* by Kay Hymowitz
* *Save the Males* by Kathleen Parker
* Ongoing writings of columnists such as Leonard Pitts, Donald Brooks, and Kathleen Parker.

These resources by experts and journalist are joined by books, articles, and blogs on boys' distress and needs that may get less notice, but are popping up on the Internet and in print nearly every day.

Ann Case and Angus Deaton, "Rising morbidity and mortality in midlife among white non-Hispanic Americans in the 21st century," *Proceedings of the National Academy of Sciences,* Vol. 112, November 2015, 15078-15083.

Chapter 2

William James, *Varieties of Religious Experience,* recently republished by CrossReach Publications, 2015.

Carol Gilligan, *In a Different Voice,* Boston: Harvard University Press, 1998.

Hanna Rosin, *The End of Men,* New York: Riverhead, 2013.

Andrew Reiner, "Teaching Men to Be Emotionally Honest," *The New York Times,* April 4, 2016.

"Citizen Science" has grown in popularity with the advancement of the Internet. While it is generally an anecdotal science, I believe it is the wave of the future for parenting and child development issues. Given how easy it is now to get access to primary science studies, and given the power of the parent to observe and study children nearby, citizen science seems a revolutionary way to discover best practices for our children. At the same time, citizen science can go awry, as it has in the anti-vaccination movement. With all science, especially given the possibility of mob rule or dominant extreme ideologies driving science, we must be rigorous and vigilant.

Gillian Flaccus, "Citizen Scientists Map Impact of El Nino," *Associated Press,* January 25, 2016.

Shirley S. Wang, "Why Medial Researchers Experiment on Themselves," *The Wall Street Journal,* January 26, 2016.

Alyssa L. Norris, et al. "Homosexuality as a Discrete Class," *Psychological Science,* 2015, Vol. 26, 1843-1853.

Baily., J.M., et al. "Genetic and Environmental Influences on Sexual Orientation and its Correlates in an Australian Twin Sample," *Journal of Personality and Social Psychology,* 2000, Vol. 78, 524-536.

Fergusson, D.M., et al. "Sexual Orientation and Mental Health in a Birth Cohort of Young Adults," *Psychological Medicine,* 2005, Vol. 35, 971-981.

Peters, M., et al. "The Effects of Sex, Sexual Orientation, and Digit ratio (2D:4D) on Mental Rotation Performance," *Archives of Sexual Behavior,* 2007, Vol. 36, 251-260.

Sanders, A.R., et al. "Genome-wide Scan Demonstrates Significant Linkage for Male Sexual Orientation," *Psychological Medicine,* 2015, Vol. 45, 1379-1388.

Jennifer Peltz, "New York Moves to Stop LGBT 'Conversion Therapy,'" *Associated Press,* February 6, 2016.

Ryan J. Foley, "States Taking Action to Keep Guns Out of Abuser's Hands," *The Spokesman-Review,* February 7, 2016.

Robert Lee Hotz, "China Genetically Modifies Monkeys to Aid Autism Study," *Wall Street Journal,* January 26, 2016.

Robert M. Sapolsky, "Sperm Can Carry Dad's Stress as Well as Genes," *Wall Street Journal,* September 6, 2014.

Simon Makin, "What Really Causes Autism," *Scientific American Mind,*

November/December, 2015.

Alpha Genomix is one of the companies that uses a DNA test to determine how medications are metabolized in each individual, producing a comprehensive list of a wide array of medications and their efficacy; medications are listed as able to be prescribed, based on genotype.: 1) able to be prescribed according to standard regimens, 2) adjusting dosages or increased vigilance while on that medication 3) potentially reduced efficacy or increased toxicity.

See the Walsh Research Institute in Illinois. *Nutrient Power* by Dr. William J. Walsh, the founder, is a very fascinating book.

23 and Me is another company that provides genetic testing. With its results in hand you can use the Genetics Genie software, with professional assistance, to interpret results. I have personally used 23 and Me for genetics study and found the company reputable and professional. Let me make clear, however, that I am not "selling" any of these companies. They are companies I know of, ones that my and some of my colleagues' clients and patients have utilized. I recommend that you get the help of psychiatrists and/or other qualified medical professionals to help you learn which tests are best and how to interpret the results. The tests need some very qualified eyes to read them and make good sense of them for the individual child/adult.

The September/October 2015 edition of *Family Therapy* is devoted to looking at a number of the issues regarding medication that I discuss in this chapter and this book. If you have a child on medication, you might especially find this article useful: "Children, Adolescents, and Psychiatric Drugs," by Dr. Jacqueline A. Sparks.

Melvin Konner, "A Better World Ruled by Women?" *The Wall Street Journal,* March 7, 2015, and Melvin Konner, "Matriarchy on the March," *The Wall Street Journal,* March 28-29, 2015. Dr. Konner, an evolutionary biologist, makes a number of important points, including the fact that the SRY chromosome, which is linked to shorter life span, a greater probability of death due to accidents, and to a greater likelihood of being both a victim and perpetrator of violence, is also present in 90 percent of our incarcerated individuals, and most of these are, of course, men.

Stephen Wilson, "IOC Relaxes Transgender Guidelines for Athletes," *Associated Press,* January 25, 2016.

Isen, Joshua D., et al. "Aggressive-Antisocial Boys Develop into Physically Strong Young Men," *Psychological Science,* 2015, Vol. 26(4), pp. 444-455.

Ronal Serpas, "Understanding Violence as a 'Contagion'," *The Wall Street Journal,* April 6, 2015.

Scott Maben, "Boy Had Thought About Killing," *The Spokesman-Review,* January 16, 2016.

Jennifer Sullivan, "Families File Claim for Shooting," *The Spokesman-Review,* January 10, 2016.

Thomas F. Denson, "Naturally Nasty," *Journal of the Association for Psychological Science,"* January 2014 – Vol 27, No 1.

Scott Maben, "Zombie Fears Fueled Slayings, CdA Teenager's Lawyer

Argues," *The Spokesman-Review,* January 14, 2016.

Editorial Staff, "How Much Do We Care About Ending the Carnage?" *The Spokesman-Review,* June 21, 2015.

Charlene M. Alexander, et al. "Adolescent Dating Violence: Application of a U.S. Primary Prevention Program in St. Lucia," *Journal of Counseling and Development,* October 2014, Vol. 92, 489-498.

Dahlberg LL, Mercy JA. "History of Violence as a Public Health Issue." *AMA Virtual Mentor,* February 2009. Volume 11, No. 2: 167-172. Available on-line at http://virtualmentor.ama-assn.org/2009/02/mhst1-0902.html.

Khullar, Dhruv and Jena, Anupam B. "Homicide's Role in the Racial Life-Expectancy Gap," *The Wall Street Journal,* April 28, 2016.

Gapp, Katharina, et al. including Isabelle M. Mansuy, "Implication of sperm RNAs in transgenerational inheritance of the effects of early trauma in mice," *Nature Neuroscience,* March 2014, Vol. 17, 667–669.

Lisa Gillespie, "Struggles Now—And Later," *Tribune News Service,* March 8, 2106.

Robert M. Sapolsky, "The Price of Poverty for a Developing Brain," *The Wall Street Journal,* April 12-13, 2016.

Jane E. Brody, "A Mysterious Rise in Type 1 Diabetes," *The New York Times,* April 21, 2015. The title of this article implies that it is only about Diabetes, but in fact the article goes into helpful depth on new genetics based research on the effects of stress on juveniles and adults, i.e. how stress affects epigenetics.

Roxanne Nelson, "Violence as an Infectious Disease," *Medscape Medical News,* April 29, 2013.

Manuel Jimenez, "Kindergartners with Traumatic Life Experiences Struggle More in School," *Healthday News,* January 15, 2016.

Brand, C.R., et al. "Personality and General Intelligence." In G.L. Van Heck, P. Bonaiuto, I.J. Deary & W. Nowack (eds.), *Personality Psychology in Europe* 4, 203-228. Tilburg University Press. 1993.

William Pollack. *Real Boys.*

Kindlon, Daniel. and Thompson, Michael. *Raising Cain.*

Chapter 3

Steven Pinker, "The Genetics of IQ," *The Wall Street Journal,* January 2, 2016.

Steven Pinker, *The Blank Slate.*

Shihui Han, "Making Sense," *Association for Psychological Science,* December 2015, Vol. 28, 10.

Frank Griffits, et al. including Kathryn Boak McPherson, *Why Teens Fail,* Phoenix: Be the One, 2012.

For more on obesity genetics, see: http://www.ncbi.nlm.nih.gov/pubmed/21717811.

Andrea Petersen, "Training the Brain to Cope with Depression," *Wall*

Street Journal, January 19, 2016.

Daniel Akst, "Delay That's in Our DNA," *The Wall Street Journal,* April 12, 2014.

Amy Dockser Marcus, "The Hard New Family Talk: Our Genes," *The Wall Street Journal,* September 28, 2015.

Lyndsey Layton, "Study Influences Achievement-Gap Debate," *The Washington Post,* April 16, 2015.

Alison Gopnik, "The Income Gap in the Growth of Children's Brains," *The Wall Street Journal,* May 16, 2015.

Blair, C., et al. "Maternal and Child Contributions to Cortisol Response to Emotional Arousal in Young Children from Low-Income Rural Communities," *Developmental Psychology,* Vol. 44, 1095-1109.

Allen, Mark S. and Laborde, Sylvain, "The Role of Personality in Sport and Physical Activity," *Current Directions in Psychological Science,* 2014, Vol. 23(6) 460-465.

Ed Riley, a physician and professor at Stanford University, has written a fascinating and helpful article for anyone whose children like football, "Research Suggests Parents Should Allow Kids to Play Football," *The Portland Tribune.* Dr. Riley goes through the data on brain injuries and mental health of NFL players, finding cause for alarm, but notes that the Mayo Clinic research on high school players shows no higher probability of mental health risks than a non-football-playing teen, with some specific gains from the team work of football in youths' lives.

Sue Lani Madsen, "State's New Gender-Restroom Rule," *The Spokesman Review,* January 16, 2016, quoting Williams' University of UCLA School of Law study, "0.3 percent of population are transgender."

See original study at: Gates, G.J., "How Many People Are Lesbian, Gay, Bisexual, and Transgender?" Retrieved from http://williamsinstitute.law.ucla.edu/qp-content/Gates.

Olson, Kristina R., et al. "Gender Cognition in Transgender Children," *Psychological Science,* 2015, Vol. 26 467-474.

The whole March/April 2016 issue of *Psychotherapy Networker* is devoted to "The Mystery of Gender."

Melissa Healy, "Study Links Autism, Anti-Depressants in Pregnancy," *The Los Angeles Times,* December 15, 2015.

Sbarra, David A, et.al. "Divorce and Health: Beyond Individual Differences," Current Directions in Psychological Science, 2015, Vol 24, 109-113.

Luc Goossens, et al. "The Genetics of Loneliness: Linking Evolutionary Theory to Genome-Wide Genetics, Epigenetics, and Social Science," *Perspectives on Psychological Science,* 2015, Vol. 10(2) 213-226.

Laurie Meyers, "The Toll of Childhood Trauma," *Counseling Today,* July 2014, 29-36.

Latvala, Antti, et al. "Paternal Antisocial Behavior and Sons' Cognitive Ability: A Population-Based Quasiexperimental Study," *Psychological Science,* 2015, Vol. 26(1) 78-88.

Alison Gopnik, "The Smartest Questions to Ask About Intelligence," *The Wall Street Journal,* February 21, 2015.

Alison Gopnik, "Genes' Unknown Role in a Vicious Circle of Poverty," *The Wall Street Journal,* September 27 – 28, 2014.

Robert Maranto and Michael Crouch, "Ignoring an Inequality Culprit: Single Parent Families," *The Wall Street Journal,* April 21, 2014.

Shanna Swan, "Parents Needn't Wait for Legislation to Shield Kids from Toxins in Products," *San Francisco Chronicle,* January 9, 2006.

In a tiny two-paragraph story off the wires, the headline reads, "Artificial Ingredient Sliced." The story is about Pizza Hut ending the use of artificial ingredients over the next year in its U.S. restaurants. Pizza Hut executives have studied the science and agree that BHA and BHT must be cut from meat to protect customers, as must artificial preservatives from cheese.

This is the kind of responsible citizenship that should make front-page news, in my humble opinion. The epigenetics issues that preservatives, artificial ingredients, red dye, artificial sweeteners, and even simple things like aluminum can cause our children should be front page news whenever possible.

To learn more about male/female brain difference, please see *Boys and Girls Learn Differently, The Minds of Boys, The Wonder of Girls,* and the books written by all of the scientists I mentioned, e.g. Louann Brizendine, and Daniel Amen. I have created a further resource, a list appearing on the website www.michaelgurian.com/Research that includes approximately 1,000 primary and secondary sources in gender neuroscience such as the study I mentioned: Diane Halpern, et al., including Camilla Benbow and Ruben Gur, "The Science of Sex Differences in Science and Mathematics," *Psychological Science in the Public Interest,* Vol 8, No. 1, August 2007.

Sex differences in the brain (what we now popularly call "gender differences") appear at all ages, including in earliest childhood and latest life-stages. For early childhood to late adolescent differences see especially:

Yu, Vickie., et al. "Age-Related Sex Differences in Language Lateralization: A Magnetoencephalography Study in Children," *Developmental Psychology,* 2014, Vol.50, 2276-2284.

Ingalhalikar, Madhura, et al. "Sex Differences in the Structural Connectome of the Human Brain," *Proceedings of the National Academy of Sciences,* 2014, Vol 111, 823-828.

Killgore, William, et al. "Sex-Specific Developmental Changes in Amygdala Responses to Affective Faces," *NeuroReport,* 2001, Vol. 12, 427-433.

Gummadavelli, Abhijeet, et al. "Spatiotemporal and Frequency Signatures of Word Recognition in the Developing Brain," *Brain Research,* 2013, Vol. 1498, 20-32.

Sacher, Julia, et al. "Sexual Dimorphism in the Human Brain," *Magnetic Resonance Imaging,* 2013, Vol 31, 366-375.

Alina Dizik, "The Secret Subtext of Menus," *The Wall Street Journal,* March 25, 2015.

Ron Winslow, "Genes May Explain Why Cancer Varies by Gender," *The Wall Street Journal,* May 17, 2016.

Bartz, Jennifer A., "Oxytocin and the Pharmacological Dissection of Affiliation," *Current Directions in Psychological Science,* 2016, Vol. 25, 104-110.

Shors, Tracey J. and Miesegaes, George, "Testosterone in Utero and at Birth Dictates How Stressful Experience Will Affect Learning in Adulthood," *Proceedings of the National Academy of Sciences 99,* no. 21 (October 15, 2002): 13955–60.

Shors, Tracey J., "Stress and Sex Effects on Associative Learning: For Better or for Worse," *Neuroscientist 4,* no. 5 (September, 1998): 353–64.

Nicolas Wade, "Peeking into Pandora's Box," *The Wall Street Journal,* May 14-15, 2016. Wade explores themes in the new book by Siddhartha Mukherjee, *The Gene,* (Scribner, 2016). He makes a point that is perhaps common sense but also can get lost as we try to understand what is "sex" and what is "gender" from a biological viewpoint.

While we can discuss "gender" as happening on a spectrum, as male/female brains do happen on a spectrum, these brains are still male and female. So, while gender can feel fluid, when we come right down to living our lives and doing our daily tasks of surviving and thriving, sex (neurobiology) is far more powerful in us than some of the present debate allows for as we talk about gender fluidity.

Everyone who has had children has peeked into this truth; parents see the genes in their own family lab. Few if any parents of boys and girls cannot tell, within five years of the child's birth, that there are gender-different brains in those gendered bodies. Even the parents of a transgender child are seeing male/female brains in a way that science observes as "exceptions prove the rule."

So, the rule here should not be to force a transgender child to develop in a gender group that does not fit his/her internal map for gender; rather, the rule is that only .3 percent of children fit this profile, which puts more than 99 percent of children in a mind/body sync regarding gender, though the spectrum of that gender includes more than 7.3 billion kinds of boys/girls.

In a 2008 study published in the *Journal of Personality and Social Psychology,* a group of international researchers compared data on gender and personality across 55 nations and confirmed that, throughout the world, women tend to be more empathically nurturing, risk averse, and emotionally expressive in words, while men are usually more competitive, risk taking, and emotionally flat in comparison (men feel fewer feelings and express fewer of those feelings in words).

These differences were obvious in all cultures, but highest in frequency between men and women in the more prosperous, egalitarian, and educated societies such as ours. According to the authors, "Higher levels of human development—including long and healthy life, equal access to knowledge and education, and economic wealth—were the main nation-level predictors of sex difference variation across cultures."

The idea, then, that male/female difference disappears in an economic democracy is patently false. The more males and females have the freedom to "be who they are," the more they evidence gender differences. While their gender roles become more parallel, their gender differences—which affect their ability to learn well, grow well, survive and thrive—are robust and must be taken into account in all social theories or we will lose huge portions of both males and females to distress.

I promised not to repeat previous books in this book so, if you would like even more in depth understanding of the male brain *as applied directly to parenting* not covered in this chapter and this book, I hope you will read:

The Wonder of Boys (for understanding, parenting, and mentoring boys in general, especially if you are raising a boy under ten years old, including assistance with discipline and other parenting issues);

A Fine Young Man (for understanding, parenting, and mentoring boys between ten and twenty, including assistance with rites of passage, media use, mentoring, and father-son/mother-son issues);

Nurture the Nature (for nurturing core personality development of each child from birth to 25, with childhood and emerging adulthood divided into seven stages matching brain development);

Raising Boys by Design (specifically connecting the science of the male brain with Christian parenting and Biblical wisdom, written in collaboration with Dr. Gregory Jantz, an evangelical Christian psychologist);

The Good Son (which reveals male brain development from birth to adulthood in two year developmental increments);

I want to thank all of my collaborators, and colleagues in nature-based theory, including co-authors from both ends of the political spectrum, who prove that gender neuroscience and theory developed from it can build bridges between us.

Conversations with Dr. Amen have been ongoing over the last decade. The conversation with Dr. Berman occurred spontaneously in 2016 on an airplane in which we were seated together on the way to conferences.

Leonard Sax, *Boys Adrift*.

Leonard Sax, *Why Gender Matters*.

Daniel Amen, *Healing ADD,* New York: Berkley, 2013. I highly recommend Dr. Amen's approach to ADD, which not only uses brain scans to aid in diagnosis and treatment, but also divides ADD into various types so that parents and professionals can fully understand the exact kind of ADD/ADHD a particular child is experiencing. Like genome testing, the use of brain scans to aid in corrective treatment can be very helpful.

Medications given for ADD/ADHD (like any brain disorder or condition) can affect the human body and brain in ways unforeseen or misunderstood until much later and so are not necessarily "benign." Even though they are needed by many of our children, they can also, ironically, cause issues with lack of motivation as well as other side effects. This is why it is so important that we deal with the over-diagnosis of ADD/ADHD. In 2013, the Center for Disease Control and Prevention noted that just under

20 percent of high school boys had received an ADD/ADHD diagnosis. That figure represents misdiagnosis of American boys at epic proportions.

Robinson, Terry and Kolb, Bryan, "Structural Plasticity Associated with Exposure to Drugs of Abuse," *Neuropharmacology*, 2004, 47:33-46.

Carlezon, William, et al. "Understanding the Neurobiological Consequences of Early Exposure to Psychotropic Drugs, *Neuropharmacology*, 2004, Vol. 47, 47-60.

Gramage, Esther, et al. "Periadolescent Amphetamine Treatment Causes Transient Cognitive Disruptions and Long-Term Changes in Hippocampal LTP," 2013, *Addiction Biology,* Vol 18, 19-29.

Robinson, Terry and Kolb, Bryan, "Persistent Structural Modifications in Nucleus Accumbens and Prefrontal Cortex Neurons Porduced by Previous Experiences with Amphetamine," 1997, *Journal of Neuroscience*, Vol. 17, 8491-8497.

Pardey, Margery, et al, "Long-term Effects of Chronic Oral Ritalin Administration on Cognitive and Neural Development in Adolescent Wistar Kyoto Rats," 2012, *Brain Sciences,* Vol. 2, 375-404.

To learn more about OPRMI genes, go to the American Psychiatric Associations, and search OPRMI genes, for example, *https://www.psychiatry. org/.../am_newrese..* See May 13, 2000 - NR654 Association of *OPRMI* +118A Allele, *Charles* A. *Cloutier*, Department of Psychiatry, Duke University.

Gillespie, Charles F., et al. "Risk and Resilience: Genetic and Environmental Influences on Development of Stress Response," *Depression Anxiety,* 2009, Vol. 26, 984-992.

Kuzelova, H., et al. "The Serotonin transporter gene (5-HTT variant) and psychiatric disorders: review of current literature," *Neuro Endocrinology,* 2010, Vol. 31, 4-10.

For more on 5-HTT and related genetic coding, see *Nurture the Nature.*

William Pollack, *Real Boys.*

Kindlon, Dan. and Thompson, Michael, *Raising Cain.*

Garwood, Philip, "Neurobiological Mechanisms of Anhedonia," *Clinical Neuroscience,* 2008, Sep; 10(3): 291–299.

Carlezon, William, "Biological Substrates of Reward and Aversion: A Nucleus Accumbens Activity Hypothesis," *Neuropharmacology*, 2009, Vol. 56, 122-132.

Cornwell, Christopher, et al. "Non-cognitive Skills and the Gender Disparities in Test Scores and Teacher Assessments: Evidence from Primary School," May 1, 2012.

This is one of many studies showing that teachers unconsciously *gender profile* males and male behavior in classrooms. This gender bias was evident using data from the 1998 - 99 ECLS - K cohort. The authors showed "that the grades awarded by teachers are not aligned with test scores. Girls in every racial category outperform boys on reading tests, while boys score at least as well on math and science tests as girls.

"However, boys in all racial categories across all subject areas are not represented in grade distributions where their test scores would predict. Boys who perform equally as well as girls on reading, math and science tests are graded less favorably by their teachers, but this less favorable treatment essentially vanishes when non-cognitive skills are taken into account. For some specifications there is evidence of a grade 'bonus' for boys with test scores and behavior like their girl counterparts."

The Gurian Institute has been creating a gentle and patient friction in this regard for twenty years. We've now trained more than 60,000 teachers in thousands of schools and gathered data showing the success of nature-based theory in all human systems—schools, homes, social services, government, faith-communities, and public policy. You can utilize this research and this training. (gurianinstitute.com)

One teacher put the need for nature-based training this way: "We are women teachers, women caregivers, women leaders. We run most of the hands-on time boys spend in their first twenty years of life. But we don't get help understanding the male brain in our college and graduate schools. So we come out of our teacher training without knowing anything about male nature or how differently the male learning brain can be from the female brain. We then create schools, homes, and communities that don't help that male brain as much as they should, and the cycle just gets worse."

As she noticed: this is unconscious not malicious. "We've saddled teachers with academic gender politics that disallow training in gender neuroscience, and it's not fair to us or to our children."

To change this, parents and professionals will have to put pressure on academic culture, especially schools of education and our Department of Education in the federal government and the individual states, to provide proper gender science training to teachers in their early teacher training. Twenty years ago, this pressure was harder to bring. Now we have success data you can use to show that the nature-based course of action works for both boys and girls. To access this data, visit www.gurianinstitute.com/success. Feel free to use that data in your own meetings, blogs, and outreach.

While most of the schools having success are co-ed (because most schools in America are co-ed), some have experimented with single-gender classes for math/science and language arts; some have experimented with single-gender classes throughout the school. This latter is a new revolution in American *public schools* that shows real promise for both male and female brains. You may have heard negative press in the Big Three about single gender classes and schools but it is mainly ideological stuff, with little merit, in which the critics have not actually studied the schools or classrooms.

The actual innovations that are altering classrooms away from creating male anhedonia were initially piloted in our Gurian Institute programs in six school districts in the late 1990s in Kansas City, Missouri. That pilot study is reported in *Boys and Girls Learn Differently*. Over these last two decades, hundreds of boy-friendly innovations have emerged. You can access more of these in the pilot study, in *The Minds of Boys,* and in *Strategies for Teaching Boys and Girls.* As you study your children's schools and classrooms, see if some of these are being used. If they are not, I hope you will think about bringing the Boys and Girls Learn Differently® training to your school (contact our team at info@gurianinstitute.com).

Make sure there are squeeze balls and other spatial objects in classrooms for both genders to use in their learning. Boys' brains in general needs these more than girls' but these tools are good for girls who need them as well. The children can toss the balls up and down while taking tests or while writing. They can also squeeze them while doing any cognitive task. This allows for both sides of the male brain to be active during verbal learning.

Encourage literacy through alternative texts—boy-friendly books, comic books, nonfiction works, technical books and any other literature boys prefer. Many boys lean so heavily toward spatial-mechanical preference they need to read at least some books about how things work. When we insist they read fiction, keep in mind that they will most enjoy stories with a heroic quest in them, i.e. stories about character and manhood development.

Create a "natural classroom" in which reading and literacy, for instance, are taught via games and children stand up a great deal when they learn (or at least have the standing desk option). Corporations across the world have proven that this innovation improves productivity and performance—it can do this for boys and girls as well. (Daniel Akst, "The Productivity of Standing Up," *The Wall Street Journal,* April 9, 2016). All of these innovations fit "the natural boy" in that these are ways boys learned for millennia. A study in France recently corroborated the notion that making reading into a game would boost boy's test scores—it made them equal, in this small cohort, to girls' literacy performance. Games are natural to boys! And they are great for girls' cognition as well. ("Boys May Beat Girls in Reading—If it's a Game," Ann Lukits, *The Wall Street Journal,* May 3, 2016).

Make sure teachers use visual-spatial modalities (such as storyboards, drawing, and graphics) before writing-time for boys who need these modalities. Many boys will not immediately be able to put words to a page if just prompted with "write a paper about…." (a verbal prompt) and so they get Cs, Ds, or Fs, but if they can draw out their content or story ahead of time, they fill many pages with the words needed to get a B or A.

Use peer and/or vertical mentoring as much as possible with every boy (a master-apprentice relationship) but especially for boys who are at risk. As boys move to puberty, make sure they have at least two male "masters" in their lives—dad/father-figure and male coach/teacher/older brother or friend.

Allow boys (and girls who wish to) the space and capacity to move around in classrooms while doing their work (including writing and test taking). For instance, let them use standing desks or rock back and forth on sitting balls or "Swedish chairs." Some boys, absent of physical movement, will only be able to use a small part of their brains (the front left part) and will fall quickly behind in grades, homework, test scores, and behavior.

Nurture and direct male aggression rather than pretending it is inherently dangerous. Notice that girls are often just as aggressive and competitive as some boys—especially in brutal verbal aggression—but the schools rarely suspend or expel girls.

As you study your school for its anti-male gender biases in behavioral standards, be ready to revolutionize behavioral and learning applications even up to the legislative level.

This latter point is crucial—we in the grassroots must press legislators to pass boy-friendly laws. For instance, I believe we will need to pressure legislators in every state to pass a "good Samaritan" type of law for school systems so that parents cannot easily sue school districts for scrape-ups, small harms, and "discomforts" their boys or girls experience in school. At present, school administrators are afraid to let boys learn, play, and grow in boy-specific ways because they worry about getting sued. For example, in a school district I just spoke in, a parent sued the teacher and recess monitor because her son broke a finger while playing tag (another boy bumped him and he fell on his pinkie finger). Now, burdened by this unreasonable suit, the school is shutting down recess and not allowing any physical contact between boys.

I am partial to the Anita Burrows and Joanna Macy translations of Rilke, but there are many wonderful translators of his work. Rilke, to me, is an example of a quintessential "new kind of man" living one hundred years before we have tried to become this kind of man.

Ann Carson, *The Beauty of the Husband*
Carl Jung, edited by Claire Douglas, *Visions*

Chapter 4

Sheryl Sandberg, *Lean In.*
Camille Paglia, "2013: The Year Men Became Obsolete?" *Time,* December 30, 2013.
Leonard Sax recently told me that Supreme Justice Ruth Bader Ginsburg pointed out in 1996 in the majority ruling in U.S. v. Virginia that sex and race are not the same.
Wendy McElroy, *Rape Culture Hysteria: Fixing the Damage Done to Men and Women.*
Statistics on the real sexual assault rates appear in these articles and on the websites I mentioned, however, you really have to dig to get through to the truth, especially because the data got changed on the sites once this "rape culture" one-in-five assessment came down from the Administration. The McElroy finding of 1 in 53 college women sexually assaulted is powerful in part because she herself was raped. She has no incentive to tell anything but the truth about sexual assault. Nor do I—I was also the victim of sexual abuse as a boy.

It is important to remember that the problem with the over-reaching way statistics are used is not that there aren't sexual assaults on campus—there are and they are reprehensible and actionable. Rather, the problem is that what the Big Three are calling "sexual assault" should be divided, more accurately, into *sexual confusion, sexual confusion while inebriated, sexual misconduct, and sexual assault* so that prevention programs can deal with alcohol use, inebriation, sexual boundaries, and relational boundaries in ways that will help our youth to grow up whole.

Of the four areas I've just listed, only sexual assault is a crime; however, at this point, people in the Big Three have forced "science" to "back up" the false "one-in-five" statistic, so that the powers-that-be can continue to group all four into one criminal act. This just perpetuates the criminalization of males that is crippling our country. Meanwhile, it costs billions as males are now, already, suing schools for gender discrimination (which they have a right to do) from false accusations of crimes by the schools.

We can protect our young women and young men much better with the truth.

Jamie Tobias Neely, "Light at End of a Bad Week," *The Spokesman-Review,* June 1, 2014. "The estimated annual rate of rape or sexual assault against females in the United States declined by 64 percent between 1995 – 2010 according to numbers compiled by the U.S. Department of Justice's Bureau of Justice Statistics. The rate dropped from 5 to 1.8 per 1,000 females ages 12 or older."

Melissa Korn, "Reports of Sexual Assaults More than Double at Colleges," *The Wall Street Journal,* May 5, 2016. This article provides another excellent example of the difference between headlines (and the emotions they create) and the statistical reality of an issue.

There is something of attack politics and distraction politics in the way science has been put aside in so many of the "headlines" that depict male despicability in the public eye. By this I mean that a few anecdotal (and brutal, sympathetic) cases of a crime (a crime perpetrated by males) become a national talking point and massive energy and focus moves to the talking point—we end up, often, attacking males in general and distracting ourselves from the most devastating crises Americans face.

In the body of the article we find that actual statistics from the National Center for Education Statistics, the Bureau of Justice Statistics, and the American Institutes for Research, regarding crime at universities, and including assault, reveal 18.4 crimes per 1,000 people on our college campuses per year—and half of those crimes are burglaries. Here is another angle, then, on the idea that assault and sexual assault are not, statistically, what certain people in the Big Three have made them out to be.

Despite the fact that this Wall Street Journal story accurately reports these statistics, the headline assists in the ideological attack on our sons. So the issue here is not that we shouldn't protect females from rape—of course we should. The issue is that we have created a climate of distraction: the statistics of distress and loss we saw in Chapter 1 are in the millions while the campus assault statistics are far lower; but we do not focus on the massive areas of harm: we focus on statistically smaller areas, especially if males can be painted as brutal or too masculine.

This is an unconscious script of the DGP in the Big Three that we must do battle with over the next decade if we are to affect important social change for all of us—male and female. Doing this battle does not mean leaving our daughters unprotected from sexual assault. It will mean just the opposite— they will be better protected when our civilization grapples with the tens of millions of males in distress and helps raise them well.

Jason Felch and Larry Gordon, "Obama Task Force to Combat Sexual Assaults on Campuses," *The Los Angeles Times,* January 23, 2014.

Cynthia M. Allen, "A Culture of Irresponsibility," *The Spokesman Review,* December 15, 2014.

Sleek, Scott, "Blurred Concepts of Consent," *Journal of the Association for Psychological Science,* December 2014, Vol 27, 20-22.

Matt Pearce, "Rolling Stone Retracts UVA Rape Report," *The Los Angeles Times,* April 6, 2015.

Kathleen Parker, "Rolling Stone Causes Lots of Damage," *The Washington Post,* April 12, 2015.

Jacob E. Gersen, "How the Feds Use Title IX to Bully Universities," *The Wall Street Journal,* January 25, 2016.

Will Creeley, "How the Sex-Harassment Cops Became Speech Police," *The Wall Street Journal,* February 20-21, 2016.

Kate Brumback and Kathleen Foody, "Campus Sex Assault Follow-Up Challenged," *Associated Press,* May 29, 2016.

Phone conversation with Ron Henry.

Jessica Gavora, "How Title IX Became a Political Weapon," *The Wall Street Journal,* June 8, 2015.

Gates, G.J., *"How Many People Are Lesbian, Gay, Bisexual, and Transgender?"* Retrieved from http://williamsinstitute.law.ucla.edu/qp-content/Gates.

Olson, Kristina R., et al. "Gender Cognition in Transgender Children," *Psychological Science,* 2015, Vol. 26 467-474.

Also see the 1994 Harvard Medical Letter on the genetics and biology of homosexuality.

Frank D. LoMonte, "Don't Silence Young (Female) Journalists, *Education Week,* February 18, 2015.

Peggy Noonan, "The Trigger-Happy Generation," *The Wall Street Journal,* May 23-24, 2015.

Michael Bloomberg and Charles Koch, "Why Free Speech Matters on Campus," *The Wall Street Journal,* May 13, 2016.

Camille Paglia, "A Defense of Masculine Virtues," *http://online.wsj.com,* December 27, 2013.

Rachel Emma Silverman, "Working Parents Share the Load, Study Says," *The Wall Street Journal,* November 5, 2015.

Kathleen Smith, "The Many Faces of Domestic Violence," *Psychotherapy Networker,* November 2014, pp 11-12.

Elizabeth Bernstein, "Domestic Abusers Can Reform, Studies Show," *The Wall Street Journal,* September 16, 2014.

Noretta Koertge, *A House Built On Sand,* Oxford University Press, 2000.

Diane Halpern, et al., including Camilla Benbow and Ruben Gur, "The

Science of Sex Differences in Science and Mathematics," *Psychological Science in the Public Interest,* Volume 8, No. 1, August 2007).

Camilla Benbow and David Lubinski, *Intellectual Talent.*

Mehl, Matthias R. et al., including James W. Pennebaker, "Are Women Really More Talkative Than Men?" *Science,* Vol. 317, p. 82, July 2007.

Joy Moses and Jacquelyn Boggess are quoted from Elizabeth Stuart, "How Anti-Poverty Programs Marginalize Fathers," *The Atlantic,* February 25, 2014.

"Mental Health Crisis," *The Washington Post* (health-science@washpost.com) June 9, 2015.

Leonard Pitts, Jr., "Insane to Reject Mental Illness," *Syndicated, The Spokesman-Review,* February 9, 2015.

Melinda Beck, "Advocates Speak on Mental Illness," *The Wall Street Journal,* August 4, 2015.

Shirley S. Wang, "To Close a Gap in Mental-Health Care," *The Wall Street Journal,* January 12, 2016.

Reed, Eva E, "Man Up: Young Men's Lived Experiences and Reflections of Counseling," *Journal of Counseling & Development,* October 14, 2014, Vol. 92, 428-437.

For information on the points made regarding the White House efforts, please see www.whitehouseboysmen.org.

Gurian, Michael *How Do I Help Him: A Practitioner's Guide to Working with Boys and Men in Therapeutic Settings.*

Chapter 5

Daniel Goleman, *Emotional Intelligence.*

Sumiya, Ahmad, et al. "Emotional Intelligence and Gender Differences," 2009, *Suhrad Journal of Agriculture,* Vol. 25, No. 1.

Amen, Daniel. *Sex On The Brain.*

Baron-Cohen, Simon. *The Essential Difference.*

Taylor, Shelley E. *The Tending Instinct.*

Gladue, B, et al. "Hormonal Response to Competition in Human Males," *Aggressive Behavior,* 1989, Vol. 15, 409-422.

The July 2008 *Anesthesia & Analgesia Journal* is devoted to the topic of Sex, Gender, and Pain Response. Fifteen clinical studies comprise the volume and make powerful reading for anyone interested in how men and women respond to pain differently. Volume 107: 1.

Also, see the work of Jay Giedd, M.D., at the National Institute of Mental Health (nimh.gov). He and his lab team have posted some of their brain scans on their site, some of which show differences in the male and female brain. According to the NIMH website, "The lab studies sexual dimorphism in the developing brain (especially important in child psychiatry where nearly all disorders have different ages of onsets, prevalence and symptomatology between boys and girls)."

For more on male/female brain difference in emotional processing, please see the resources listed in the Notes for Chapter 3; my previous books on this topic; and the work of neuroscientists Louann Brizendine, Leonard Sax, and Daniel Amen.

Jeffrey Mogil appears in Sumathi Reddy, "The Problems of Treating Several Chronic Conditions," *The Wall Street Journal,* August 11, 2015.

Daniel Goleman, *Emotional Intelligence.*

Kivlighan, Katie, et al. "Gender Differences in Testosterone and Cortisol Response to Competition," *Psychoneuroendocrinology,* 2005, Vol. 30, 58-71.

Cashdan, E., "Are Men More Competitive Than Women?" *British Journal of Social Psychology,* 1998, Vol. 34, 213-229.

Geary, David and Flinn, M.V., "Sex Differences in Behavioral and Hormonal Response to Social Threat," *Psychological Review,* 2002, Vol. 109, 745-750.

David Brooks, "Is Chemistry Destiny?," *The New York Times,* September 17, 2015.

Bushman, Brad, "Does Venting Anger Feed or Extinguish the Flame? Catharsis, Rumination, Distraction, Anger, and Aggressive Responding," *Personality and Social Psychology,* 2002, Vol. 28, 724-731.

Lyubomirsky, S., and Nolen-Hoeksema, S. "Effects of Self-Focused Rumination on Negative Thinking and Interpersonal Problem Solving. *Journal of Personality and Social Psychology.* 1995, Vol. 69, 176-190.

Bushman, Brad, et al. "Chewing on it Can Chew You Up: Effects of Rumination on Displaced Aggression," *Journal of Personality and Social Psychology,* 2005, Vol. 88, 969–983.

Laura Landro, "Why Learning to Be Resilient is Good for Your Health," *The Wall Street Journal,* February 16, 2016.

Judy Foreman, "The Discomfort Zone," *The Wall Street Journal,* February 1 – 2, 2014.

Hawley, Patricia H., "The Duality of Human Nature: Coercion and Pro-sociality in Youths' Hierarchy Ascension and Social Success," *Current Directions in Psychological Science,* Vol. 23(6) 433-438.

Jena MacGregor, "Study Finds More American Workers Would Rather Work for a Male Boss," *The Washington Post,* November 14, 2013.

Russ Deniston, "'Crime' Struck Chord with Teen Nonconformist," *The Spokesman Review,* January 1, 2016.

Donna Tartt, *The Goldfinch.*

C.K. Williams, *Collected Poems.*

Tim Booth, "Hawks Won't Let Road Trip Interfere," *The Spokesman-Review,* December 21, 2015.

William Pollock, *Real Boys.*

Chapter 6

The story of Billy Cody appears in Meghan Cox Gurdon, "When Children Truly Ranged Free," *The Wall Street Journal,* December 26, 2025.

Michael Gurian, "Disappearing Act," *The Washington Post,* November 2005. To read the full article, please visit www.michaelgurian.com/articles.

Leonard Sax tells this story in *Boys Adrift.*

Geller, A.M., et al. "Gender-Dependent Behavioral and Sensory Effects of a Commercial Mixture of Polychlorinated Biphenyls," *Toxicological Science,* 2001, Vol. 59, 268-277.

Palanza, Paola, et al. "Effects of Developmental Exposure to Biphenol A on Brain and Behavior in Mice," 2008, *Environmental Research,* Vol. 108, 140 -157.

The May and June 2015 *Scientific American* provides a number of very readable and powerful articles on the workings of genetics, gene expression, and effects of neuro-toxins on genes. Diana Maron is quoted from this volume. Frank Biro is quoted from May 2015, "The Science of Health." We introduced this topic in Chapter 2 and Chapter 3, and those Endnotes include more references for this section. Also, Leonard Sax has updated *Boys Adrift* with further analysis of this topic.

Grandjean, Phillippe, et al. "Neurobehavioral Effects of Developmental Toxicity," *Lancet Neurology,* Vol. 13, 333- 338, March 2014.

See also the online summary: "Endocrine-disrupting Chemicals Pose Threat to Male Reproductive Health" in *News Medical: Science and Health,* December 11, 2015.

Colborn, Theo, et al. "Developmental Effects of Endocrine-Disrupting Chemicals in Wildlife and Humans," *Environmental Health Perspectives,* 1993, Vol. 101, 378-384.

Fisher, Jane, "Environmental Anti-androgens and Male Reproductive Health: Focus on Phthalates and Testicular Dysgenesis Syndrome," *Reproduction,* 2004, Vol. 127, 305-325.

Golub, Mari, et al. "Endocrine Disruption in Adolescence," *Toxicological Sciences,* 2004, Vol.82, 598-607.

Travison, Thomas, et al. "A Population-Level Decline in Serum Testosterone Levels in American Men," *Journal of Clinical Endocrinology and Metabolism,* 2007, Vol. 92, 196-202.

Ozen, Samim and Darcan, Sukran, "Effects of Environmental Endocrine Disruptors on Pubertal Development," *Journal of Clinical Research in Pediatric Endocrinology,* 2011, Vol. 3, 1-6.

Masuo, Yoshinori and Ishido, Masami, "Neurotoxicity of Endocrine Disruptors: Possible Involvement in Brain Development and Neurodegeneration," *Journal of Toxicology and Environmental Research,* 2008, Vol. 14, 346-349.

Aksglaede, Lise et al. "The Sensitivity of the Child to Sex Steroids:

Possible Impact of Exogenous Estrogens," *Human Reproduction Update,* 2006, Vol. 12, 341-349.

"Chemicals Present in Clear Plastics Can Impair Learning and Cause Disease," March 28, 2005, retrieved from www.yale.edu/opa/newsr/05-30-28-02.all.html.

Hojo, R., et al. "Sexually Dimorphic Behavioral Responses to Prenatal Dioxin Exposure," *Environmental Health Perspectives,* 2002, Vol. 110, 247-254.

Roy, Jonathan, et al. "Estrogen-like Endocrine Disrupting Chemicals Affecting Puberty in Humans—A Review," *Medical Science Review,* 2009, Vol. 15, 137-145.

Makin, Simon, "What Really Causes Autism," *Scientific American Mind,* November/December, 2015.

Thomas E. Brown, "ADHD: From Stereotype to Science," *Educational Leadership,* October 2015.

Daniel Amen, *Healing ADD.*

Yoshinori, Masuo, et al. "Motor Hyperactivity Caused by a Deficit in Dopaminergic Neurons and the Effects of Endocrine Disruptors," *Regulatory Peptides,* 2004, Vol. 123, 225-234.

Swan, Shanna H., et al. "Decrease in Anogenital Distance Among Male Infants with Prenatal Phthalate Exposure," *Environmental Health Perspectives,* 2005, Vol. 11, 1056-1061.

Duty, S.M, et al. "Phthalate Exposure and Reproductive Hormones in Adult Men," *Human Reproduction,* 2005, Vol. 20, 604-610.

Duty, S.M., et al. "Phthalate Exposure and Human Semen Parameters," *Epidemiology,* 2003, Vol. 14, 269-277.

McEwen, Bruce, "Steroid Hormones and Brain Development: Some Guidelines for Understanding Actions of Pseudo-hormones and Other Toxic Agents," *Environmental Health Perspectives,* 1987, Vol. 74, 177-184. As far back as the 1980s, we knew estrogen receptors could harm our children, but we did not act with scientific rigor.

MacLusky, Neil, et al. "The Environmental Estrogen Bisphenol A Inhibits Estradiol-Induced Hippocampal Synaptogenesis," *Environmental Health Perspectives,* 2005, Vol. 113, 675-679.

Fisher, Claire I, et al. "Women's Preference for Attractive Makeup Tracks Changes in their Salivary Testosterone," *Psychological Science,* Vol. 26(12) 1958-1964.

Michael Hawthorne, "Exposed: Studies Show Link Between Childhood Lead Levels and Violent Crime Years Later," *Chicago Tribune,* June 15, 2015.

Kris Maher, "City Urges Aid after Lead Found in Water," *The Wall Street Journal,* December 16, 2015.

Cameron McWhirter and Mike Vilensky, "Water Contamination Found in Vermont Wells," *The Wall Street Journal,* March 16, 2016. Flint, Michigan is not the only area of the country that must look carefully at the water our children drink. PFOA (perfluorooctanoic acid), which is used in various industrial products, joins chemicals in aluminum, lead, and other metals as potentially toxic to the brains of our children.

Anna Gorman, "Doctors Encourage Shoppers to Skip 'Bad Food'," *Tribune News Service,* January 5, 2016.

Andrew Reiner, "Teaching Men to Be Emotionally Honest," *The New York Times,* April 4, 2016.

Roets, Arne, et al. "Can Authoritarianism Lead to Greater Liking of Out-Groups? The Intriguing Case of Singapore," *Psychological Science,* 2015, Vol. 26, 1972-1974.

Lee Alan Dugatkin and Matthew Hasenjager, "The Networked Animal," *Scientific American,* June 2015.

The Winter 2015-2016 edition of *American Educator* is devoted to exploring changes that are needed in interventionist school discipline procedures and paradigms.

Tyrone Howard, "Decriminalizing School Discipline," *Education Week,* April 1, 2015.

Dr. Yuko Munakato's research can be found in Amy Drew, "Under New Management: Executive Control Across the Lifespan," *Observer: Association for Psychological Science,* Vol 28, No. 9, November 2015.

Rebecca Skloot and Ted Dawe appear in the Author's Guild Bulletin, Fall 2015, p. 5.

For much more about how to activate, achieve, and protect a Three Family System, please see my trilogy of books on raising boys, *The Wonder of Boys, The Minds of Boys,* and *The Purpose of Boys.*

Proceedings of the National Academy of Sciences are reported in Robert M. Sapolsky, "Brain Reflexes That Monitor the Pecking Order," *The Wall Street Journal,* December 12 – 13, 2015.

Discussion of winning and losing is found in Nina Sovich, "The Hardest Game for Parents," *The Wall Street Journal,* December 17, 2015.

These articles provide illustrations of the kind of aggression nurturance dads often provide. As has been noted by many researchers over the last five decades, and as we've noted throughout this book, the issue of fatherlessness is a crucial one for both boys and girls, and it is one to which some powerful DGP adherents in the Big Three have attached neither their rancor nor their indifference. Family Courts are caught in the middle, not sure if protecting women and children is the same as protecting men and fathers.

Ned Holstein, M.D., National Director of the National Parents Organization, has thoroughly studied the family court system and made these powerful points in a recent blog on our Commission to Create a White House Council listserve. I hope you will find these helpful and go to www.nationalparentsorganization.org to see the combination of grassroots and legislative effort the NPO provides.

"Unfortunately, family courts announce loudly and clearly that fathers are useful as payers of child support, but otherwise their participation as fathers in the rearing of their children is purely optional— nice if it happens, but really of very little value. Here are a few among numerous data points:

1. Our federal government spends close to $5 billion on enforcing child support, and only about $10 million on fatherhood programs (most of which are, in fact, child support programs, since child support collection is the most commonly used outcome measure of these programs).
2. According to the U.S. Census Bureau, about 83 percent of all children whose parents are apart are in the sole custody of mothers, and there is a near-complete lack of enforcement of 'visitation' orders, even though they have been adjudicated as being in the best interest of the child and are valid court orders.
3. According to a report of the Urban Institute, many children are put into foster care as a result of maternal abuse or neglect without any attempt to identify or locate the fathers to determine if they might be a suitable placement, even when the fathers are paying child support and are thus readily found.
4. There are endless discussions in family court and in academic papers about whether it is safe to allow children to be with their fathers, but no similar discussion about mothers, even though mothers commit more child abuse than fathers do.
5. A number of scholarly studies show that majorities of both men and women, and even family law attorneys, believe there is gender bias in the family courts, yet the bias, unfortunately, has not significantly diminished.
6. Studies also show that family court judges decide hypothetical cases differently when presented with two scenarios, the only difference between them being the gender of the parent.
7. There is a national readiness to issue millions of restraining orders that separate fathers and children without any evidence other than the mother's accusation; this indicates a belief that fathering is of not enough value to require even a minimal show of evidence.
8. As recently emphasized by the federal Office of Child Support Enforcement, there is a significant promulgation of child support orders for poor parents that are clearly unpayable; these have the effect of turning poor fathers into fugitives. This process is only reinforced by the extraordinarily high interest rates and penalties that are piled on top of unpaid child support. Thus, children lose the only potential benefits available from indigent fathers, namely, their love, guidance, support and occasional overcoat or bag of groceries."

The court system is filled with good people trying to do good work who are burdened by a Dominant Gender Paradigm that pits women and men against one another. Hopefully the next two decades of American social change will evolve toward a deeper understanding of male emotional intelligence.

If we can get to this new place in social reform, we will rescue fathering and thus rescue our children. In doing this, the mother's love of her children will also be uplifted because the partnership with the father will ensure her children's health and well-being—which is, ultimately, her primary and loving goal as a mom.

Maggie Gray, "Interview with Michael B. Jordan," *Sportsillustrated.com,* December 7, 2015.

Austin Murphy, "You're My Boy, Blue!", *Sports Illustrated,* March 9, 2015.

Aggression Nurturance even appears in "It's A Wonderful Life" in a way that is central to the beautiful and general tenderness of the film. I hadn't realized this until I read Froma Harrop's commentary, "Eerie Parallels to 'Wonderful Life," in *The Spokesman-Review,* December 20, 2014.

Sue Shellenbarger, "Moms, Let Dads Be Dad," *The Wall Street Journal,* June 17, 2015.

Further online research on the need for fathers appears in these online resources. These links may be archived but should remain easily accessible for a long time so that you can use them as social media blasts and discussions immediately.

Larry Elder says the problem in the black community is fatherlessness. https://www.facebook.com/federalistfox/videos/261321660906306/

BYU research finds link between father absences and declining male college enrollment. http://www.heraldextra.com/news/local/education/college/byu/byu-research-finds-link-between-father-absences-and-declining-male/article_7cafa756-967a-5399-a9a1-596db17bbd83.html.

Fathers play a large role in their children's development, from language and cognitive growth in toddlerhood to social skills in fifth grade, according to new findings from Michigan State University scholars.https://www.sciencedaily.com/releases/2016/07/160714110912.html.

Barbara Kay, "Want to help society? Let kids know their fathers," *National Post,* June 16, 2016 http://news.nationalpost.com/full-comment/barbara-kay-want-to-help-society-let-kids-know-their-fathers.

Megan Daley, "Five Things Pediatricians Want Dads to Know about Fathering," *The Los Angeles Times,* June 13, 2016, reporting multiple studies in Science and other journals corroborating the importance of fathers in building emotional intelligence, social success, and cognitive development in boys and girls.

Martin Daubney, "How Dad Deprivation May Be Eroding Society," *The Daily Telegraph,* June 22, 2016.

Lack of healthy father influence leads to poorer behavior among boys and, as new studies have confirmed, poor behavior early in life leads to significant issues later. For a very accessible glimpse into the research see Nick Morrison, "Poor Behavior Hits Boys Hardest," *Forbes Magazine,* Jun 22, 2016.

"Paternal Nurturance" can appear in the most unlikely places. Elizabeth Bernstein, in 'Self-Talk,' (*The Wall Street Journal,* May 6, 2014), tells a wonderful story of her father's motivational techniques.

Carlos Lozada, "The Art of Bromance," *The Washington Post,* May 31,

2015.

Carlos Lozada, "Trump and Our Stone-Age Brain," *The Washington Post.*
Paul Tournier, *The Whole Person in a Broken World,* New York: Harper, 1964.

Chapter 7

To delve even deeper into male and female maturation see my previous books on this subject, noted in the chapter, and also the studies earlier noted in brain biology and gender differences.

Jay N. Giedd, "The Amazing Teen Brain," *Scientific American,* June 2015.

Jaffe, Eric, "Portrait of Self-Control as a Young Process," *Journal of the Association for Psychological Science,* July/August 2015, Vol. 28, No. 6.

Casey, B.J., "Beyond Simple Models of Self-Control to Circuit-Based Accounts of Adolescent Behavior, *Annual Review of Psychology,* 2015, Vol 66, 295-319.

Matt Richtel, "A Silicon Valley School that Doesn't Compute," *The New York Times,* October 22, 2011.

Jim Taylor, "Is the American Academy of Pediatrics Copping Out on Screens," *Psychology Today,* October 13, 2015.

Please also see the American Academy of Pediatrics new guidelines of October 2016.

Up-to-date "blue light" research is referenced in Alexia Elejalde-Ruiz's "Harsh on the Eyes," *Chicago Tribune,* January 12, 2016.

Catlin Tucker, "Creating a Safe Digital Space," *Educational Leadership,* October 2015.

Kevin Clark, "The NFL'S Laboratory for Millennials," *The Wall Street Journal,* September 15, 2015.

Joel Cooper and Kimberlee Weaver, *Gender and Computers: Understanding the Digital Divide.*

George, Madeleine J. and Odgers, Candice L., "Seven Fears and the Science of How Mobile Technologies May Be Influencing Adolescents in the Digital Age," *Perspectives on Psychological Science,* 2015, Vol. 10(6) 832-851

Sue Shellenbarger, "We Want Our Children to Code, Even if We Can't," *The Wall Street Journal,* February 10, 2016. In this article is an example of a family in which children are introduced to intense computer use through coding by age 6. If we could study children longitudinally, especially young males, I believe we will find, in 20 years, a high probability of later social-emotional issues for children whose brains are linked to technologies so young.

Charlie Wells, "Smartphones Go to School," *The Wall Street Journal,* February 18, 2016.

Deborah Perkins-Gough, "Secrets of the Teenage Brain," *Educational Leadership,* October 2015.

Casey, B.J., et al. "Behavioral and Neural Correlates of Delay of

Gratification 40 Years Later," *Proceedings of the National Academy of Sciences,* 2011, Vol. 108, 14998-15003.

Galvan, A., et al. "Earlier Development of the Accumbens Relative to Orbitofrontal Cortex Might Underlie Risk-Taking Behavior in Adolescents," *The Journal of Neuroscience,* 2006, Vol. 26, 6885-6892.

Amy Ellis Nutt, "Loneliness Can Be Lethal Health Risk, Scientists Say," *The Washington Post,* February 1, 2016.

You can learn more about obesity genetics and the new trend of genetic testing in workplaces in Rachel Emma Silverman, "Genetic Testing May Be Coming to Your Office," *The Wall Street Journal,* December 16, 2015.

See also:

Mead, Nathaniel, "Origins of Obesity: Chemical Exposures," *Environmental Health Perspectives,* 2004, Vol.112, A344.

Berkey, Catherine, et al. "Activity, Dietary Intake, and Weight Changes in a Longitudinal Study of Preadolescent and Adolescent Boys and Girls," *Pediatrics,* 2000, Vol. 105, e56.

Mario, Stervo, et al. "Frequent Video Game Playing in Young Males is Associated with Central Adiposity and High-Sugar, Low-Fibre Dietary Consumption," *Eating and Weight Disorders,* 2014, Vol. 19, 515-520.

Vandewater, Elizabeth, et al. "Linking Obesity and Activity Level with Children's Television and Video Game Use," *Journal of Adolescence, 2004,* Vol. 27, 71-85.

Bob Granleese, "Why Are British Kids So Unhappy? Two Words: Screen Time," *The Guardian,* January 16, 2016.

Lindsay Holmes, "Sneaky Ways Technology Is Messing with Your Body and Mind," Huffington Post, December 5, 2014.

Joel M. Moskowitz and Larry Junck, "Do Cellphones Need Warning Labels?" *The Wall Street Journal,* May 23, 2016.

Susan Pinker, "To Beat the Blues, Visits Must Be Real, Not Virtual," *The Wall Street Journal,* June 4-5, 2016. This is a pithy and very powerful article on the science of loneliness—and the necessity of real life to combat it. Virtual life can often amplify depression, not help it.

Matsuda, Goh and Hiraki, Kazuo, "Sustained Decrease in Oxygenated Hemoglobin During Video Games in the Dorsal Prefrontal Cortex: A NIRS study of Children," *Neuroimage,* 2006, Vol. 29, 706-711.

Hummer, Tom, et al. "Short-Term Violent Video Game Play by Adolescents Alters Prefrontal Activity During Cognitive Inhibition," *Media Psychology,* 2010, Vol. 13, 136-154.

Bartholow, Bruce, et al. "Chronic Violent Video Game Exposure and Desensitization to Violence," *Journal of Experimental Social Psychology,* 2006, Vol. 42, 532-539.

Gentile, Douglas, et al. "The Effects of Violent Videogame Habits on Adolescent Hostility, Aggressive Behaviors, and School Performance," *Journal of Adolescence,* 2004, Vol. 27, 5-22.

David Williamson Shaffer, *How Computer Games Help Children Learn.*

Sadie Dingfelder, "Your Brain on Video Games," February 2007, *Monitor on Psychology,* http://www.apa.org/monitor/feb07/yourbrain.html.

A somewhat different view than mine on technology and electronics appears in Danah Boyd's "Let Kids Run Wild Online," *Time,* March 24, 2014.

A very good use of video games for the brain appears in "Videogames So Tough They Teach You to Win in Life," by Chris Suellentrop, *The Wall Street Journal,* May 14-15, 2016.

Zilioli, Samuele, et al. "Interest in Babies Negatively Predicts Testosterone Responses to Sexual Visual Stimuli Among Heterosexual Young Men," *Psychological Science,* 2016, Vol 27(1) 114-118.

The January/February 2016 edition of the *Psychotherapy Networker* is dedicated almost exclusively to Sex and Sexuality. I highly recommend this issue of the magazine for anyone interested in learning more about pornography, male/female differences in sexual interest, and the hook up culture among our teens and young adults.

Erin Anderssen, "Our Porn-Saturated Media Landscape is Wreaking Havoc on Teen Boys, too," *The Globe and Mail,* April 14, 2016.

Joanna Ellington, *Slippery When Wet.*

Julie Schwartz Gottman and John Gottman, "Lessons from the Love Lab," *Psychotherapy Networker,* November/December, 2015.

Cynthia M. Allen, "Faith, Education Dovetail After All," *Forth Worth Star-Telegram,* April 20, 2014.

Tim Wright, *Searching for Tom Sawyer,* Phoenix: TWM Press, 2014. For much more about these powerful rite of passage programs please visit www.timwrightministries.org.

Hafiz's *The Gift* is translated by Daniel Ladinsky.

Abraham Joshua Heschel, *The Sabbath.*

William Watson, S.J., *Sacred Story.* To learn more about Fr. Watson's Forty Weeks Program visit www.sacredstory.net.

Michael Gurian, *How Do I Help Him?*

Michael Gurian, *A Fine Young Man.*

E-school News reported the gap in February, 22, 2016 based on federal data. "Low-income students enroll in school having heard 30 million fewer words than their peers from more affluent homes, researchers have found. The gap is even wider for English-language learners."

Robert J. Samuelson, "Jobless Young Pose Global Risks," *The Wall Street Journal,* June 9, 2015.

WDAF – TV reported the EMT program on February 18, 2016, "Missouri School District Creates EMT Program," saying: "Kansas City Public Schools in Missouri is teaming up with Metropolitan Community College and the Kansas City Fire Department to offer a training program for high-school students interested in becoming emergency medical technicians or paramedics. Students will be able to take the EMT class during the school year, and some students may be hired as apprentices as soon as they complete the program, officials say."

Special thanks are due my longtime collaborator, Gary Plep, who helped gather comments from Silicon Valley executives on the immaturity of much of the young male workforce.

Chapter 8

Gerald Skoning, "The Mythical 'Pay Equity' Crisis," *The Wall Street Journal,* October 14, 2014.

Jim Puzzanghera and Evan Halper, "Obama Moves to Close Gap in Women's, Minority Pay," *Chicago Tribune News Service,* January 30, 2016.

Sherry Jones and Janet Chung, "Pregnant Workers Measure Overdue," *The Spokesman-Review,* February 13, 2016.

Amartya Sen, "Women's Progress," *The Wall Street Journal,* January 2-3, 2016.

Joanna L. Krotz, "Being Equal Doesn't Mean Being the Same," joannakrotz.com, January 21, 2016.

The 2013 national poll on modern parenthood was conducted by the Pew Research Center. The study asked mothers and fathers to identify their "ideal" working arrangement. Fifty percent of mothers said they would prefer to work part-time and 11 percent said they would prefer not to work at all. Fathers answered differently: 75 percent preferred full-time work. *And the higher the socio-economic status of women, the more likely they were to reject full-time employment.* Among women with annual family incomes of $50,000 or higher, only 25 percent identified full-time work as their ideal.

W. Bradford Wilcox, "The Matrimony Gap," *The Wall Street Journal,* June 21-22, 2014.

Christina Sommers and Warren Farrell, mentioned earlier, are two social thinkers who bolster the "choice" and "freedom" movement.

June Carbone & Naomi Cahn, *Marriage Market.*

Christina Zander, "Even Scandinavia Has a CEO Gender Gap," *The Wall Street Journal,* May 22, 2014.

Julie Rovner, "NIH May Not Be Sorting Clinical Trial Data by Sex," *Kaiser Health News,* November 29, 2015.

Sue Shellenbarger, "When the Only Thing Holding You Back is Self-Doubt," *The Wall Street Journal,* April 15, 2015.

Darcy Walker, "The Anguish and Value of the Stay-at-Home Feminist," *The Wall Street Journal,* May 9-10, 2015.

Kay Hymowitz, "Fractured Families," *The Wall Street Journal,* January 6, 2015.

Joe Palazzolo, "Prison Population Cuts Catch On," *The Wall Street Journal,* January 2-3, 2016.

Henry C. Jackson, "Texas Aims to Make Inmates into Entrepreneurs," *Associated Press,* January 18, 2015.

The *Times* Staff, "Executions across the U.S. Decline to 24-year Low," *Los Angeles Times,* January 3, 2016.

Aida Midgett, "Bullying: How Counselors Can Intervene," *Counseling Today*, June 2016.

Bullying statistics vary depending on the source because what is defined as bullying differs between sources. Because some of what I have defined as aggression nurturance now counts as bullying, I would estimate that the commonly accepted statistics of one in four or one in five children bullied at school to be high.

Check out the Center for Disease Control, for instance, http://americanspcc.org/bullying/statistics-and-information/?gclid=Cj0KEQjwy um6BRDQ, and you can find further statistics at http://americanspcc.org/bullying/statistics-and-information/.

Any bullying at all is too much, obviously. I have written extensively on bullying and provided resources to prevent bullying in such works as *The Minds of Boys*, and will continue to assist communities in dealing with bullying and cyber-bullying.

Simultaneously, I also believe we must become more realistic about what is bullying and what is not. By some present definitions of bullying, every child is bullied, and if you spend time on Google, you can even find reputable "studies" that claim exactly that. If that is the case, then every sibling has bullied his/her sibling repeatedly and been bullied repeatedly. To me, this approach to bullying trivializes the actual and dangerous bullying that goes on among our children and adults.

Stephen Moore, "President Obama, Are You Listening?" *The Wall Street Journal*, May 2-3, 2015.

Corey Mitchell, "Boys-Only Programs Raise Legal Concerns," *Education Week*, March 4, 2015.

These articles refer to the ACLU and Executive Office attacks on single gender schools. I have supported the ACLU over the years on free speech issues but on gender issues, both the ACLU and the Obama Administration fell on the wrong side of science and common sense.

The ACLU began this trend by deciding to align with a few people who formed the "American Council for Coeducational Schooling (ACCS)" to attack the single-gender classroom movement in public schools. These people use the "gender equality requires gender sameness" myth to team up with the ACLU to accuse single-gender teachers and schools of illegal activity (gender discrimination) and severe danger to children's psyches via "gender stereotypes." Some of the schools the Gurian Institute works with are coeducational schools that utilize single-gender classes to teach math/science and language arts, and we work with single-gender academies.

These schools (see www.gurianinstitute.com/success) are having great success in closing achievement gaps and educating our nation's children, both female and male, but the ACLU and the ACCS attack them and us with rhetoric that 1) shows no proof of danger to children in single gender classes, and 2) pretends success of these classrooms doesn't exist. These ideologues even pretend the science of gender doesn't exist! This is attack politics at its worst; it closes down these programs and schools not because the attacker is right but because the attacker is well-funded.

Two schools under siege by these people are Gurian Institute Model Schools (schools in which all personnel have been trained in nature-based theory and male/female brain difference) located in Hillsboro Country Public Schools. Their predecessor institutions were failing and nearly shut down. Now the schools are A schools with some of the best test scores and graduation rates in the state. They serve mainly disadvantaged populations and their brave teachers and staff have literally saved many young lives from crime and early death. Despite their clear success for (and lack of harm to) their hundreds of students, the ACLU manipulated Title IX and other laws to attack their single-gender option.

If you would like to witness the ACLU straw man arguments, go to the aclu.org website and obtain its "Teach Kids, Not Stereotypes" document. Reading that very slick document you'll want to shut every person in America down who even thinks about a single sex classroom! Until you realize: wait a minute, this is all ideological air. The "harm" only makes sense if you buy the DGP ideology that anything "boy" or "girl" is gender stereotyping and thus, inherently, harmful because "boy" and "girl" are just patriarchal social constructs that damage children.

But if you don't start from the extreme DGP position, the ACLU position crumbles. Once you use cost-benefit analysis to determine if the old gender equity paradigm is still working, you'll see how much disservice this kind of document does to children. Millions of dollars are spent in the school districts such as Hillsboro to answer 60,000 pages of ACLU and OPR (Office of Public Review) attack/inquiry. This is taxpayer money spent to defend against not a valid or proven claim, but an ideology that focuses nearly always on what a certain group (the ACLU funders) think is good for girls (or not good). Notice, too, that they keep us focused on their ideology by creating hobgoblins—generally male—so people remain scared, androphobic, and paralyzed.

As I made these points at one particular governmental meeting, one of the supervisors opened a very thick book, *What Is a Man?* by sociologist Walter R. Newell, who wrote in 2001 about the irony of righting social wrongs through equity enhancement that use a limited paradigm of equity.

"The last thirty years have witnessed a prolonged effort at social engineering throughout our public and educational institutions. Its purpose is to eradicate any psychological and emotional differences between men and women, on the grounds that any concept of manliness inevitably leads to arrogance and violence toward women, and to rigid hierarchies that exclude the marginalized and powerless. This experiment was meant to reduce violence and tensions between the sexes. And yet, during this same period, 'macho' violence and stress between men and women has increased. Recent crime statistics suggest as much in the United States, Canada, and the UK— the countries where the feminist social experiment stigmatizing manliness has had the greatest latitude to prove itself."

After he read this aloud we talked about it and some people reacted negatively but most did not. Most agreed. That alerted me, the facilitator, that, in fact, a new gender equity conversation might not be impossible in this room so I gave the quote from Garrison Keillor: "Manhood was once an opportunity for achievement; now, it is a problem to be overcome." What does everyone think of that? I asked.

A discussion ensued. Because the majority of people in the room were actually open to discussing new gender equity possibilities, the "paralysis" some people noticed before was recognizable now as more of a loud attack by a few individuals that most people—especially those in the room who have children—did not share at a deep level. From here we could look at a social revolution against imprisoning ideologies.

So we moved to other straw man arguments. Someone in the room brought up the "rape culture" and we moved into the material in Chapter 4. Quickly, most people in this meeting saw the games being played with the statistics. We all agreed that even a single rape is too many, but once we deconstructed that straw man argument, we had a foothold to use more science and less attack politics. We moved now to PET, fMRI, and SPECT scans of the male and female brains.

This moment in a meeting room is always electric. Most people in the room like this one have masters, doctorates, or MDs, but they sit back in amazement when they see the brain scans. They had not seen these scans in undergraduate or graduate school. In the room that day were also some people who had been very anti-science before, claiming that admitting male and female brain difference is "junk science" but now they could barely raise an objection; the pictures were too powerful.

So I asked people in the room to give me the other areas of gender inequity against females that they sense are flawed straw man arguments. They responded: "Women don't have equal pay for equal work—77 cents on the dollar is unfair to females."

I pointed out the political complexity of that statement, as we noted in this chapter. According to decades of research through the American Enterprise Institute, women's and men's pay *for equal work* is generally equal with some exceptions (for instance, the Women's World Cup Soccer team was paid less than male World Cup team members even though the women won the World Cup). These cases must clearly be redressed and various laws are being enforced to address them. When enforcement of those laws is not enough, tort and court systems under federal and state law provide the avenue for redress.

Meanwhile, my own work as a gender consultant in various Fortune 500 corporations, as well as the work of Barbara Annis who has provided consulting to dozens of these companies, show these issues beneath the surface: women are less likely to self-promote or negotiate for raises than men (less naturally aggressive in the pay process); and women tend to work fewer hours than men in the same job, choosing not to travel away from home as much as men do. Our gender consulting is set up to help women self-promote better and more aggressively so that they can be better paid. At the same time, if men put two more hours a day into their job via travel and commute, there will always be some pay gap that favors the longer-hour workday.

But perhaps most politically unfair in the 77 cents on the dollar figure is the fact that, while it is meant by politicians to stand for a major discrepancy in wages for equal work, this *aggregate income during work years* gap will never close since males tend to stay in the money-earning workforce throughout their lifetimes, gaining a higher aggregate income. The majority of their wives/partners, once children come, have chosen (if possible), as noted in the chapter, to take many years off from full money-earning in order to care for children in the home. Thus there is a pay gap of 77 cents on the dollar.

Given that the very men who earn more money during child-raising years give that money in partnership with their spouse to support women and children, simplifying the gender conversation to "77 cents on the dollar" does a grave disservice to women who have chosen their lives and men who help them make that life-choice by supporting them.

While protecting women who really are discriminated against in wage earning is sacred work and will continue via law and tort, the 77 cents on the dollar is a straw man argument we must rethink if we are to fully support our children and our families.

Another person said, "Most funding in America is spent on things that help boys and men not girls and women."

This statement got answered by others in the room who pointed out that this is a false statement, though politically useful, as we noted in the chapter.

Other statements in the room:

"Until girls and women get the engineering and CEO jobs that males have, we won't have gender equity."

"Most of American education, from Pre-K through college is still about white males, so gender equity isn't even close to happening in America."

"Gender stereotypes favoring males and masculinity permeate American culture and oppress females; until we get rid of them there is no gender equity for women."

"The highest levels of government and business are run mainly by men thus we can't do anything but see 'gender equity' as something women need, not men."

To help with each of these I provided some of the analysis in this book. I also suggested the teams use short video clips by Christina Hoff Sommers at the American Enterprise Institute. These are on YouTube and you can use them in your meetings. They provide a visual counterpoint to some of the usual straw man arguments.

http://conversationswithbillkristol.org/video/christina-hoff-sommers/?start=15&end=376

http://www.youtube.com/playlist?list=PLytTJqkSQqtr7BqC1Jf4nv3g2y Dfu7Xmd

A final "straw man" was: "Well, we don't know what will work to help boys, so we should wait to do anything until we study everything further." While close study of an issue is generally very useful, the straw man isn't true.

We do know a great deal about what works, as this book and many other resources have shown. Sometimes this straw man is used just as evidence of lazy reporting or lack of knowledge, but sometimes it is used as a way of paralyzing social change—keeping the revolutionary conversation about boys on a back burner.

Ultimately in that room, after all straw man arguments were answered, the final takeaway regarding gender equity in the new millennium became: every governmental, legal, academic, and social organization must move forward toward new ways of discussing gender that involve *science*. Once they do, they have a framework for understanding gender that is as potentially powerful as the DGP. Until then, I don't think they will be able to advance full gender equity.

We must remember: the feminist movement and the DGP assessment of males were created "pre-science" (around 1960) before the brain sciences found full form. Now, we can move gender equity out of old paradigms, whether patriarchal or DGP, to fully protect women and girls, and boys and men in ways that are equitable, complementary, and ultimately help our females as much as our males.

Isaac Cohen, "An 'Ether of Sexism' Doesn't Explain Gender Disparities in Science and Tech," *Forbes Magazine*, July 30, 2014.

Betty Friedan, *The Feminine Mystique*.

Epilogue

Ella Wheeler Wilcox, "Protest," *Poems of Problems*, 1914.

Christina Sommers, "The Boys at the Back," *The New York Times*, February 3, 2013. Also please see Dr. Sommers' *The War on Boys* and *Freedom Feminism*.

The quotation about misandry in 2016 is taken off a private listserv.

E.O. Wilson, *The Meaning of Human Existence*.

E.O. Wilson, *Consilience*.

Rilke is quoted from "Man Watching."

Bibliography

Amen, Daniel. (2013) *Unleashing the Power of the Female Brain.* Bantam. New York .

_____. (2010) *Change Your Brain, Change Your Life.* Bantam. New York.

_____. (2006) *Healing A.D.D.* Bantam. New York.

_____. (2005) *Sex on the Brain.* Bantam. New York.

Arnot, Robert. (2001) *The Biology of Success.* Little Brown & Company. Boston, MA.

Baron-Cohen, Simon. (2003) *The Essential Difference.* Basic Books. New York.

Bear, Mark; Connors, Barry; Paradiso, Michael. (1996). *Neuroscience.* Williams and Wilkins. Baltimore, M.D.

Benbow, Camilla and Lubinski, David. (1997) *Intellectual Talent.* Johns Hopkins University Press.

Blum, Deborah. (1998) *Sex On the Brain.* Penguin Books. New York.

Borba, Michelle. (2016). *Unselfie.* Touchstone: New York.

Brizendine, Louann. (2007) *The Female Brain.* Three Rivers Press. New York.

_____ (2011). *The Male Brain.* Harmony: New York.

Brott, Armin. (2010) *The Expectant Father.* Abbeville Press. New York.

_____. (2009) *The Military Father.* Abbeville Press. New York.
Browne, Rollo and Fletcher, Richard. (1994) *Boys in Schools.* Finch Publishing. Sydney.

Bly, Robert. (1996). *The Sibling Society.* Addison-Wesley Publishing. Boston, MA.

Bly, Robert; Meade, Michael; Hillman, James. (1993) *The Rag and Bone Shop of the Heart.* Harper. San Francisco.

Carbone, June and Cahn, Naomi. (2014) *Marriage Markets.* Oxford University Press. Oxford.

Carr-Morse, Robin. (1998) *Ghosts from the Nursery*. Atlantic Monthly Press. New York.

Carson, Ann. (2002) *The Beauty of the Husband*. Vintage. New York.

Carter, Rita. (1998) *Mapping the Mind*. U. of CA Press. Los Angeles, CA.

Cooper, Joel and Weaver, Kimberlee. (2003). *Gender and Computers*. Lawrence Erlbaum: Mahwah, NJ.

Deak, JoAnn (2003) *Girls Will Be Girls*. Hyperion. New York.

Diamond, Jed. (2005) . *The Irritable Male Syndrome*. Rodale: New York.

Ellington, Joanna. (2015) *Slippery When Wet,* JDK Publications. Spokane.

Faludi, Susan. (2000) *Stiffed*. Harper Perennial. New York.

Farrell, Warren. (2000). *The Myth of Male Power*. Berkeley. New York.

Flinders, Carol. (2002). *The Values of Belonging*. HarperSanFrancisco. San Francisco.

Friedan, Betty (1963) *The Feminine Mystique*. Norton. New York.

_____ (1981/1998). *The Second Stage*. Harvard University. Cambridge.

Fogarty, Robin. (1997) *Brain Compatible Classrooms*. Skylight Professional Development. Arlington Heights, IL.

Garbarino, James. (1999) *Lost Boys*. The Free Press., New York.

Gilligan, Carol. (1998). *In A Different Voice*. Harvard University Press: Boston.

Gilmore, David. (1990). *Manhood in the Making*. Yale University Press. New Haven.

Golden, T. R. (2000). *Swallowed by a Snake*. GH Publishing, LLC. Gaithersburg, MD.

Goleman, Daniel. (1995). *Emotional Intelligence*. Bantam. New York.

Griffits, Frank, et.al., including Kathryn Boak McPherson. (2012). *Why Teens Fail*. Be the One: Phoenix, AZ.

Gurian, J.P. & J. (1983) *The Dependency Tendency*. Rowman and Littlefield.

Gurian, Michael. (2011) *How Do I Help Him?* Gurian Institute. Spokane, WA.

Gurian, Michael, with Kathy Stevens. (2005) *The Minds of Boys*. Jossey-Bass. San Francisco.

Gurian, Michael., et.al. (2011) *Boys and Girls Learn Differently! A Guide for Teachers and Parents*. Jossey-Bass. San Francisco, Tenth Anniversary Edition.

_____. (2006) *The Wonder of Boys*. Tarcher-Putnam. New York, Tenth Anniversary Edition
_____. (2002) *The Wonder of Girls*. Pocket Books. New York.

_____. (1998) *A Fine Young Man*. Tarcher-Putnam. New York.

Harris, Judith R. (1998) *The Nurture Assumption*. Free Press. New York.

Hallowell, Edward and Ratey, John. (1994) *Driven to Distraction*. Touchstone. New York.

Heschel, Abraham Joshua. (2005) *The Sabbath*. Farrar Straus: New York.

Hymowitz, Kay. (2012). *Manning Up*. Basic Books: New York.

Jantz, Gregory; Gurian, Michael; MacMurray, Ann. (2013) *Raising Boys by Design*. Waterbrook/Multnomah: New York.

Jensen, Eric. (1995, 200 Rev.) *Brain-Based Learning*. The Brain Store. San Diego, CA.

Jessel, David and Moir, Anne. (1989) *Brain Sex*. Dell. New York.

Johnson, Steven. (2004). *Mind Wide Open*. Scribner. New York.

Jung, Carl, edited by Claire Douglas. (1997) *Visions*. Princeton University Press. Princeton.

Kandel Eric; Schwartz, James; Jessell, Thomas. (1995). *Essentials of Neural Science and Behavior*. Appleton & Lange. Norwalk, Connecticut.

Karges-Bone, Linda. (1998) *More Than Pink & Blue*. Teaching and Learning Company, 1204 Buchanan St., Carthage, IL.

Kipnis, Aaron. (1999) *Angry Young Men*. Jossey-Bass. San Francisco.

Kiselica, Mark; Englar-Carson, Matt; Horne, Arthur M. (Editors) (2007) *Counseling Troubled Boys*. Routledge Publishers. New York..

Kindlon, Dan. and Thompson, Michael. (2000) *Raising Cain*. Ballantine. New York.

Koertge, Noretta. (2000) *A House Built On Sand*, Oxford University Press. Oxford.

Kundtz, David. (2004). *Nothing's Wrong*. Conari Press: Boston.

Ladinsky, Daniel, trans. (1999) *The Gift by Hafiz*. Penguin Compass. New York.

Ladner, Joyce. (2003). *Launching Our Black Children for Success*. Jossey-Bass/John Wiley. San Francisco.

Levine, Mel. (2002) *A Mind at a Time*. Simon & Schuster. New York.

McElroy, Wendy. (2016). *Rape Culture Hysteria: Fixing the Damage Done to Men and Women*, CreateSpace.

Moir, Anne and Bill. (1999). *Why Men Don't Iron*. Citadel. New York.

Moir, Anne and Jessel, David (1990) *Brain Sex*. Laurel. New York.

Murphy, Shane. (1999) *The Cheers and the Tears: A Healthy Alternative to the Dark Side of Youth Sports Today*. Jossey-Bass/John Wiley. San Francisco.

Newell, Walter R. (2000) *What is a Man?* Regan Books. New York.

Nylund, David. (2000) *Treating Huckleberry Finn*. Jossey-Bass/John Wiley. New York.

Paglia, Camille. (1991) *Sexual Personae*. Vintage: New York.

Parker, Kathleen. (2010) *Save The Males*. Random House: New York.

Payne, Ruby. (2000) *A Framework for Understanding Poverty*. AhaProcess, Inc. Highlands, Texas.

Pease, Barbara and Allan. (1999) *Why Men Don't Listen, And Women Can't Read Maps*. Broadway Books. New York.

Pinker, Steven. (2003) *The Blank Slate*, Penguin: New York,

Pollack, William. (1998) *Real Boys*. Henry Holt, New York.

Ratey, John and Eric Hagerman. (2008) *Spark*. Little Brown. New York.

Ravitch, Diane. (2003) *The Language Police: How Pressure Groups Restrict What Children Learn*. Alfred A. Knopf. New York.

Real, Terrence. (1997). *I Don't Want to Talk About It*. Fireside. New York.

Rhoads, Steven E. (2004) *Taking Sex Differences Seriously*. Encounter Books. San Francisco.

Rilke, Rainer Maria, trans. Anita Barrows. (2005). *Books of Hours*. Riverhead: New York.

Rosin, Hanna. (2013). *The End of Men*, Riverhead: New York.

Salomone, Rosemary C. (2003) *same, different, equal*. Yale University Press. New Haven.

Sandberg, Sheryl. (2013). *Lean In*. Knopf: New York.

Sax, Leonard. (2005). *Why Gender Matters*. Doubleday. New York

_____ (2009, updated 2016). *Boys Adrift*. Basic Books. New York.

Shaffer, David Williamson. (2006) *How Computer Games Help Children Learn*, Palgrave Macmillan. New York.

Siegel, Daniel J. (1999). *The Developing Mind*. Guilford Press. New York.

Slocumb, Paul. (2004). *Boys In Crisis*. Aha Process, Inc. Highlands, Texas.

Smith, Michael W. and Wilhelm, Jeffrey D. (2002) *Reading Don't Fix No Chevy's: Literacy in the Lives of Young Men*. Heinenmann. Portsmouth.

Sommers, Christina Hoff. (2000) *The War on Boys*. Touchstone. New York.

_____(2013) *Freedom Feminism*. AEI Press. Washington, D.C.

Sousa, David. A. (2001) *How the Brain Learns*. Corwin Press. Thousand Oaks, CA.

Sprenger, Marilee. (2002) *Becoming A "Wiz" at Brain-Based Teaching: How to Make Every Year Your Best Year*. Corwin Press. Thousand Oaks, CA.

Stephenson, Bret. (2004) *Slaying the Dragon*. www.adolescentmid.com. Stein, David. (1999) *Ritalin Is Not The Answer*. Jossey-Bass. San Francisco.

Sykes, Bryan. (2003) *Adam's Curse*. W.W. Norton & Company. New York.

Szalavitz, Maia. (2016) *Unbroken Brain*. St. Martin's Press. New York

Tannen, Deborah. (1991) *You Just Don't Understand*. William Morrow. New York.

Taylor, Shelley E. (2002). *The Tending Instinct*. Times Books. New York.

Tartt, Donna. (2013) The Goldfinch. Back Bay Books: New York.

Thompson, Michael. (2009) *It's a Boy!* Ballantine. New York.

Verhaagen, David A. (2010). *Therapy with Young Men*. Routledge. New York.

Watson, William, SJ. (2012) *Sacred Story.* Seattle. Sacred Story Press.

Walsh, William. (2014) *Nutrient Power*. New York: Skyhorse Publishing.

Wexler, David. (2009) *Men in Therapy*. Norton. New York.

Whitmire, Richard. (2010) *Why Boys Fail.* AMACOM. New York.

Williams, C.K. (2007). *Collected Poems*, Farrar Strauss. New York.

Wilson, E.O. (2015) *The Meaning of Human Existence*, Liveright. New York,

_____ (1999) *Consilience*, Vintage: New York.

Wiseman, Rosalind. (2014) *Masterminds and Wingmen*. Harmony: New York

Wolfe, Patricia. (2001) *Brain Matters*. Assoc. for Supervision and Curriculum Development.

Woody, Jane DiVita. (2002) *How Can We Talk About That?* Jossey-Bass. San Francisco.

Wright, Tim. (2014) *Searching for Tom Sawyer* TWM Publishers. Phoenix, AZ.

Zeff, Ted. (2010) *The Strong Sensitive Boy.* Prana Publishing. San Francisco.

Appendix

HERE IS A SHORT blog you can distribute without having to get my own or my publisher's permission as long as you credit the blog "By Dr. Michael Gurian, from *Saving Our Sons.*"

If I Were a Parent of a Boy…

By Dr. Michael Gurian, Author of *Saving Our Sons*
(www.michaelgurian.com)

In working with her family therapy clients over the last thirty years, my wife, Gail, has said, "If I were a parent of a boy, I would really be worried." She is referring to her fear for the social, economic, emotional, and spiritual lives of America's boys.

As we raised our daughters, we asked our girls what they thought of the gender landscape around them. Gabrielle (then 16) came home from school in 2006 and said, "We had a discussion in social studies about boys and girls—everyone was talking like girls had it hard but boys had it easy. They were in denial."

Davita (then 19) came home from college for the holidays a few years ago and reported a discussion with her college friends. "I'm really glad I'm a girl, not a boy. The boys aren't sure what to do, but the girls are doing everything."

These discussions were anecdotal, of course. Both girls and boys, and women and men, can experience suffering in our world. Girls don't have it easy. Women don't have it easy.

But it is also true that boys and men are in substantial trouble today. They increasingly fill our principal's offices, ADD/ADHD assessment clinics, and rolls of the homeless and unemployed. Boys and men are more likely to be victims of violence than girls and women, commit suicide at four times the rate of females, and suffer emotional disturbance, behavioral and other brain-related disorders in higher numbers than females. They are suspended or expelled from school in much higher numbers than girls, receive two-thirds of the Ds and Fs in schools, and lag behind girls in standardized test scores throughout the nation. They abuse substances and alcohol at higher rates than girls and are incarcerated at exponentially higher rates (for more data in all these areas, please see *Saving Our Sons*).

Especially telling, the majority of government and philanthropic funding for gender-friendly programming goes to programs and innovations to help girls and women. The existence of this funding is to be celebrated, but the disconnect between the reality males face and the social justice attention males get needs to be examined by each of us.

We are in denial about our males.

I believe this denial will continue (and we will ultimately rue and mourn the dangerous, socially debilitating consequences) unless we change our academic, media, governmental, and philanthropic programming to include a new truth: just as the traditionalist paradigm regarding girls and women needed to be deconstructed and replaced by the feminist paradigm in the last century, *the now dominant gender paradigm of privileged males needs to be deconstructed and, at least in part, replaced if we are to meet the needs of both genders.*

Why does it need to change? Because it posits that females are victims of a privileged masculine society that systematically and universally oppresses them, and this isn't true in the developed world anymore. While individual girls and women can be dominated and demeaned by individual boys and men (and vice versa), we do not live in a culture that systematically teaches girls and women that they are second-class citizens and boys and men that they are superior.

While some areas of life are still populated by more males (mechanical engineering, senior leadership at some corporations and some areas of government), other areas of life and work are female dominant (management, health care, education, mental health professions). The original feminist paradigm posited systemic male dominance in our culture, but male dominance is only systemic in small pockets of the culture and female dominance also exists in others.

Can our culture open its mind to our new reality? To answer yes, we will need to make a distinction between gender issues in the developed world and the developing world. In many countries in the developing world, systemic and brutal patriarchy does prevail and the feminist model of male dominance/female victimization is essential for encouraging social justice. My own parents, while they served in the State Department, helped build schools for girls in Afghanistan against impossible odds. In that world, systemic degradation of females was and is prevalent.

But in the developed world, we can't keep operating out of a gender lens that blinds us to reality. If we do continue to remain blind, we will continue to avoid fulfilling our most human of imperatives: to take care of our children. If we do not fix what ails our sons—if we do not love them in the ways they need to be loved—we will create an increasingly dangerous society for girls and women, too.

No parent of either gender wants that.

Copyright Michael Gurian 2016

Question: Can you provide me with a ready-to-use, short blog I can customize and then send to my social media that might capture this issue of maturity?

Answer: Here is a model of a blog you could write after starting it with your own stories of your own sons.

I've discovered that, for many well-meaning academics, celebrities, and journalists, the painful state of boyhood in America can be summed up in looking at the discomfort our boys can experience when they are put down or called names. I agree that we must help boys feel feelings and express emotions in healthy ways. I agree that we must protect boys, especially our most sensitive and vulnerable boys, from hurt feelings. If a boy or girl is in danger, we must get right in there and protect that child immediately.

However, as a parent of sons, I also think we're oversimplifying things. We've created a huge industry around bullying but spend almost no time realizing all the subtle things our boys and girls are actually doing as they try to mature, grow up, become adults, and develop real resilience with which to face a very tough existence.

Personally, as a parent of sons, I believe advocacy for boys now requires that we reshape the debate toward major priorities, not just hurt feelings and the ability to talk about repressed emotions. If a child is in trauma, getting at the repressed feelings is crucial, but we can't let that model completely overshadow the subtleties of growing our boys into good men.

Feelings are good, they're fine, they're important, but they are not at the top of the list for most males in the way that they may be for lots of females. Every mom of adolescent sons knows this. Most of our social critics and commentators, though, seem to avoid this truth.

I know in writing about this in this way I'll be called insensitive, as if I want to pull back on protecting boys and girls from bullying or hyper-masculinity, or as if I'm some throwback to male dominance and the patriarchy and all that.

Let me say, just the opposite is true. I'm a good mom and I'm not insensitive—rather, I'm very sensitive to what boys need—they need character development, purpose-development, fathering, mothering, positive workplaces, shared custody of children, a safe home and hearth. These are the themes we need to talk about to save our sons from continuing to disappear into prisons, basements, and unemployment.

You might get flack for this kind of blog (and please do change the language to fit your voice), but you will also help our culture see a healthier future for our boys and young men.

About the Author

DR. MICHAEL GURIAN is a marriage and family counselor in his twenty-fifth year of private practice and a *New York Times* bestselling author of twenty-eight books, with more than one million copies in print (www.michaelgurian.com) The Gurian Institute, which he cofounded in 1996, conducts research internationally, launches pilot programs, and trains professionals (www.gurianinstitute.com).

Dr. Gurian has been called "the people's philosopher" for his ability to bring together people's ordinary lives and scientific ideas. Gurian provides between twenty and thirty keynotes and trainings per year and provides consulting to community organizations, schools, governmental agencies, corporations, medical personnel, and faith communities.

Dr. Gurian previously taught at Gonzaga University, Eastern Washington University, and Ankara University. His more recent academic speaking engagements include Harvard University, Johns Hopkins University, Stanford University, Morehouse College, the University of Colorado, the University of Missouri–Kansas City, and UCLA. His multicultural philosophy reflects the diverse cultures (European, Asian, Middle Eastern, and American) in which he has lived, worked, and studied.

Dr. Gurian's work has been featured multiple times in nearly all the major media, including *the New York Times, the Washington Post, USA Today, Newsweek, Time, Psychology Today, AARP Magazine, People, Reader's Digest, the Wall Street Journal, Forbes Magazine, Parenting, Good Housekeeping, Family Therapy Magazine, Redbook,* and others. Gurian has also made multiple appearances on *Today, Good Morning America, CNN, PBS, National Public Radio,* and many others.

Dr. Gurian lives in Spokane, Washington, with his wife, Gail, a family therapist in private practice. The couple has two grown daughters, Gabrielle and Davita.

About The Gurian Institute

The Gurian Institute, founded in 1996, provides professional development, training services, and pilot programs in gender diversity and gender dynamics. All of the Institute's work is science-based, research-driven, and practice-oriented.

The Institute staff, trainers, and coaches work with parents, mental health professionals, teachers, counselors, school districts, corporations, the legal system, medical professionals, and others who serve boys and girls, and women and men. The Institute has trainers throughout the world.

The Institute also provides products such as DVDs, books, workbooks, newsletters, and a user-friendly website at www.gurianinstitute.com.

The Institute has also developed training, consulting, and coaching programs specifically for therapists, social work professionals, corrections and law enforcement, and all other therapeutic professionals working in areas of male and female mental and social health. (Please see www.michaelgurian.com/how-do-I-help-him.html.)

The Gurian Institute staff of certified trainers is committed to not only training professionals and parents but also to helping ensure that participant agencies, schools, corporations, organizations, and individual practitioners can be self-sufficient in their ability to provide ongoing assets to their communities.

The Gurian Institute Corporate Division provides training and consulting in gender diversity for businesses, corporations, and government agencies. This work has inspired the book *Leadership and the Sexes*, which looks at both women and men in our workforce from a gender science perspective. For more about this work, see www.genderleadership.com.

Helping Boys Thrive® Initiatives

The Helping Boys Thrive® Initiative generally begins as a Helping Boys Thrive Summit® then can become an ongoing community-wide collaboration. It requires a small team of dynamic individuals—both in the private and public sectors—to take on the responsibility of putting on a Helping Boys Thrive Summit®; then, from there, an initiative can build in local schools, community organizations, government agencies, and non-profits.

The Gurian Institute provides all materials needed to put on a successful Summit and partners with local resources to facilitate initiatives.

To learn more or bring a Summit to your community, please visit www.helpingboysthrive.org. For further information on initiatives, please contact Dr. Gurian, Katey McPherson, and the Gurian Institute staff at info@gurianinstitute.com.

The Gurian Foundation

The Gurian Foundation was co-founded by Michael and Gail Gurian. It is a 501c3 corporation that can take donations and help with grant funding. Please go to www.gurianfoundation.org to learn more.

If you feel so moved, please donate toward Summits, Initiatives, and community work in your area through the Foundation. Donations and some grant funds are eligible for tax deduction.

To reach the Foundation directly, please contact Gail Reid-Gurian or Michael Gurian at michaelgurian@comcast.net.

Index

A

ACLU 299, 300
ADD 7
ADD/ADHD 39, 67, 82, 107, 159, 183, 195, 226, 281, 282, 311
Adderall 58
aggression 30, 31, 36, 37, 42, 43, 46, 47, 48, 49, 63, 65, 71, 78, 81, 119, 128, 130, 136, 137, 162, 163, 201, 240, 248, 284
aggression nurturance 137, 162, 169, 172, 216, 250, 292, 294, 299
Alpha Genomix 49, 276
Amen, Daniel 67, 120, 139, 279, 289, 291
Amen, Dr. 107, 281
American Medical Association 43
androphobia 99, 100, 101, 103, 110, 120, 126, 178
anterior cingulate cortex 202
Army and Navy Academy 84, 85, 250
Assassin's Creed 230
Autor, David 10, 15, 16, 270

B

Baron-Cohen, Simon 288, 305
Bartell, Art 84
Basista, Lisa 84
Benbow, Camilla 64, 106, 257, 279, 287, 288, 305
Bible 100, 138
Big Three x, 24, 28, 30, 31, 81, 82, 94, 95, 97, 108, 109, 113, 135, 174, 175, 178, 181, 235, 236, 238, 242, 245, 262, 271, 283, 285, 286, 292
bisphenol A 158, 291
bi-strategic 129, 130, 131, 132, 171, 175, 176, 179, 181
black males 19, 241, 270
Blue Bloods 133, 134
blue light 198, 295
Bly, Robert 270, 305

Boggess, Jacquelyn 110, 288
book banning 169
Boys and Girls Learn Differently 8, 80, 283, 284, 279, 307
Boy Scouts 172
boys of color 6, 7, 19, 110, 241
brain differences 64, 65, 121, 122, 126, 190, 226, 279, 289, 300, 301
brain scans 51, 108, 120, 139, 140, 176, 185, 226, 227, 281, 288, 301
bridge brains 66, 68
Brizendine, Louann 64, 107, 279, 289, 305
bullying 30, 31, 49, 50, 131, 133, 134, 135
Bushman, Brad 138, 139, 289

C

Cahn, Naomi 298, 305
Carbone, June 298, 305
Carroll, Pete 147, 148
cell phones 200, 203
Central Catholic 84, 267
choice theory 242, 243, 255
chromosomes 40, 43, 171
Cohen, Isaac 255-257, 303
Cole, Robert 131
colleges 17, 91, 97, 98, 103, 223, 224, 226
Commission to Create a White House Council on Boys and Men 93, 110
competition 5, 81, 85, 86, 127, 128, 141, 173, 197, 240
Congress 20, 233, 270
Cooper, Joel 295, 306
criminalization of males 286

D

Dawe, Ted 170, 292
de-criminalize 245, 248
Deniston, Russ 141, 142, 289
Department of Education 18, 90, 96, 97, 283
developmental milestones xi, 172, 231, 236
digital 183, 187, 203, 209, 213, 227, 228
Dire, Gene 238
DNA 28, 39, 40, 158, 159, 230, 235, 276

dopamine 75-78, 186, 201-203, 221, 223

drugs 17, 41, 76, 248

E

early childhood 8, 29, 81, 279

educators xi, 59, 79, 83-86, 174, 175, 226

Ellington, Joanna 207, 297, 306

emotional intelligence 119, 121-123, 127, 136, 169, 229, 235, 264, 294

empathy 28, 30, 86, 118-121, 125, 127, 128, 130, 168, 169, 172, 214, 228

endocrine disruptors 31, 158, 159, 161, 162

epigenetics 36, 37, 39-41, 49, 53, 60, 235, 267, 277, 279

equal pay 237, 239, 301

estrogen receptors 160, 291

F

Facebook 137, 240

Faludi, Susan 274, 306

Farrell Girls Preparatory Academy 83

Farrell, Warren 9, 93, 96, 97, 274, 298, 306

female brain 256

female brain 16, 38, 57, 64-66, 79-81, 93, 108, 120-123, 149, 157, 165, 202, 223, 226, 227, 235, 255, 256, 279, 280, 283, 288, 289, 300, 301

female emotional intelligence 119, 122, 127, 135, 138

feminism 92, 95, 224, 239, 257, 258

5-HTT 70, 160, 282

football 41, 85, 127, 128, 130, 258, 264, 278

Franklin Boys Preparatory Academy 83

Friedan, Betty 259, 260, 303, 306

frontal lobe 65, 164, 166, 202

G

GABA receptors 70

Garro, Paul 84, 267

gay gene 100

gender differences 64, 106, 108, 193, 242, 256, 257, 273, 279, 281, 295

gender equity 18, 91, 92, 94, 111, 233-239, 242-244, 252-254, 258-260, 262, 300-303

gender fluidity 280

gender gap 9, 10, 15, 16, 79, 82, 93, 255, 256, 271
gender identity 38
gender norms 25, 27, 32, 33, 52
gender profiling 99, 245-247, 273
gender symbiosis 120, 231, 259, 262, 264
genetics ix, 28, 31, 37, 38, 40, 41, 43, 46, 61, 62, 68, 70, 72, 76, 77, 114, 150,
     159, 182, 193, 194, 226, 261, 262, 276, 277, 287, 290, 296
genetic testing 47, 60, 185, 194, 276, 296
Giedd, Jay 201, 288, 295
Gilligan, Carol 24, 25, 32, 275, 306
Goleman, Daniel 120, 125, 127, 288, 289, 306
Google 194, 195, 225, 299
Gore, Deb 239, 242, 244
grandparents 72, 172, 180, 214, 259
gray matter 65, 121, 147, 156, 195, 211, 223
Gurian Institute 7, 8, 29, 31, 57-59, 67, 80, 82, 84, 86, 133, 170, 267, 269, 270,
     272, 283, 299, 306, 315-317
Gur, Ruben 140, 261, 279, 287

H

Hafiz 218, 219, 297
Halo 205
Halpern, Diane 64, 279, 287
Hawley, Patricia 129, 130, 289
Helping Boys Thrive 17, 18, 236, 317
Heschel, Abraham Joshua 219, 297, 307
Hillsboro County Public Schools 83, 250, 267, 300
homeschool 83
homosexuality 99, 100, 287
Hymowitz, Kay 274, 298, 307

I

immaturity 91, 101, 104, 130, 150-152, 154, 156, 159, 161, 178, 209, 222, 224,
     227, 236, 298
incarceration ix, 6, 15, 112, 248, 251
insula 121, 125, 126, 128

J

Jantz, Gregory 76, 267, 281, 307
Jung, Carl 87, 149, 285, 307

K

Keillor, Garrison 178, 301
Kemp, Troy 85, 267
Kerns, Kathryn 131, 132
Kindlon, Daniel 75, 274, 277, 282, 307
Koertge, Noretta 104, 287, 308
Konner, Melvin 42, 276

L

Ladinsky, Daniel 218, 297, 308
learning disabilities 241
LGBT 99, 100, 275
limbic system 122, 164, 176
literacy 7, 79, 81, 109, 113, 130, 162, 163, 188, 284
Lubinski, David 257, 288, 305

M

male behavior 52, 104, 155, 245, 248, 250, 282
male brain 38, 53, 62-66, 69-71, 77, 79, 81, 82, 114, 121-124, 126, 140, 143,
       145, 147, 149, 155, 157, 158, 168, 170, 173, 175, 176, 187, 189, 190,
       193, 195, 199, 201, 202, 204, 209, 211, 212, 222, 223, 226, 227, 256
male emotional intelligence 94, 117, 119-122, 124, 126, 127, 133-135, 137, 138,
       147, 149, 163, 164, 176, 235, 293
male/female brain difference 57, 64, 279, 289, 300, 301
male maturity xi, 32, 153, 164, 171, 195
male mental illness 110, 113, 227
male motivation 151, 154, 163, 164, 168
mental illness 16, 29, 50, 235
meta-analysis 9, 25, 29, 36, 154, 269, 270
micro-aggressions 101-105, 110, 112, 224
mirror neurons 128
misandry 32, 261, 303
misdiagnosis 67, 109, 235, 282
Mogil, Jeffrey 125, 289

Montessori 162, 163, 164, 165

Mortenson, Tom 10, 14, 15, 271

Moses, Joy 109, 288

motivation 5, 7, 25, 29, 62, 63, 65, 67, 75, 81, 94, 98, 150, 152-157, 159, 169, 176, 178, 181, 228, 235, 281

Munakato, Yuko 292

My Brother's Keeper 110

N

National Center for the Development of Boys 85, 267

natural boy ix, xi, 59, 63, 64, 66, 71, 72, 79, 80, 82, 83, 87, 154, 156, 163, 187, 202, 231, 236, 284

natural girl 63, 202, 236

nature-based theory 31, 57, 59, 60, 61, 79, 80, 92, 211, 262, 281, 283, 300

neurobiology 75, 80, 235, 280

neuroscience x, 36, 57, 59, 62, 100, 106-108, 127, 171, 197, 204, 226, 227, 267, 279, 281, 283

Neuroscience 165

neurotoxins ix, 28, 31, 36, 40-42, 60, 79, 154-161, 194, 235

Newell, Walter R. 300. 308

non-intervention 119, 162, 164, 167, 211

nucleus accumbens 75, 77, 201. 282

Nurture the Nature 61, 164, 190, 281, 282

nutrition 40, 60

O

Obama, President 95, 97, 110, 298, 299

obesity genetics 61, 277, 296

OECD 8, 269, 271

OPRMI 69, 70, 282

over-medication 80

oxytocin 65, 121, 128, 129, 280

P

Paglia, Camille 95, 285, 287, 308

Parker, Kathleen 274, 287, 308

patriarchy 105, 109, 252, 312, 314

Pell Institute 10, 15, 269, 270, 271, 272

Phthalates 290
Pinker, Steven 55, 257, 277, 308
PISA 8, 271
plastics 31, 157, 158, 162, 291
Plep, Gary 153, 267, 297
Pollack, William 277, 282, 308
pornography 17, 170, 206, 297
prefrontal cortex 75, 77, 282, 296
preschool 17, 168, 191, 193, 240, 249
prison 6, 30, 50, 51, 58, 62, 63, 66, 67, 142, 177, 248, 251, 263, 273, 298
pruning 201, 202, 211

Q

Qu'ran 100, 215

R

rape culture 95, 97, 105, 107, 224, 237, 238, 285, 301
red dye 31, 47, 279
resilience 68-70, 76, 81, 87, 128-135, 137, 179, 247, 248, 249, 313
resilience 127, 282
Rilke, Rainer Maria 82, 264, 285, 303, 309
Ritalin 7, 67, 184, 282, 309
rites of passage 30, 156, 208, 211, 212, 229, 281
role models 29, 63, 148, 155, 175, 176
Rosin, Hannah 25, 32, 105, 106, 275, 309
rumination 121, 139, 289

S

safe container 168, 172-175, 217
safe emotional container 171, 173
Sandberg, Sheryl 94, 95, 285, 309
Sapolsky, Robert M. 275, 277, 292
Sax, Leonard 67, 153, 160, 274, 281, 285, 289, 290, 309
science-based xi, 8, 31, 32, 67, 83-85, 97, 111, 113, 137, 188, 194, 196, 238, 268, 316
screen time 48, 156, 188, 189, 191, 193, 194, 196-198, 200, 203, 210, 222, 223, 296
Seattle Seahawks 144, 147, 148, 264

self-esteem 81, 124, 125, 128, 135, 257

sensitive boys 25, 123

sex differences 64, 279, 288, 289, 309

sexism 30, 303

Shaffer, David Williamson 296, 309

Shiver, Sanders 130

Shors, Tracey 64, 280

Skloot, Rebecca 170, 292

smartphones 188, 209, 210, 220, 295

social science 104, 105, 256-278

Sommers, Christina Hoff 96, 97, 261, 274, 298, 302, 303, 309

Sparks, Carla 83, 267

spatial-mechanical 186, 190, 255, 284

sports 41, 68, 71, 124, 125, 130, 149, 173, 196, 209

stages 125, 188-190, 193, 222, 281

standardized tests 79

statistics 8, 9, 13, 14, 18, 26, 36, 79, 97, 239, 241, 270, 271, 273, 274, 285, 286, 299-301

STEM 93, 239, 254-257

stereotypes ix, 5, 24, 25, 30, 32-34, 37, 51, 52, 150, 161, 178, 234, 235, 237, 259, 299, 302

straw man arguments 236, 300-303

stress 62, 64, 65, 76, 121, 139, 162, 198, 257, 277, 280, 300

suicide 6, 7, 11, 17, 19, 25, 30, 51, 110, 111, 137, 240, 241, 259, 311

Supertramp 141, 142, 145

Szalavitz, Maia 273, 309

T

Tartt, Donna 144, 289, 310

Taylor, Shelley E. 288, 309

technology 30, 76, 94, 156, 173, 182, 184, 186-188, 190, 193, 195, 197, 199, 200, 202, 203, 209-211, 213, 217-220, 222, 225-227, 229, 231, 236, 297

temporal lobe 204, 205, 219

testosterone 41, 42, 44, 62-65, 75, 121, 128, 129, 136, 145, 155, 159, 160, 161, 173, 186, 289, 290

Thompson, Michael 75, 274, 277, 282, 307, 310

Three Family System 172-174, 178, 179, 181, 208, 211-223, 250, 292

Title IX 18, 92, 96, 97, 287, 300

Tournier, Paul 181, 295

toxic masculinity 25, 27, 30, 44, 50, 161, 164
transgender 30, 38, 42, 66, 276, 278, 280
trauma 28, 30-32, 36, 41, 49-51, 62, 65, 69, 70, 73, 74, 77, 79, 80, 111, 114, 117, 155, 160, 172, 187, 208, 227, 228, 235, 277, 313
Travison, Thomas 160, 290
Trueman, Terry 170, 267
Trump, Donald 20, 270
23andMe 49, 276

U

under-motivation 159, 161
universities 78, 93, 95, 103, 112, 224, 226, 256, 286

V

ventral striatum 75, 77, 176
verbal centers 65, 143
verbal literacy 79, 109, 130
victimology 98
video games 3, 27, 33, 49, 50, 51, 77, 136, 152, 153, 173, 184-189, 203-206, 208, 213, 227, 297
violence ix, 7, 9, 24-33, 36, 37, 41-43, 49-53, 59, 62, 78, 80, 102, 103, 135, 159, 161, 178, 235, 237, 240, 246, 248, 271, 276, 300, 311
Violence 10, 277, 296
violent genes 43
Vyvanse 183, 184

W

Waldorf 194
Walken, Christopher 214, 215
Walsh, William J. 276, 310
Washington, Denzel 213
Wasserman, Melanie 10, 15, 16, 270
Watson, William (Bill) 219, 267, 297, 310
White House 9, 90, 93, 110, 111, 233, 269, 270, 288, 292
white males 6, 19, 20, 49, 224, 270, 271, 274, 302
white matter 65, 121, 157, 202
Whitmire, Richard 274, 310
WHO 9, 269, 271, 272

Wilcox, Ella Wheeler 261, 303
Williams 310
Williams, C.K. 145, 289
Wilson, E.O. 24, 261, 262, 303, 310
Wilson, Russell 147, 148
women and children 110, 146, 231, 235, 239, 252, 253, 260, 264, 292, 302
words-for-feelings 5, 21, 108, 122, 138
workplace 14, 60, 63, 93, 104, 128, 130, 131, 137, 140, 148, 222, 224, 244, 253, 296, 314
Wright, Tim 211, 253, 267, 297, 310

Y

Y chromosome 64, 173, 190, 195
YouTube 140, 202, 213, 270, 302

Made in the USA
Middletown, DE
20 May 2018